MASSIF CENTRAL

Aurillac

Valence

Conques

LANGU

OF THE C

D0554554

Rodez

CÉVENNES

Ardèche

Cèze

Millau

Tarn

Gard

Avignon

Durance

ALBIGEOIS

Nîmes

Beaucaire

Combers

St. Gilles

PROVENCE

Hérault

Montpellier

Arles

to Marseilles

Castres

Agout

Rhône

Saint Pons

Orb

MONTAGNE NOIRE

Servian

MINERVOIS

Béziers

Cabaret

Minerve

Carcassonne

Aude

Narbonne

MEDITERRANEAN SEA

Villerouge-
Termenès

Fontfroide

Pieusse

Termes

CORBIÈRES

Peyrepertuse

Quéribus

Termes

Perpignan

ROUSSILLON

ATLANTIC
OCEAN

BRITTANY

NORMANDY

ILE DE
FRANCE

HOLY

ROMAN

AQUITAINE

NAVARRA

Area of Detail

EMPIRE

LEON

LANGUEDOC

PROVENCE

PORTUGAL

ARAGON

CASTILE

CORSICA

DOMINIONS OF THE ALMOHADES

SARDINIA

MEDITERRANEAN SEA

Ter

to Barcelona

The Perfect Heresy

Also by Stephen O'Shea

Back to the Front

STEPHEN O'SHEA

The Perfect Heresy

The Revolutionary Life and Death of the Medieval Cathars

DOUGLAS & McINTYRE

VANCOUVER/TORONTO

Douglas & McIntyre Ltd.
2323 Quebec Street, Suite 201
Vancouver, British Columbia
V5T 4S7

Published simultaneously in the United States of America by Walker Publishing Company, Inc.

Canadian Cataloguing in Publication Data
O'Shea, Stephen, 1956–
The perfect heresy

Includes bibliographical references and index.
ISBN 1-55054-776-3

1. Albigenses—History.   2. Heresies, Christian—France—
Languedoc—History—Middle Ages, 600–1500.   3. France—Church
BX4891.2.O74   2000   272'.3   C00-910535-2

Book design by Ellen Cipriano

Printed and bound in the U.S.A.

We gratefully acknowledge the financial support of the Canada Council for the Arts, the British Columbia Ministry of Tourism, Small Business and Culture, and the Government of Canada through the Book Publishing Industry Development Program (BPIDP) for our publishing activities.

To
Jill, Rachel, and Eve

Contents

Principal Figures in the
Cathar Story

SPIRITUAL FOES

Arnold Amaury (d. 1225): Head of the Cistercian order of monks. Papal plenipotentiary in Languedoc, he was later appointed archbishop of Narbonne. Arnold led the Albigensian Crusade at the infamous sack of Béziers in 1209.

Peter Autier (c. 1245–1309): Cathar holy man. Until middle age a wealthy notary in the mountain town of Ax-les-Thermes, Autier received heretical religious instruction in Italy and returned to Languedoc to spread the faith.

William Bélibaste (d. 1321): The last Languedoc Perfect. Sought by the authorities on charges of heresy and murder, Bélibaste exercised his ministry for over a decade among fellow exiles in Catalonia.

Bernard of Clairvaux (1090–1153): Cistercian monk, founder of the abbey of Clairvaux in Champagne in 1115, canonized in 1174. Bernard advised popes, preached the Second Crusade, and sounded the alarm about the growth of Catharism.

Blanche of Laurac: The greatest matriarch of Languedoc Catharism. Two of her daughters made prominent marriages, then became Perfect; another ran a Cathar home in Laurac. Blanche's fourth daughter and only son were murdered at Lavaur in 1211.

Domingo de Guzmán (1170–1221): Founder of the Order of Friars Preachers, or Dominicans, canonized as St. Dominic in 1234. A native of Castile, Dominic preached tirelessly in Languedoc in the years preceding the crusade. During the Cathar wars he became a confidant of Simon de Montfort.

Esclarmonde of Foix: Sister of Raymond Roger, the count of Foix. Esclarmonde embraced Catharism in 1204 at a ceremony attended by Languedoc's leading families. She ran a heretical convent and, centuries later, became the object of an erotico-historical cult.

Jacques Fournier (c. 1280–1342): Cistercian monk of Languedoc peasant stock. Fournier, a peerless inquisitor uncovered the Cathar revival at Montaillou. He was elected pope Benedict XII in 1334.

Fulk of Marseilles (1155–1231): Bishop of Toulouse from 1205 until his death. Immortalized by Dante in canto IX of the *Paradiso*, Fulk showed uncommon eloquence and ruthlessness in combating Catharism.

Gregory IX (1170–1241): Ugolino dei Conti di Segni, elected pope in 1227. His appointment, in 1233, of the Dominicans to lead the fight against heresy is usually cited as the founding act of the Inquisition.

Guilhabert of Castres (d. c. 1240): The greatest of the male Languedoc Perfect. Although in constant danger as the Cathar bishop of Toulouse, Guilhabert eluded capture and organized the strategic retreat of the faith into the Pyrenees.

Innocent III (1160–1216): Lotario dei Conti di Segni, elected pope in 1198. He launched the Albigensian Crusade in 1208 and convoked the Fourth Lateran Council in 1215. One of the most feared and admired medieval pontiffs, Innocent died in Perugia en route to brokering a peace between Genoa and Pisa.

Peter of Castelnau (d. 1208): Cistercian monk and papal legate whose demise prompted the call to crush the Cathars.

TEMPORAL RIVALS

Amaury de Montfort (1192–1241): Eldest son of Alice of Montmorency and Simon de Montfort. Embattled lord of Languedoc from 1218 until the cession of his rights to King Louis VIII of France. Captured by the Muslims at Gaza in 1239, held captive in Babylon for two years, Amaury died in Calabria on his homeward journey.

Blanche of Castile (1185–1252): Queen of France, then regent after the death of Louis VIII and during the minority of her eldest son, Louis IX (St. Louis), as well as during his extended crusading absences in Palestine. Arguably, France's greatest thirteenth-century ruler.

Bouchard de Marly (d. 1226): First cousin of Alice of Montmorency and comrade-in-arms of her husband, Simon de Montfort. Held hostage for a time by Cathars in Cabaret, Bouchard subsequently led the second corps of cavalry at the battle of Muret.

Louis VIII (1187–1226): King of France after the death of his father, Philip Augustus, in 1223. Louis ordered the massacre of Marmande and launched the decisive royal crusade of 1226.

Pedro II (1174–1213): Monarch of the unified kingdom of Aragon and county of Barcelona, victor over the Moors at the battle of Las Navas de Tolosa. King Pedro the Catholic allied himself to the cause of Languedoc and led the greatest army ever assembled to fight the crusaders.

Philip Augustus (1165–1223): King of France. He successfully whittled down the Plantagenet continental presence of Kings Richard (Lionheart) and John (Lackland) of England to a small corner of Aquitaine. Philip's barons were the principal leaders of the Albigensian Crusade.

Raymond VI (1156–1222): Count of Toulouse. Three times excommunicated and five times married, the leader of Languedoc was formally dispossessed at the Lateran Council of 1215.

Raymond VII (1197–1249): The last count of Toulouse of the Saint-Gilles clan. Despite having driven the French from his lands, Raymond was eventually forced to agree to a harsh peace that obliged him to subsidize the Inquisition.

Raymond Roger of Foix (d. 1223): The most belligerent of the southern nobles opposed to the French invasion. Brother and husband of Cathar holy women, he distinguished himself for ferocity on the battlefield and bluntness before the pope.

Simon de Montfort (1165–1218): Champion of the Catholic cause in the south. After showing conspicuous bravery in battle, he was made viscount of Béziers and Carcassonne in 1209. Years of brilliant, brutal generalship led to his becoming lord of all of Languedoc.

Raymond Roger Trencavel (1188–1209): Viscount of Béziers and Carcassonne, suspected of strong Cathar sympathies. He stood alone during the summer of 1209 against the might of the north.

The Perfect Heresy

Introduction

ALBI, AS IN ALBIGENSIAN, the most notorious heresy of all time. On a bright summer afternoon several years ago, I found myself walking the silent streets of Albi in the company of my brother, surprised at having stumbled across a town whose name was familiar. We had come to Albi by chance, having rented a car in Paris a week earlier for an aimless drive southward through the French countryside. It was our version of what the English call "a mystery tour," a trip with an unknown destination. Once the slate roofs and off-white walls north of the Loire had given way to the warm terra-cotta of the Midi, we began feeling pleasantly disoriented. In Clermont-Ferrand, we had our first confirmed beret sighting; in Aurillac, we backed into an accident; in Rodez, we watched as our waitress fell out of her dress. We had reached Languedoc, France's Mediterranean southwest.

After a long lunch at a truck stop, we cruised into Albi, the town with a whiff of infamy to its name. The Albigensian Crusade, we knew, was a cataclysm of the Middle Ages, a ferocious campaign of siege, battle, and bonfire during which supporters of the Catholic Church sought to eliminate the heretics known as the Albigenses, or the Cathars. That thirteenth-century crusade, directed not against Muslims in distant Palestine but against dissident Christians in the heart of Europe, was followed by the founding of the Inquisition, an implacable machine expressly created to destroy the Cathar survivors of the war. As a result of the upheaval, Languedoc, once a proudly independent territory, was annexed to the kingdom of France. Crusade, Inquisition, conquest—Albi's place in history, if not in fond memory, was assured.

To our eyes on that summer day, the town looked as if it had opted for drowsy amnesia about its past. We strolled through a deserted old quarter, past siesta-shuttered shops and homes, the wine-red bricks of walls and windowsills bathing us in a rosy glow. A white cat slept on a doorstep, undisturbed by any ghosts. It was hard to square Albi's blush of forgetful well-being with its singular legacy. I needed only think back a decade or so to remember a college instructor describing the Albigensian Crusade as nascent colonialism and, in a more obsessive vein, a potheaded roommate rambling on and on about how the heretics had been hunted down by the original thought police. Now that I was actually in Albi, such recollections seemed inappropriate, a rude intrusion into the town's pink dream.

On a height above the River Tarn, the narrow streets opened up into a wide plaza. My brother and I glanced at each other. This was more like it.

There, looming over a terraced tumble of riverside dwellings, stood a red fortress, monolithic and menacing, a stupendous

The Cathedral of Ste-Cécile, Albi

mountain of bricks piled 100 feet high and 300 feet wide. Sullenly rectangular, its windows little more than elongated slits, the building looked indestructible, like a glowering anvil hurled from the heavens. Its thirty-two buttresses, shaped like smokestacks cut in half lengthwise, ringed cyclopean walls on all four sides and rose as far as the flat line of an impossibly distant roof. In silhouette, it resembled an appallingly large change dispenser, of the type once worn by bus conductors and waitresses—one buttress holding pennies, another nickels, and so on. Yet that homely comparison was spoiled by an even taller structure, a tower, a red-brick rocket shooting 100 feet higher than the roof alongside the west wall.

The tower held bells that toll on Sunday. The building was a church.

We had been dead wrong about Albi's amnesia. The fearsome oddity that is the Cathedral of Ste-Cécile will never let the townspeople forget their Albigensian connection. Erected from 1282 to 1392, the building is a massive bully that dwarfs and dominates its neighbors. There is no transept; thus the church does not even have the redemptive shape of the cross. For centuries, it had just one small door. Unlike the other great French cathedrals in Paris, Chartres, Rheims, Bourges, Rouen, and Amiens, there were no messy markets under Ste-Cécile's soaring vault, no snoring wayfarers on its floor, no livestock droppings to slop out in the mornings, no grand portals to let in the air breathed by ordinary men. The church's exterior was—and still is—a monument to power.

Bernard de Castanet was the medieval bishop who approved the plans, raised the money, and started the construction. As he was doing this in the 1280s, Castanet was also accusing many prominent townspeople of heresy, even though the Albigensian Crusade had ended two generations earlier and the inquisitors had been assiduously intimidating the populace ever since. The bishop's opponents, particularly one outspoken Franciscan friar named Bernard Délicieux, claimed that Castanet was using the threat of Inquisition prisons to silence free men and to extort funds. Whatever the truth, the fortress church rose, brick by unforgiving brick, until its larger message became clear: Submit or be crushed.

There was nothing subtle about the appearance of Ste-Cécile, nothing that demanded a specialized monograph detailing gargoyles, grace notes, and the like. We walked around the hulking giant, marveling that the midafternoon silence of Albi had been so deceptive. The red cathedral was, in the end, an enraged bellow from Bishop Castanet and his successors. They had seen their world—their power, privileges, beliefs—imperiled by the subversive creed of the Cathars, and they had roared out their anger in this monstrous mountain of brick. It filled our eyes and our ears. Only a disagreement over something as fathomless as the soul of a civilization could elicit a shout so loud that it was still audible across a chasm of 700 years.

Not surprisingly, that afternoon echoed for a long time in my memory. In the years to follow, the Cathars and Albi came to mind again and again, appearing unbidden in books and magazines and the conversations of the Parisians in whose midst I lived. A lot of people had heard the shout. I began haunting the booksellers' stalls by the Seine. Friends reached into their bookshelves, invariably producing yet another French-language study of the Cathars for me to discover. Specialized libraries contained hard-to-obtain translations of chronicles, correspondence, and Inquisition registers. In 1997, years after my first glimpse of Ste-Cécile, I moved to southwestern France to look—and listen—more closely in the places where the Cathars had lived and died. *The Perfect Heresy*, it turned out, was the destination of my mystery tour.

"Kill them all, God will know his own." The sole catchphrase of the Cathar conflict to be handed down to posterity is attrib-

uted to Arnold Amaury, the monk who led the Albigensian Crusade. A chronicler reported that Arnold voiced this command
outside the Mediterranean trading town of Béziers on July 22,
1209, when his crusading warriors, on the verge of storming the
city after having breached its defenses, had turned to him for
advice on distinguishing Catholic believer from Cathar heretic.
The monk's simple instructions were followed and the entire
population—20,000 or so—indiscriminately murdered. The sack
of Béziers was the Guernica of the Middle Ages.

Whether Arnold Amaury actually uttered that pitiless order
is still a matter for debate. What no one doubts, however, is that
the phrase neatly illustrates the homicidal passions at work during the Albigensian Crusade. Even in an era commonly considered barbarous—"a thousand years without a bath," runs a
benign putdown of the Middle Ages—the campaign against the
Cathars and their supporters stands out for its stark cruelty. The
stories of Béziers and other Church-sponsored atrocities shock at
first, then play into the belief that the millennium lying between
antiquity and Renaissance was an unrelieved nightmare. Popular
culture, drawing on the Gothic imagination of the nineteenth
century, has exploited that notion; in Quentin Tarantino's *Pulp
Fiction*, to take a well-known example, an enraged mobster hisses
at an enemy, "I'm gonna get *medieval* on yo' ass!" Just the word
makes us wince.

In this sense, the story of the Cathars is surpassingly medieval. The Albigensian Crusade, which lasted from 1209 to 1229,
was launched by the most powerful pope of the Middle Ages,
Innocent III, and initially prosecuted by a gifted warrior, Simon
de Montfort, under the approving eye of Arnold Amaury. A
mail-fisted response to the questions posed by a popular heresy,
the crusade set baleful precedents for Christendom's approach to

dissidence by laying waste to Languedoc, the great arc of land stretching from the Pyrenees to Provence and including such cities as Toulouse, Albi, Carcassonne, Narbonne, Béziers, and Montpellier.

The crusade's two decades of salutary slaughter then gave way to fifteen years of fitful revolt and repression, which culminated in the siege of Montségur in 1244. A lonely fortress atop a needle of rock, Montségur eventually surrendered, and more than 200 of its defenders, the leaders of the embattled Cathar faith, were herded into a snowy clearing to be burned alive. By then the Inquisition, guided since its founding in 1233 by the steely intellects of the Dominican order, had developed the techniques that would torment Catholic Europe and Latin America for centuries to come and, in the process, provide the model for latter-day totalitarian control of the individual conscience. By the middle of the fourteenth century, the Inquisition had razed any residual trace of the Albigensian heresy from the landscape of Christendom, and the Cathars of Languedoc had vanished. The stations of their calvary—the mass burnings, blindings, and hangings, the catapulting of body parts over castle walls, the rapine, the looting, the chanting of monks behind battering rams, the secret trials, the exhuming of corpses, the creakings of the rack—match our phantasmagoria of the medieval only too well.

Were the tale just that, a sort of pulp nonfiction for the prurient, then the Cathars should be relegated to a footnote in the annals of terror. Yet their rise and fall call up other connotations of the medieval—the sublime, mysterious, and dynamic Middle Ages that often gets obscured by the flash of armored knights. The Cathar heresy, a pacifist brand of Christianity embracing tolerance and poverty, rose to prominence in the middle of the so-called renaissance of the twelfth century, the time when

Europe shook off the intellectual torpor that had afflicted it for hundreds of years. It was a period of change, experimentation, and broader horizons. After 1095, the year Pope Urban II had urged Christendom to retake Jerusalem, tens of thousands had gone charging off to Palestine in search of adventure and salvation—and returned as men and women who had seen, if not understood, that life was organized differently elsewhere. At home, the towns began to grow for the first time since the fall of the Roman Empire, and the great era of cathedral building got under way. Schools formed, as yet unfettered by the strictures of a watchful hierarchy. The spread of new ideas and the birth of new ambitions often led to dissatisfaction with an early medieval Church more suited to a benighted age of huddled monks and shivering peasantries. The great awakening of the twelfth century ushered in an era of spiritual longing that searched and often found the sublime outside the fortress of orthodoxy. The Cathars were joined by other heretical groups—notably the Waldensians, or the "Poor Men of Lyons"—in lashing out at the mainstream religion.

Catharism thrived in regions farthest along the road from the Dark Ages: the merchant cities of Italy, the trading centers of Champagne and the Rhineland, and, especially, the fractious checkerboard of familial holdings and independent towns that made up Languedoc at the end of the twelfth century. The fate of the Cathars became wedded to the destiny of Languedoc, for it was there where the heretics prospered most and won disciples in every quarter of society, from mountain shepherd and hillside yeoman to lowland noble and urban merchant. When attacked, the creed's small priestly class—that is, the ascetics known as the *Perfect*—found a militant multitude of protectors from among its far-reaching network of kinsman, convert, and anticlerical

sympathizer. The Perfect heresy was ideally, indeed perfectly, suited to the tolerant feudalism of Languedoc, and for that its people would pay a terrible tribute. The region entered the thirteenth century a voluble anomaly in the chorus of European Christianity, its culture enlivened by poetic troubadours and revolutionary Cathars; 100 years later, Languedoc had been swallowed whole by the kings of France, its fearful towns the proving grounds for ambitious inquisitors and royal magistrates.

Without the Cathars, the nobles beholden to the Capet mon-

archy and its small woodland territory around the city of Paris—
the Ile de France—might never have found a pretext to swoop
down on the Mediterranean and force the unlikely annexation of
Languedoc to the Crown of France. Languedoc shared a culture
and language with its cousin south of the Pyrenees, the kingdom
of Aragon and Barcelona, one of the Christian fiefs that would
eventually roll back the Muslim Moors from the rest of the Iberian Peninsula. Arguably, Languedoc "belonged" with Aragon,
not with the Frankish northerners who would someday create
the entity known as France.* Without the convulsion of the Albigensian Crusade, the map and makeup of Europe could very
well have been different.

Although firmly anchored in the politics and society of its
era, the story of the Cathars also forms an important—and har-
rowing—chapter in the history of ideas. The heresy hinged upon
the question of Good and Evil. Not that one side in the struggle
over Languedoc was good and the other bad, even if propagandists for both sides claimed that such was the case. Rather, the
fundamental disagreement between Catholic orthodoxy and
Cathar heterodoxy, their irreducible bone of contention, concerned the role and power of Evil in life.

For the Cathars, the world was not the handiwork of a good
god. It was wholly the creation of a force of darkness, immanent
in all things. Matter was corrupt, therefore irrelevant to salvation. Little if any attention had to be paid to the elaborate systems set up to bully people into obeying the man with the
sharpest sword, the fattest wallet, or the biggest stick of incense.
Worldly authority was a fraud, and worldly authority based on

---

*In the interest of brevity, *The Perfect Heresy* will use such terms as *France* and *England* to describe
the twelfth- and thirteenth-century constellations of feudal arrangements that would not evolve into
states until much later.

some divine sanction, such as the Church claimed, was outright hypocrisy.

The god deserving of Cathar worship was a god of light, who ruled the invisible, the ethereal, the spiritual domain; this god, unconcerned with the material, simply didn't care if you got into bed before getting married, had a Jew or Muslim for a friend, treated men and women as equals, or did anything else contrary to the teachings of the medieval Church. It was up to the individual (man or woman) to decide whether he or she was willing to renounce the material for a life of self-denial. If not, one would keep returning to this world—that is, be reincarnated—until ready to embrace a life sufficiently spotless to allow accession, at death, to the same blissful state one had experienced as an angel prior to having been tempted out of heaven at the beginning of time. To be saved, then, meant becoming a saint. To be damned was to live, again and again, on this corrupt Earth. Hell was here, not in some horrific afterlife dreamed up by Rome to scare people out of their wits.

To believe in what is called the Two Principles of creation (Evil in the visible, Good in the invisible) is to be a dualist, an adherent to a notion that has been shared by other creeds in the long course of humanity's grappling with the unknowable. Christian Cathar dualism, however, posited a meeting place between Good and Evil: within the breast of every human being. There, our wavering divine spark, the remnant of our earlier, angelic state, waited patiently to be freed from the cycle of reincarnations.

Even a cursory description of the Cathar faith gives an idea of how seditious the heresy was. If its tenets were true, the sacraments of the Church necessarily became null and void, for the very good reason that the Church itself was a hoax. Why then, the Cathars asked, pay any attention to the Church? More concretely, why pay any taxes and tithes to it? To the Cathars, ecclesiastical trappings of wealth and worldly power served only to show that the Church belonged to the realm of matter. At best, the pope and his underlings were merely unenlightened; at worst, they were active agents of the evil creator.

Neither was the rest of society spared the revolutionary ramifications of Cathar thought. This was particularly true of the movement's treatment of women. The medieval sexual status quo would have been undermined if everybody had believed, as the Cathars did, that a nobleman in one life might be a milkmaid in the next, or that women were fit to be spiritual leaders. Perhaps even more subversive than this protofeminism was the Cathar repugnance to the practice of swearing oaths. Minor though this may seem to us now, medieval man thought otherwise, for the swearing of an oath was the contractual underpinning of early feudal society. It lent sacred weight to the existing order; no kingdom, estate, or bond of vassalage could be created or transferred without establishing a sworn link, mediated by the clergy, between the individual and the divine. As dualists, the Cathars believed that trying to link the doings of the material world with the detachment of the good god was an exercise in wishful thinking. With startling ease, the Cathar preacher could portray medieval society as a fanciful and illegitimate house of cards.

Catharism was, in short, perfect heresy to the powers-that-were, and it consequently inspired a loathing that knew few bounds. Rome could not allow itself to be publicly humiliated by the success of the Cathars. Although their teachings were often misunderstood by their opponents, fantastic slanders were concocted and repeated—in good faith—about their practices. Their name, once thought to mean "the pure," is not their own invention; *Cathar* is now taken as a twelfth-century German play on words implying a cat worshiper. It was long bruited about that Cathars performed the so-called obscene kiss on the rear end of a cat. They were said to consume the ashes of dead babies and indulge in incestuous orgies. Also common was the epithet *bougre*, a corruption of *Bulgar*—a reference to a sister church of heretical dualists in eastern Europe. *Bougre* eventually gave English *bugger,* which is yet another proclivity once ascribed to Cathar enthusiasts. The term *Albigensian,* snubbed by modern historical convention for circumscribing the geographic reach of Catharism, was the invention of a companion of the crusade who related that the heretics believed that no one could sin from the waist down. We now know that the Cathars referred to themselves, rather soberly, as "good Christians."

Yet rumors about cat fondling and baby burning found listeners, as did more accurate accounts about the rise of an alternate Christian creed. The might of feudal Europe fell upon Languedoc in a righteous fury. In many ways, the hatred aroused by the heretics masked a deeper antipathy, one that pitted the twelfth century's spiritual ebullience against the thirteenth century's culture of lawmaking and codification. In its largest sense, then, the Cathar wars arose because Western civilization had reached a crossroads—historian R. I. Moore has provocatively seen the years around 1200 as a watershed that led to "the formation of a persecuting society." Choices were made that would take centuries to undo. Less grandly, the fate of the Cathars can be viewed as the story of a dissidence unprepared for the vigor of its opponents. The Languedoc of the Cathars was too weakened by tolerance to withstand the single-minded certainties of its neighbors.

This telling of the Cathar drama, intended for nonspecialists, relies on the diligent research conducted by academic historians in the last half century. The principal primary sources behind the story will vary according to which act is unfolding. For the rise of the heretics from the 1150s on, the documentary record is spotty, and those documents that do exist—principally letters and the acts of Church councils—were penned by their enemies. If the Cathars had a written corpus at that time, it was destroyed by the Dominican inquisitors charged with extirpating the heresy 100 years later. Ironically, it took a twentieth-century Dominican friar, Antoine Dondaine, to dispel the fog of calumny and guesswork surrounding early Catharism by scouring archives to uncover heretical catechisms and treatises previously unknown to historians.

As for the twilight years of the heresy, the Dominicans again played a role crucial to our understanding. However destructive they were of Catharism in general, the medieval friars proved splendid curators of its decline by taking down the proceedings of their investigations. The transcripts of Inquisition interrogations, the spoken words of long-vanished peasants and burghers, have been made widely available in recent years and form an inestimable boon to students of the period. One need only refer to *Montaillou: The Promised Land of Error*, Emmanuel Le Roy Ladurie's classic work on one of the last redoubts of Catharism, to see the value of Inquisition registers in reconstructing the past.

The heart of the story, however, takes place between the Cathars' rise and fall, in the momentous time of open conflict that began with the sack of Béziers in 1209 and ended at the fall

of Montségur in 1244. Fortunately, there were four contemporary chroniclers—only one of whom took the side of Languedoc—to witness and record the sudden triumphs and
reversals of this eventful period, as well as several later medieval
commentators who quite rightly found the tale to be compelling.
Taken together—the manuscripts bequeathed to us by chroniclers, commentators, inquisitors, clergymen, and lords—the
sources offer a detailed and complex picture of a time abounding
with people of great conviction and courage. The Church and
its allies counted, among others: Lotario dei Conti di Segni, the
charismatic Roman baron crowned Pope Innocent III; Domingo
de Guzmán, the barefoot St. Dominic crying out in the Cathar
wilderness; Simon de Montfort, a devout warrior intent on building an empire; Bishop Fulk of Toulouse, a troubadour turned
persecutor; and Arnold Amaury, the papal legate lacking even
the ghost of a scruple. In the other camp stood Count Raymond
VI of Toulouse, the leading lecher, diplomat, and nobleman of
Languedoc; Raymond Roger of Foix, a mountain lord given to
exacting horrific revenge; Guilhabert of Castres, a prominent
Cathar fugitive who eluded both crusader and inquisitor; Peter
Autier, a wealthy notary turned heretical ringleader; and William
Bélibaste, a murderous holy man whose burning in 1321 marked
the disappearance of the faith.

Cathar missionaries walked the pathways of rural Languedoc two full centuries before the era of Joan of Arc; three,
before Martin Luther; four, before the *Mayflower*. The immense
distance between us and them would be even more daunting
were it not for the truth behind the axiom enunciated by a disciple of David Hume: "The past has no existence except as a
succession of present mental states." The epilogue of this work
will therefore survey the luxuriant oddness of Catharism in our

own day, which has seen the Cathars come in from the shadow-land of the recondite and enter the unruly marketplace of Euro-pean memory. Indeed, the Cathars have been championed, with varying degrees of seriousness, by vegetarians, nationalists, feminists, treasure hunters, New Agers, civil libertarians, Church bashers, and pacifists. Their former hideouts—shattered castles in the foothills of the Pyrenees—have become hiking destinations. Their less benign admirers have included Nazis and, more recently, self-immolating members of the Order of the Solar Temple. A recent French novel even has neo-Cathars combating the forces of American corporate imperialism. In some quarters, the Cathars inspire the same mixture of awe and occult respect surrounding the native peoples of the New World. The heretics of Montségur have become European stand-ins for the Hopis, their beliefs pointing to a spiritual choice etched not against the dreamscape of the desert but against the background of medieval nightmare. Despite the great gulf of centuries, the Cathars still haunt the timeless highlands of Languedoc.

1.

Languedoc and the Great Heresy

LANGUEDOC'S PATCHWORK OF olive groves and vineyards stretches from the sea to the mountains, an arc of hard-won prosperity reaching from the salty mouth of the Rhône to the lazy flood of the Garonne. The land, scorched by the sun and scoured by the wind, seems created for a tale of sudden change. In the reedy marshes of the Mediterranean coast stand the cities of Nîmes, Montpellier, Béziers, and Narbonne, already lively outposts of empire when the centurions of Rome called the area the *provincia Narbonnensis*. By the time of the Cathars, these centers of rough civility had long since come in out of the night of chaos following the collapse of the classical world. Their dockside warehouses overflowed anew with wine and oil, wool and leather; their richer townspeople, clad in costly silks and brocades, traded with their counterparts in Spain, Italy, and beyond.

The warm littoral plain of the traders quickly gives way to

more rugged surroundings. Close to the shore rise the bleached heights of the Corbières, a range of limestone peaks that stretches inland to the south of the River Aude. The summits of these mountains, now crowned with ruined castles, were ideal for watching the tramp of armies in the river valley below. There, in the Aude's rumpled geometry of field and village, ranks of cypress trees compete with grapevines in giving order to the landscape. Far away to the north loom the rocky plateau of the Minervois, its parasol pines teetering over steep ravines, and the Montagne Noire (the black mountain), a brooding forested prominence that lies across the countryside like some great beached whale.

Beyond the turrets and ramparts of Carcassonne, some forty miles from the coast, the Corbières and the Montagne Noire disappear, and the earth fans out into a succession of gentle ridges. In the summer, the land bakes and the cicadas sing; irregular swatches of cultivation soften the long hogbacks in the rolling panorama. This fertile area comprised the heartland of Catharism. In such towns as Lavaur, Fanjeaux, and Montréal, dualism won its largest following.

To the west of these sleepy settlements lies the broad rich plain of Toulouse, leaden green in the heat. The great city, surpassed in size only by Rome and Venice in the Latin Christendom of 1200, sits on a bend of the River Garonne as it uncoils slowly on its long journey to the Atlantic. The river rises far in the south, in the rock and snow that separate France from Spain. The bleak black majesty of the Pyrenees marks the limit of Languedoc with a towering finality. It was within sight of their summits that such outposts as Montségur and Montaillou witnessed the ultimate stages of the Cathar story.

Wedged between more celebrated cousins—to the east,

Provence; to the west, Aquitaine; to the south, Aragon and Catalonia—Languedoc has never been redeemed from its original sin of sheltering heresy. Incorporated by force into the kingdom of France as a result of the Albigensian Crusade, the region took generations to rediscover the nascent nationalism that northern knight and Dominican inquisitor first aroused, then crushed, in the thirteenth century. Today, it is still more an imaginary construct than a cohesive entity. It doesn't exist as a full-fledged nation or province, all of which suits its role as standard-bearer of the Cathar invisible.

Even its name reflects the chimerical. Languedoc is a contraction of *langue d'oc*, that is, the language of yes—or rather, the languages in which the word *yes* is *oc*, not *oui*. The patois of Paris and its surrounding Ile de France eventually evolved into French; the languages of oc, or Occitan and its related dialects—Languedocien, Gascon, Limousin, Auvergnat, Provençal—were far closer to Catalan and Spanish. Over time Occitan was decisively exiled to the outermost fringes of the Romance conversation, and the butter-smooth tongue of the French northerners came to dominate Languedoc. Yet the memory of the displaced idiom abides, if only in the twangy way French is now spoken in the south. Whereas the hubbub of café debate in say, Normandy, sounds like a mellifluous exchange between articulate cows, the tenor of the same discussion in Languedoc is akin to a musician tuning a large, and very loud, guitar. This, the echo of old Occitan, can be heard everywhere.

It was in the Occitan language that troubadour poetry first flowered in the twelfth century. In the fields and groves of Languedoc, love was discovered and the erotic rekindled. Jongleurs—the performers of troubadour works—sang of a coy, courtly game of deferred pleasure, exalted sublimation and, ultimately, adulterous fulfillment. The idea of *fin'amors* was a fresh, heady breeze of individual transcendence imbued with the spirit of medieval Languedoc. While beyond the Loire and the Rhine noblemen were still stirred by epics about the viscera dripping from Charlemagne's sword, their counterparts in the sunny south were learning to count the ways. The ethos of amorous longing, so much at odds with the mix of rapine and piety that passed for normal behavior everywhere else, gave a different cast to Languedoc's life of the mind.

The region's distinctiveness showed up elsewhere during this period. In the coastal cities, the Jews of Languedoc were inventing and exploring the mystical implications of the Kabbalah, proving that spiritual ferment was by no means confined to the Christian majority. In the more material world, the burghers of Languedoc were wresting power from the feudal families who had ruled the land since the time of the Visigoths. Money, the enemy of the agrarian caste sysem, was circulating again, as were ideas. On the paths and rivers of the Languedoc of 1150, there were not only traders and troubadours but also pairs of itinerant holy men, recognizable by the thin leather thong tied around the waist of their black robes. They entered villages and towns, set up shop, often as weavers, and became known for their honest, hard work. When the time came, they would talk—first, in the moonlight beyond the walls, then out in the open, before the fireplaces of noble and burgher, in the houses of tradespeople, near the stalls of the marketplace. They asked for nothing, no alms, no obeisance; just a hearing. Within a generation, these Cathar missionaries had converted thousands. Languedoc had become host to what would be called the Great Heresy.

The small town of St. Félix en Lauragais, huddled on its prow of granite in a sea of waving green, teemed with visitors in early May of 1167. From the windows of their hostelries, the newcomers could look out over fields of spring wheat and be thankful for the felicity of a time without famine. Not that they thought the good god had had a hand in such material good fortune, for the guests of St. Félix were dualist grandees—heresiarchs—from distant lands. They had gathered here to talk, openly, without fear of persecution or contradiction, at a great conclave in the castle of a local noble. It was the first and only meeting of its kind, a Cathar International of spiritual dissent. The Catholic bishop in his palace in Toulouse, a day's ride to the west, would not have received an invitation.

The townspeople no doubt greeted the robed heresiarchs by bowing deeply and reciting a prayer that asked for assurance of a good end to their lives. This ritual, known as the *melioramentum*, marked the supplicants as believers in the Cathar message. These believers, or *credentes*, were not, properly speaking, Cathars but rather sympathizers who bore witness and showed deference to the faith. The credentes had to await a future life to accede to the status of the Cathar elect.

Throughout Languedoc the believers overwhelmingly outnumbered the holy few, whom the Church would later label the *Perfect*—as in perfected, or fully initiated, heretics. It was the Perfect, the black-robed visitors to St. Félix, who were the true, seditious Cathars. An austere class of monks-in-the-world, the Perfect showed by example alone that there was a way out of the cycle of reincarnation. Their holiness made them living saints, equal in stature, in the view of the credentes, to Jesus' apostles. Having arrived at the last phase of worldly existence, the Perfect prepared for a final journey; their lives of self-denial ensured that at their death they would not return. Rather, their imprisoned spirit would at last be freed to join the eternal, invisible Goodness. Eventually, all people would be among the Perfect, in the sere and spartan waiting room of bliss. In the meantime, the simple Cathar believers could conduct themselves as they saw fit, but it was best to follow the teachings of the gospels: Love your neighbor and the peace that goodness and honesty bring.

The Perfect in St. Félix acknowledged the homage of the credentes with a ritual response to the melioramentum. Normally, the utterances would have been exclusively in Occitan, the lingua franca of the rolling farmland in which St. Félix was just one of many small settlements. But, given the uniqueness of the occasion, some of the Perfect answered in the *langue d'oïl*, the ancestor of French. A certain Robert d'Epernon, leader of the Cathar faith in northern France, had come to the meeting along with several of his fellow Perfect. The melioramentum response was also given in the tongue that would mature as Italian. This was spoken by a Milanese gravedigger named Mark, one of the pioneers of Catharism in Lombardy, where the growing towns were wracked by strife between the pope and the Germanic emperor. In this year of 1167, the towns and the papacy founded the defensive Lombard League to thwart the designs of Emperor Frederick Barbarossa. In the cracks caused by this power struggle, the heretical faith of Mark and his fellows was allowed to flower.

Mark had come to St. Félix as an escort. Nicetas, his traveling companion, spoke Greek, a language not heard in these peasant surroundings since the local Latin gentry recited it in their literary academies some 800 years previously. Nicetas, whose identity has never been fully established, was most probably the bishop of Constantinople for the Bogomil faith, a dualist creed that had arisen in eastern Europe when a tenth-century Macedonian monk known as "Beloved of God" (*Bogomil*, in Slavonic) started spreading the good-and-evil news. Dualism, a metaphysic known to Christianity since the gnostics of antiquity, had a following in several lands controlled by the Byzantine Empire. Although mystery surrounds the genesis of the Cathars, it is reasonable to assume that the Bogomils* may have initially acted as mentors to the Western heresy, especially as the contacts between Greek East and Latin West increased after the turn of the first millennium.

As a heresiarch from the East, Nicetas brought an impressive pedigree of dissent to the meeting in St. Félix. One of his predecessors, a certain Basil, had openly tried to convert the Byzantine emperor to the ways of dualism in the year 1100. The emperor was not amused, and Basil the Bogomil was burned for his temerity just outside the hippodrome of Constantinople. For the Cathar Perfect, however, the martyrdom suffered by the Bogomils, no matter how glorious, mattered less than the conduit of legitimacy they represented.

Through Nicetas's fingers passed the power of the *consolamentum*, the sole dualist sacrament. It transformed the ordinary believer into one of the Perfect, who then, in turn, could "console" others ready to live their final, holy life. Baptism, confirmation, ordination, and, if received at death's door, extreme unction all rolled into one, the consolamentum entailed the laying-on of hands and repeated injunctions to live a flawlessly chaste and ascetic existence. The Perfect had to abstain from any form of sexual intimacy, pray constantly, and fast frequently.

---

*The very last of the Bogomils, many of whom converted to Islam, were reported in Bosnia, in 1867.

When allowed to eat, they had to avoid all meat or any by-product of reproduction, such as cheese, eggs, milk, or butter. They could, however, drink wine and eat fish, as the latter was believed by medieval man to be the product of spontaneous generation in water. One slip in this strictly enforced regimen—be it as minor as a nibble of veal or a stolen kiss—and the status of Perfect vanished. The backslider had to receive the consolamentum again, as would all others whom the imperfect Perfect had "consoled" in his or her career. The Catholic precept of *ex opere operato, non ex opere operantis* ([grace] results from what is performed, not who performs it), through which a sacrament remains valid no matter how corrupt its celebrant, was rejected out of hand by the Cathars. The consolamentum had to be immaculate.

For the Perfect in St. Félix that day, there was no ecclesiastical hierarchy, no church as such, not even a building or chapel. The northern French Cathars would have shrugged at the laying of the cornerstone of Paris's Notre Dame Cathedral four years earlier. To the dualists, the continuity of the consolamentum from the time of the apostles was the invisible edifice of the eternal, literally handed down from one generation to the next as a kind of supernatural game of tag. The sacrament was the lone manifestation of the divine in this world. The Cathars believed that Jesus of Nazareth, an apparition rather than a gross material being, had come to Earth as a messenger carrying the dualist truth and as the initiator of the chain of the consolamentum. The Nazarene's death, if indeed he did die, was almost incidental; certainly it was not the unique redemptive instant of history as proclaimed by the Church.

The Perfect maintained that the cross was not something to be revered; it was simply an instrument of torture, perversely glorified by the Roman faith. They also looked on aghast at the cult of saintly relics. Those bits of bone and cloth for which churches were built and pilgrimages undertaken belonged to the realm of matter, the stuff created by the evil demiurge who fashioned this world and the fleshy envelope of the human. He had created the cosmos, tempted the angels out of heaven, then trapped them in the perishable packages of the human body. What counted, in the greater scheme of things, was only one's spirit, that which remained of one's nature as a fallen angel, that which remained connected to the good. To think otherwise was to be deluded. The sacraments dispensed by the Church were nothing more than codswallop.

The pious outlaws of 1167 referred to the majority faith as "the harlot of the Apocalypse" and "the church of wolves." Not for them Rome's claims to temporal and spiritual preeminence. It had been ninety years since Hildebrand, the Tuscan radical elected as Pope Gregory VII, pronounced papal supremacy over all other powers. Kings, bishops, cardinals, and princes had been bickering ever since. Three years after the meeting at St. Félix, the thuggish confidants of Henry II of England broke into Canterbury Cathedral and murdered Thomas Becket, the archbishop who defied the royal demand to bring felonious priests to trial in secular courts. The assassination would be medieval Europe's most notorious, but for the Cathars the act, aside from its abhorrent savagery, was totally without further meaning, having occurred in a void. There could be no legitimate kingdom, or church, of this Earth; thus the array of legal arguments presented by both Church and Crown amounted to utter casuistry.

The credentes were told to ignore other yarns spun in Rome. Catharism held that man and woman were one. A human being had been reincarnated many times over—as peasant, prin-

cess, boy, girl—but again what counted was one's divine, imma-
terial, sexless self. If the sexes insisted on coming together and
thereby prolonging their stay in the world of matter, they could
do so freely, outside of marriage, yet another baseless sacrament
invented by a priestly will to power. The so-called Petrine commission, by which the pope still claims authority through direct
descent from the apostle Peter, could also be ignored. The most
fateful pun in Western history—"You are Peter, on this rock
[*petra*] I will build my church" (Matthew 16:18)—failed to edify
the Perfect. For them, the pope teetered atop a rickety fiction,
his pronouncements a perpetual source of pointless mischief. The
mania for crusades, begun in 1095, was a recent example. The
journey to Jerusalem, with swords shamefully raised against
other hapless prisoners of matter, had to be renounced for the
journey within. All violence was loathsome.

There can be no doubt that these men and women of St.
Félix were well and truly heretical, by every definition except
their own. Nicetas would "reconsole" some of them who had
journeyed there from Champagne, Ile de France, and Lombardy,
so that they could be absolutely sure of their otherworldly credentials. To them, he was not a pope, or even a bishop in the
traditional sense, but just a distinguished elder who had received
the consolamentum properly and who should thus be treated
with respect. Individual Cathars had their differences—some
were more radically dualist than others—just as Catharism did
not completely dovetail with Nicetas's Bogomil creed. But that
hardly mattered. The news of St. Félix's extraordinary days of
May proved something else, something far more disturbing to
the exponents of orthodox Christianity. The heretics were now
united in a novel, ominous way.

Prior to the meeting in 1167, heresy had seemed a sporadic affair, launched by charismatic loners taking advantage of a continent-wide upsurge in religious longing. Throughout the twelfth century, there were calls for a clergy more responsive to the spiritual needs of the growing towns. Religion was becoming personal again, and ephemeral messiahs and cranky reformers sprouted like weeds in an untended garden.

In Flanders in the 1110s, a certain Tanchelm of Antwerp rode roughshod over wealthy prelates, attracting an army of followers who, it is said, revered him so much that they drank his bathwater. Peasant Brittany fell under the sway of an illiterate visionary named Eudo. His disciples sacked monasteries and churches before he was declared a lunatic and thrown in prison. Nearby, in Le Mans, France, a wayward Benedictine monk called Henry of Lausanne profited from the bishop's absence to turn the whole town into an anticlerical carnival. When the bishop returned and at last managed to reenter his city, the voluble Henry took to the road and headed south, accompanied by a retinue of smitten women. One commentator noted, in the lively metaphorical idiom of the day, that Henry "has returned to the world and the filth of the flesh, like a dog to its vomit."

Tanchelm, Eudo, and Henry could at first be shrugged off by the Church as merely misguided in their enthusiasms. After all, orthodoxy had its own eccentric firebrands in this heyday of spiritual exaltation. The unkempt Robert of Arbrissel, a monk the equal of Henry for his preaching prowess, padded around in a skimpy loincloth wowing and winning female followers before finally being prevailed upon to found an abbey for women and men at Fontevrault, in the Loire Valley. Another, Bernard of Tiron, was so given to producing and inducing fits of weeping that his shoulders were said to be perpetually soaking.

These men gradually gave way to less conciliatory preachers. Peter of Bruis unleashed an orgy of church pillaging and crucifix burning reminiscent of the iconoclasts of Byzantium. Like the Cathars, he was dismissive of Church wealth and the imagery of the cross. Unlike the Cathars, Peter was careless. At a bonfire of statuary near the mouth of the Rhône on Good Friday of 1139, he turned his back one time too many, and some enraged townspeople tossed him into the flames. More alarming yet was Arnold of Brescia, a former student of the great Peter Abelard. A rabble-rouser determined to save the Church from itself, Arnold proclaimed Rome a republic in 1146 and chased the terrified pope from the city. It would take eight long years before Nicholas Breakspear, the sole Englishman to be the pontiff, could move back to his residence at the Lateran Palace, thanks to the self-interested help of Emperor Barbarossa. Arnold was duly arrested, strangled, and burned, and his ashes were thrown into the Tiber, so that none of his large Roman following could start a cult with his corpse.

Yet even these extreme instances of Church-baiting could be ascribed, charitably, to an excess of reformist zeal. Such was patently not the case with the Cathars. They stood aloof from orthodoxy, and, as soon became obvious, they did not stand alone. Whereas there were few with enough physical stamina to live as Perfect, there were credentes by the thousands.

Bernard of Clairvaux
(Musée Condé, Chantilly/Giraudon)

In 1145, the influential Bernard of Clairvaux traveled to Languedoc to put the fear of God back into the followers of Henry of Lausanne. Mystical, anorexic, brilliant, eloquent, and polemical (he penned the sick dog trope cited earlier), Bernard was the greatest churchman of the century, a monk who was feared, admired, and obeyed more than any mere pope of the time. He proceeded in quiet triumph, feted and flattered everywhere as he wrested a few people away from Henry's histrionics of protest. But Bernard was no fool; he sensed that there were other, more serious subversions afoot. At Verfeil, a market center northeast of Toulouse, the unthinkable occurred. Mounted knights pounded on the doors of the church and clashed their swords together, rendering Bernard's sermon inaudible and turning his golden tongue to dust. The great man was laughed out of town.

Once safely back home in his monastic cell in Champagne, Bernard recovered his voice and sounded the alarm. A prodigious letter writer, the great man informed his correspondents that what had previously only been suspected was now confirmed: Down-to-earth reform was being supplanted by the metaphysical rebellion of heresy. Like thunderstorms on a hot and unsettled summer's day, dualists were sighted everywhere in western Europe. England, Flanders, France, Languedoc, Italy—no place seemed safe for the traditional Christian faith. In Cologne, Germany, in both 1143 and 1163, fires were lit under the feet of dualist believers, and a German monk who witnessed their torment labeled the unfortunates *Cathars*.

Understandably, the dualists were given to discretion. In 1165, several were brought before an audience in Lombers, a town ten miles to the south of Albi. In attendance were six bishops, eight abbots, the viscount of the region, and Constance, a sister of the king of France. Everyone in Lombers on that day knew that there was dry wood in the vicinity.

The Perfect, led by a certain Olivier, were cagey enough to cite the New Testament at soporific length. Wisely, they did not state that they entirely rejected the Hebrew Bible, or Old Testament, in keeping with their belief that the somewhat headstrong god described therein was none other than the Evil One, the creator of matter. In this, they rejoined the gnostics of antiquity. As for Jesus of Nazareth, they avoided saying that he was a mere apparition, a hallucination who could not possibly have been a being of flesh and blood. That—a heretical opinion known as Docetism—would have constituted a whopping contradiction of the orthodox doctrine of the Incarnation and given them away immediately.

Eventually, the Cathars at Lombers were flushed out on the question of oath taking. Citing Christian Scriptures, they said it was forbidden to swear any oath whatsoever, which was a red flag in a society where sworn fealty formed the Church-mediated bond of all feudal relations. This aversion to oaths was a hallmark of Cathar belief, a logical extension of the clear-cut divide they saw between the world of humanity and the ether of the Good. When the role of the Church in the world was evoked, the veil dropped entirely, and Olivier and his fellow Cathars attacked the bishops and abbots at Lombers as "mercenaries," "ravening wolves," "hypocrites," and "seducers." Although offensive in the extreme to the churchmen, leveling such charges may have secretly pleased the assembled laity, who harbored no great love for the tax-gathering clergy. In the end, despite the universal sentiment that Olivier and his friends were heretics, everyone was allowed to go home unharmed. The lord of Lombers no doubt sensed that it would be impolitic to put local heroes to death.

The memory of that showdown was only two years old when the Cathars gathered in St. Félix, some thirty miles south of Lombers. Nicetas and the assembled Perfect, unmolested and unafraid, undertook the task of organizing the growing faith. Cathar dioceses were drawn up, and "bishops"—coordinators rather than feudal overseers like their Catholic counterparts— were appointed or confirmed. We know the names of the men in charge of the Cathar homeland: Sicard Cellerien got Albi; Bernard Raymond, Toulouse; Guirald Mercier, Carcassonne. Quietly, without the theatrics of earlier heretics, the Cathars were laying the foundations of a revolution. After St. Félix, the greatest fear of the orthodox—the rivalry of a powerful counter-church—came closer to being a reality.

2.

Rome

ON FEBRUARY 22, 1198, a generation after the Cathar conclave in St. Félix, the leaders of the Church gathered in
Rome as Lotario dei Conti di Segni was crowned Pope Innocent
III. Lotario's solemn procession made its way from its assembly
point on the hill of the Vatican past the churches and fortified
mansions of the city. The snaking ceremonial moved from out
of the shadow of Hadrian's mausoleum and through the *abitato*,
the warren of streets in the bend on the left bank of the Tiber.
Robed men yanked on ropes in dozens of belfries to rend the air
with a deafening din of celebration; thousands lined the parade
route to watch. All eyes were on the thirty-seven-year-old pope,
mounted on a white charger and clad in the regalia of his office.
He wore the pallium, a lambskin cloth draped over his shoulders,
and the tiara, a bejeweled coronet affixed to a silken skullcap.

A millennium earlier in the Eternal City, a man of his caliber
might have been made emperor of the known world. For Lota-

rio, there was little difference in the two positions—except that the supreme pontiff of Latin Christendom was by far the superior one. The pope was the sole earthly guardian of absolute, irrefragable truth. Disagreement with him was not dissent, it was treason.

Even before his election on the second ballot, Lotario had had no doubts about the sanctity of his new role. He became, in his words, "higher than man, but lower than God." As Innocent III, he proclaimed for all the world to hear in a sermon, "We are the successor of the Prince of the Apostles, but we are not his vicar, nor the vicar of any man or Apostle, but the vicar of Jesus Christ himself." He had looked downward in the morning as the cardinals at St. Peter's trooped before him and performed the proskynesis, the kissing of his feet. The more abject the posture, the more correct was the gesture. In this, Lotario trod the theocratic trail blazed in the eleventh century by Hildebrand, who, as Pope Gregory VII, had affirmed the pontiff's superiority over all the crowned heads of Christendom. Previously, kingship was thought divinely ordained; Hildebrand and his successors had informed a misguided medieval world that it was up to the pope, and the pope alone, to decide who could rule. The man wearing the bishop's miter in Rome was mightier than any bearded ruffian with a leafy family tree.

Well-traveled and well-informed, Lotario was aware, however, that what looked splendid sealed with a leaden *bulla* (hence a papal "bull") often ended up a dead letter in the royal chanceries of the north. A new century was about to dawn, and Lotario wanted to make sure that the next 100 years would be rosier than the last. The 1100s had not been a happy time for the vicars of Christ. Prior to Innocent, eleven of the sixteen twelfth-century pontificates saw popes forcibly kept out of Rome by rioters, re-

Pope Innocent III
(Thirteenth-century fresco in the monastery Sacro Speco, Subiaco)

publicans, or agents of distant kings. The Roman commune led by Arnold of Brescia at midcentury was a particularly vivid episode in a recurring nightmare. In 1145, Pope Lucius II died of wounds incurred in a battle for control of the Capitol; thirty years earlier, a frail old Gelasius II was seated backward on a mule and forced to endure the jeers of his enemies. "Antipopes" were regularly elected by rival Roman clans and by churchmen in the thrall of the German emperor, the single biggest threat to the papacy's independence.

At the beginning of the 1190s, the man on the German throne, Henry VI, the son of Barbarossa, had seemed poised to take over all of central Europe and, more important, the entire Italian peninsula. An ambitious and arrogant young monarch, he bestrode the continent like a latter-day Caesar; Celestine III, the aging pope in a besieged Rome, could do little else but try to have the man murdered. The plot was discovered, and Henry dispatched the papal assassin by nailing a red-hot crown into his skull. Then, in September 1197, Henry fell ill, most probably with malaria, and died in Messina, Sicily. It was a blessed mosquito for the papacy. Five months later, Henry's infant son, Frederick, had become the ward of none other than Lotario dei Conti, the child's birthright soon to be occulted by the skirted intrigues skillfully conducted by the new pope. The future looked bright for theocracy.

But as Lotario guided his horse through the straw-strewn streets, past dwellings proud and humble, he had to know that the Roman skies over his papacy were not cloudless. Hundreds of forbidding stone towers, constructed by the powerful families of the city, loomed over him like a forest of menace. As a Conti, Lotario had to contend with such clans as the Frangipani, Colonna, Annibaldi, and Caetani, all of whom counted cardinals and rich barons in their midst. The Vassaletti had cornered the market on quarrying classical Roman statuary into chunks of marble to be sold throughout Europe. It was the Frangipani who had made Gelasius take his shameful mule ride. And it was they and their allies who viewed this upstart Conti pope with misgiving.

To their patrician Roman noses, Lotario and his kinsmen still had a lingering scent of the barnyard to them. The Conti were from the Campagna, the rolling hinterland to the southeast of the city. Their rough-hewn castle, which still crowns the hilltop village of Gavignano, overlooked a quilted valley that had known the hand of man since the time of the Etruscans. A few miles to the west, tucked behind steep green slopes, stood the larger town of Segni. It was between there and Gavignano that the estates of the Conti di Segni produced the wealth that fueled social striving.

Sometime around the middle of the century, Lotario's father, Trasimondo, had wooed and won Claricia, a Roman heiress of the influential Scotti family. Given an exalted station in society through his highborn mother, the young Lotario eventually left the hills and valleys around Gavignano and rode toward Rome to make his mark in the world. Most probably, he took the Appian Way into the city, passing the hulking ruins of antiquity guarded by rows of pencil-thin cypress trees. Destiny smiled on him in 1187 when his mother's brother became Pope Clement III and ensured his talented nephew's rise to prominence. Lotario studied theology in Paris and learned the law in Bologna, and wrote several closely argued treatises. One of these, *De miseria condicionis humanae* (The wretchedness of man's lot), won him lasting recognition among learned pessimists throughout Europe. His fierce and never idle legalistic intellect, wedded to the diplomatic guile of an Italian aristocrat, would make Lotario a redoubtable opponent to any who dared stand in his way.

Like the pilgrims who flocked to the sights described in *Mirabilis Urbis Romae* (The wonders of the City of Rome), a popular twelfth-century guidebook, Lotario's procession would have passed through the neighborhood built over the Roman Forum. Tradition dictated that papal coronation parades stop at intervals along their route to receive the acclaim of the crowds and to distribute alms. No doubt at the arch of Septimius Severus, then 995 years old, Lotario's retinue came to halt. Of the two tall towers that medieval Romans had seen fit to build on the antique archway, the southernmost served as a belfry for the church of SS. Sergio and Bacco, where Lotario had served his cardinalate. The area of the Roman Forum had been the young man's home in the city, where he had mastered the intricacies of its turbulent civic politics. A few hundred yards from the church of SS. Sergio and Bacco, midway between Trajan's Column and the Colosseum, the new pope would commission a tower, the Torre dei Conti, as a great statement on the ambitions of his family. Lotario's brother Riccardo would build the tower to protect the Conti's new turf on the slopes leading to the Viminal Hill. The brown-brick monolith, called "unique in the world" by an astonished Petrarch, dominated the Capitol and the Quirinal, and would still do so if an earthquake in 1348 had not cut its height by half. Today it continues to loom over Nerva's Forum, a reminder that Lotario not only raised his family from obscurity to greatness but also gave Rome the fleeting impression of once again being the capital of the world.

Beyond the Colosseum, past the flank of the Celian Hill, the procession headed to its final destination amid the well-tended fields of the papacy's private domains. The basilica of St. John Lateran, the grandest and oldest of Rome, was built some 850 years earlier by the emperor Constantine, who donated the land and the adjoining palace to the Church from the private estate of his wife, Fausta. It was Constantine who decreed Christianity a legitimate Roman cult. His mother, Helena, had the staircase from Pontius Pilate's quarters in Jerusalem hauled to the Lateran Palace. The pope could climb the twenty-eight steps of the Scala Santa in imitation of Jesus whenever the responsibility of his office weighed too heavily.

His parade finished, Lotario dismounted and entered St. John Lateran, his cathedral as the bishop of Rome. The church was a treasure house of relics, the celebrity memorabilia of an age when faith outshone fame. Lotario had no doubt seen the Lateran's collection: the heads of St. Peter and St. Paul; the Ark of the Covenant; the Tablets of Moses; the Rod of Aaron; an urn of manna; the Virgin's tunic; five loaves and two fishes from the Feeding of the Five Thousand; and the dinner table from the Last Supper. The pope's private chapel held the foreskin and umbilical cord of Jesus. Lotario's beliefs, like those of the millions he now led, were rooted firmly in the material.

The Lateran Palace, where a banquet awaited the procession's participants, had been the principal residence of the popes since Constantine's Fausta was forced to find other lodgings some eight centuries earlier. Yet Lotario was aware that the Lateran now stood marooned in an archipelago of Frangipani strongholds around the Celian Hill. He was determined not to be cowed or held captive here; thus it was he who definitively nudged the papal court to where his triumphant day had begun, near the tomb of St. Peter on the grounds of the Vatican.

From summers of childhood in the Campagna to this portentous day in the winter of 1198, Lotario's life had shaped him into a leader of unshakable convictions. He had been a boy when, in 1173, a pope in temporary residence in his hometown of Segni had proclaimed the murdered Thomas Becket a saint. Just thirteen, living with his family atop Gavignano, Lotario must have absorbed the lesson behind that beatification: No one must ever trifle with the Church. Becket went on to become the supernova of the medieval clerical firmament; when the apostate King Henry VIII robbed his tomb in the sixteenth century, he would make off with almost 5,000 ounces of gold. Lotario's destiny lay between the base calculations of ordinary monarchs and the exalted peaks of sainthood.

As Pope Innocent III, he had now been given, in his words, "not only the universal church but the whole world to govern." In many quarters of Europe, his beloved Church, buffeted by the changes of the twelfth century, had been left disorganized, discredited, or, worse still, corrupted. When he looked to the east, he saw Jerusalem still in the hands of the Muslims. On the Italian peninsula, years of turmoil had deprived the papacy of the lands from which it once drew income and temporal prestige. And to the west lay Languedoc, where the wound of heresy had been allowed to fester. A new pope had been chosen for a new century.

3.

The Turn of the Century

"To be always with a woman and not to have intercourse with her is more difficult than to raise the dead." So wrote a candid if frustrated Bernard of Clairvaux of the threat posed by the female to his pursuit of holiness. In this, the saint was roundly seconded by his fellow churchmen of the twelfth century. The days of powerful, pastoral abbesses, such as the Rhineland's Hildegard of Bingen, or even of joint foundations like Robert of Arbrissel's abbey for men and women at Fontevrault, were a distant memory in the era of Innocent III. Male monasteries that had sister convents began cutting ties of affiliation and withdrawing support. By the year 1200, the Church was turning its back on women. Henceforth they were to be nowhere near altar, school, conclave, or council. In the latter stages of the Middle Ages, the Virgin Mary would be tapped as a body double for all banished women of influence, her stature of semidivinity, arguably, a bone thrown to the metaphysically dispossessed. For many women, shut out of the sacristy and shut in the cloister, this was hardly enough.

As in so many other things, Catharism differed radically from the majority creed in its attitude toward women. In the three decades that lay between the meeting at St. Félix and Innocent's procession in Rome, the dualist faith had spread unchecked throughout Languedoc, its message transmitted by a determined matriarchy of revolt. It was no longer like some heterodox hot potato, to be juggled artfully by a showman before an awestruck crowd. Instead, Catharism had migrated to the home, its beliefs deeply interwoven into the fabric of Languedoc family life. The women Perfect had been hard at work.

Female Cathars, unlike their male counterparts, rarely traveled to proselytize. Instead they established group homes for the daughters, widows, and dowagers of the local petty nobility and artisan classes. Girls would be raised and educated in these homes and then go out into the world to marry and rear children who would, inevitably, become believers in the faith of their mothers. The number of credentes grew accordingly with each generation, as did the number of females opting for the rigors of life as a Perfect. Many of the latter did so as middle age approached.

Once they had survived the rigors of serial childbirth and done their dynastic duty, nothing prevented the ladies of Languedoc from receiving the consolamentum and taking up an honored position in the community. The quasi divine status of a Perfect—the Church offered nothing as remotely prestigious to women—came coupled with the commitment of Cathar homes to stay open and welcoming to the world at large. There was no cloister, for there were labors, both manual and spiritual, to be undertaken. Instead of inspiring miracles, visions, pogroms, and all the other trappings of popular Christian enthusiasms, Catharism became devastatingly domestic. When Bishop Fulk of Toulouse, one of the most determined enemies of the Cathars, reproached a Catholic knight for failing to punish heretics, the man replied, "We cannot. We have been reared in their midst. We have relatives among them and we see them living lives of perfection." It was asking too much of anyone to hunt down his mother.

The maverick faith could not fail to appeal to beleaguered medieval womanhood. Not since the time of the gnostics had women had such a say in the affairs of the hereafter. Simple credentes could bask in the reflected glory of their stronger sisters and, more important, take solace in the knowledge that they were not some sort of afterthought of the divine mind. In any event, the Evil One had created the world, so the shibboleths of its organization—including its sexual pecking order—were there to be endured, not endorsed. Like the Kabbalists who were their neighbors in Languedoc, the Cathar women found comfort in the notion of metempsychosis, the transmigration of souls.

Not that the Cathars were entirely free of the prejudices of the time. Some believers questioned by the Inquisition in the fourteenth century spoke of male Perfect teaching that one's last incarnation had to be as a man, if one were ever to leave this Earth for good. Clearly, this was a misogynist twist on earlier Cathar precepts. A few former female credentes, again under Inquisition questioning, told of being called sinks of corrupting temptation and blamed for encouraging procreation, an act which produced yet another prisoner of matter. Here, at least in its first proposition, was the familiar complaint of the medieval male ascetic, no matter what his faith. In this, some of the Cathar Perfect must have agreed with St. Bernard of Clairvaux.

Yet given the importance of women in spreading the faith, it is unlikely that such female-baiting formed a majority opinion in Catharism. The role of women was further enhanced by Languedoc's system of partible inheritance, whereby families split legacies evenly. Unlike the north's system, where everything went to the eldest son and the remainder of his siblings had to fend for themselves, the south's splintering of estates gave many women a slim margin of independence that they would not have enjoyed elsewhere. Noblewomen, especially, founded, managed, and led Cathar homes. Raymond Roger, the count of Foix, a mountain capital at the foot of the Pyrenees, would applaud in 1204 as his sister, Esclarmonde, received the consolamentum from Guilhabert of Castres in a ceremony held in Fanjeaux, a town near Carcassonne. With her, in a ceremony attended by most of Languedoc's nobility, were three ladies of equally exalted birth who would pledge their lives to spiritual perfection. When Raymond Roger's wife, Philippa, decided that she too wanted to be a Perfect, the count offered no objections.

In the numerous small fortified settlements dotting the landscape between Toulouse, Albi, and Carcassonne, Catharism touched a third to a half of the population. A network of religious women, whether Cathar grandmothers or daughters-in-law, was supporting the work of the itinerant men. In the prescribed absence of church buildings or even chapels, credentes gathered in homes run by female Perfect to listen to the visiting male Cathars from the cities. The most influential Perfect hostesses—Blanche of Laurac, Esclarmonde of Foix—had previously resided in the local castle. There, in the evening, the troubadours and jongleurs would come to entertain the same people who had been uplifted by the Cathars in the afternoon. The Perfect and the troubadours coexisted in the hearths of the

Languedoc nobility. From the dualists' love your neighbor to the jongleurs' love your neighbor's wife all in the course of a day, the Occitan culture of piety and fine feeling was slipping the traces of traditional Christianity. *Amor* was indeed the opposite of *Roma*. The consensual scholarly guess puts the number of Perfect at 1,000–1,500 in the Languedoc of the year 1200. Among the most effective of these were what one Occitan troubadour called, admiringly, *bela eretga*—the fair heretics.

None of Languedoc's spiritual eccentricity would have been possible without the tacit assent—or fecklessness—of its overlords. By the year 1200, the cause of religious sedition was well served by the region's fractured feudalism. The consolidation of power between king and clergy that would soon hoist the Ile de France and its dependencies into the first rank of medieval nations was singularly lacking in the south. Instead, Languedoc's nobles and churchmen fought like fishwives, often over the revenues that the merchants of the towns were appropriating for themselves. In such an anticlerical environment, an alternate faith like Catharism could prosper.

At the top of the shaky ladder of precedence was Raymond VI, count of Toulouse. His mother, Constance, who had attended the public hearing of the Cathars at Lombers in 1165, was the sister of the king of France. Raymond's father, Raymond V, appears to have been the last in his line to evince open support of the Church. In 1177, the elder man invited a bevy of prelates to sniff out Catharism in his capital of Toulouse, only to have the churchmen quickly discouraged by the immensity of the task. The one man convicted, a rich merchant, was forced to go on a

Seal of Raymond VI of Toulouse
(Archives Nationales, Paris)

pilgrimage to Palestine; on his return three years later, he was acclaimed a hero and given a position of high civic responsibility. In the household of the count, the younger Raymond no doubt failed to notice this outrage to the faith. Just turned twenty, he had already embarked on a precocious career of stealing his father's mistresses. His mother, citing marital mistreatment, had by that time fled Languedoc for the court of her brother in Paris, and her marriage to Raymond's father was annulled.

By the year 1200, Raymond VI was in his early forties, having inherited his title six years earlier. He had just buried his fourth and penultimate wife, Joan of England, the sister of Richard Lionheart and John Lackland. To the horror of the orthodox, Raymond's court was a cosmopolitan mix of Cathar, Catholic, and Jew, and his friends were not distinguished for their piety. One, a troubadour named Peire Vidal, once disguised himself as a wolf to woo the loveliest woman in Languedoc, Etiennette de Pennautier, whose licentious nickname was Loba, or she-wolf.

Although unsuccessful in winning the favors of Loba (unlike Raymond Roger, the count of Foix), Vidal won fame for his exploits and composed songs for the edification of his noble patron. It is not recorded whether Count Raymond courted Loba.

Presumably, Raymond had other compensations; certainly, he had other worries. In theory, his family held sway from the hills of Provence to the lowlands of the River Garonne; in practice, the situation was a dog's breakfast of conflicting allegiances, power-sharing arrangements, and hotly contested sources of money. After the ninth-century breakup of Charlemagne's empire, which had stretched from Saxony to Catalonia, the lands of Languedoc were parceled out among a myriad of warring factions. The noble families of the region, approximately 150 in all at the turn of the millennium, fought obscure territorial skirmishes for generations, ensuring that the countryside bristled with castles and defensive fortifications. Through shrewd marriages and successful sieges, Raymond's family, the Saint Gilles, had by the turn of the twelfth century established its preeminence, if not its dominion, in Languedoc.

Yet they were never to develop into a putative royal family of the south. Any chance the Saint Gilles clan had of increasing its power at home was squandered by its fondness for foreign adventure. Raymond's great-grandfather, Count Raymond IV, answered the call for the First Crusade and in 1099 led the Christian armies into Jerusalem. He then decided to stay in the East, carving out a kingdom for himself in what is now Lebanon,* and consigning a bastard son to look after the family possessions at home. Years of fitful struggle ensued in Languedoc, during which the Saint Gilles lands became fair game for neighboring

---

*There is still a St. Gilles Citadel in the harbor of Tripoli. It is known locally as Qal'at Sinjil.

clans, including those from Aquitaine, to the west, and Aragon, to the south. By the time a legitimate Saint Gilles had grown to manhood and moved from Palestine—Alfons-Jordan, so named for his baptism in the River Jordan—the family had let slip the opportunity to increase its power and lay the groundwork for a future kingdom. Elsewhere in the early twelfth century, such prominent families as the Capets of France had begun the long process of reining in their fractious barons, and the Plantagenets of England and Hohenstaufens of Germany hovered in the wings of power. Closer to Languedoc, the ruling families of Barcelona and Aragon had merged to form a coherent, powerful kingdom just south of the Pyrenees.

The years of absentee landlordship by the Saint Gilles would cost them dearly. As the twelfth century progressed, the south saw repeated disputes over jurisdiction as the rising clans of the north pressed claims to areas under the weak control of the Saint Gilles. Strategic marriages forestalled any great armed conflict—although Raymond's father had to undertake a series of minor defensive fights—so that by 1200 the Saint Gilles held territory in Provence as vassals of the Holy Roman emperor, land in the Toulousain from the king of France, and property in Gascony from the king of England. The king of Aragon had won control over much of the Mediterranean coast of Languedoc, including the important town of Montpellier. Given the rivalry between these overlords, the threat of war hung heavily over Languedoc. The balancing act required of Raymond VI was extremely delicate, especially as he, unlike northern barons and monarchs, did not own huge estates outright on which to rely for revenue or armed knights.

Raymond fared little better as liege lord of the greater noble families of the region. In the rugged foothills of the Pyrenees,

Toulouse

Allies of Toulouse

Aragon

Trencavel

© 2000 Jeffrey L. Ward

mulish independence was the rule, not the exception. The count of Foix, the man whose sister and wife became Perfect and who won the heart of the she-wolf Loba, exemplified the type of miscreant whose excesses Raymond was expected to curb. Whenever Raymond Roger of Foix murdered a priest or besieged a castle, as he sometimes did, Raymond of Toulouse was powerless to punish him, even had he been so inclined. The other mountain lords were similarly independent.

The prickliest thorn in Raymond's side came from the Trencavel family. They sat squarely in the middle of Languedoc, firmly ensconced behind the battlements of Carcassonne. Their vast holdings around the city, stretching as far as Béziers, sundered the Saint Gilles lands in two. To ensure their independence from Toulouse, the Trencavels had made themselves vassals —and thus protégés—of Aragon in 1150. Raymond, showing his usual preference for the bedroom over the battlefield, tried to neutralize the threat from Carcassonne by taking a Trencavel trophy wife, Beatrice of Béziers. Instead of founding a new dynasty, the couple eventually had their marriage annulled, and Beatrice became a chaste Cathar holy woman. It is unknown whether she went willingly or was shoved aside by Raymond, whose infatuation with the daughter of the king of Cyprus led to his third marriage. The result was that the patchwork of Trencavel and Saint Gilles loyalties remained as motley as ever.

The Church made the situation in Languedoc even more complex. Bernard of Clairvaux's Cistercian monastic movement— the reforming wing of the Benedictine family—had spread from its founding house in Cîteaux, Burgundy, to the south, attracting the talents of such men as Fulk of Marseilles, who would become the bishop of Toulouse. Its zealot monk-farmers, still in that period of grace when successful monasticism did not mean excessive waistlines, amassed thousands of acres of property through a combination of hard work and bequests of land from people hedging their bets on the hereafter. Visitors to present-day France, marveling at the picturesque ubiquity of villages no matter how steep the slope, wet the marsh, or barren the moor, are often admiring of the handiwork of the monks. They tamed the last wildernesses, enticed peasant pioneers into newly founded settlements, and became a tonsured gentry managing enormous estates. Given the absence of legitimate offspring among monks, these estates would not be subdivided in later generations.

Such wealth did not go unnoticed. First in line for a share of the riches were the Cistercians' fellow churchmen, the secular clergy—that is, priests living in lay society as opposed to the regular clergy, monks following some prescribed communal rule. Among Languedoc's secular clergy, there were breathtaking differences in levels of piety, liturgical literacy, and financial solvency. Bishops feuded with abbots over money, sometimes leaving parish churches vacant for years, their taxes and tolls the subject of acrimonious dispute. The office of bishop was a position very much of this world—as the Cathars never failed to deplore.

The strife between the monastic regular clergy and the secular clergy paled in comparison to the woes inflicted on them by the Languedoc laity. Attacking the property and persons of priests was something of a national pastime. The "Peace of God" movements, essentially oaths by which rambunctious nobles swore not to despoil defenseless clerics, had been started as early as the tenth century. In Languedoc, with its chronic lack of central authority, there was no force powerful enough to ensure that these oaths would be upheld. The glue of medieval society was coming unstuck. Hard-strapped counts, viscounts, and members of the petty nobility seldom came to the aid of embattled bishops—who, in any event, were rarely paragons of virtue. Tithes were routinely diverted to the coffers of secular grandees or simply not paid at all. In 1178, the Trencavels had thrown the bishop of Albi in prison; the following year, they added insult to injury by extorting a whopping 30,000 sols from the monastery of St.-Pons-de-Thomières.* Count Raymond of Toulouse made it something of a hobby to harass the abbots of the monastery near his ancestral seat of St. Gilles, a town in the Rhône delta.

Often the conflicts verged on the macabre. In 1197, the Trencavels contested the election of a new abbot in the highland monastery of Alet. Their emissary, Bertrand of Saissac, a nobleman with several Cathar Perfect in his family, came up with a novel solution to the dispute. He dug up the body of the former abbot, propped it upright in a chair, then called upon the horrified monks to listen carefully to the corpse's wishes. Not surprisingly, given such ghoulish encouragement, a friend of the Trencavels easily carried a new election. To make the proceedings legal, the consent of the Catholic hierarchy was needed, so Bertrand turned to the archbishop of Narbonne, the preeminent churchman of Languedoc. He was also its preeminent grifter. Innocent III would write of the Narbonne clergy in exasperation: "Blind men, dumb dogs who can no longer bark . . . men who will do anything for money . . . zealous in avarice, lovers of gifts, seekers of rewards. . . . The chief cause of all these evils is the archbishop of Narbonne, whose god is money, whose heart is in his treasury, who is concerned only with gold." The Trencavel request for confirmation of the new abbot's election came augmented by a handsome payoff, and approval was promptly given. A Catholic chronicler noted somberly that many people in Languedoc, when refusing to do a particularly unpleasant task, reflexively used the expression "I'd rather be a priest."

Although such anticlericalism existed elsewhere, Lan-

---

*The coup de grâce would come in the 1930s, when the cloister of St. Pons was moved to Toledo, Ohio.

guedoc's quarrels were endemic, not episodic, and came to be played out in a society that did not have just nobility and clergy competing for prizes at the expense of the peasantry. For, like Lombardy in northern Italy and Flanders by the English Channel, Languedoc of the year 1200 had become a landscape of towns, full of obstreperous burghers elbowing their way into what was once thought a divinely ordained procession of priest, knight, and serf. *Stadtluft macht frei* (City air makes men free) would run the later German byword about medieval towns, and Languedoc's precocious experience proved the axiom fully. The main centers—Montpellier, Béziers, Narbonne, Albi, Carcassonne, Toulouse—teemed with energy, most of them recovering the vigor they had known a millennium earlier under the Romans.

Toulouse, the most important of the lot, was self-governing, having purchased its freedoms from Raymond's father and elected consuls, called *capitouls*, to legislate in a new town hall built in 1189. In any city where a consular system took root, civic truculence became automatic. In 1167, the year of the Cathar meeting at St. Félix, the merchants of Béziers had even gone so far as to murder their Trencavel viscount. The capitouls of Toulouse, perhaps reflecting the diplomacy and disposition of their count, preferred to legislate reasonably about their pursuit of wealth and pleasure. An observer noted that in the city, a married person could not, by a law of the capitouls, be arrested "for reason of adultery, fornication or coitus in any store or house he or she rented, owned or maintained as a residence." Clearly, Languedoc's mix of troubadour and trader culture was cocking a snook at the Church.

The towns also began tolerating ideas and people usually kept outside the confines of the feudal Christian commonwealth.

Groups at the margin of society—and not just heretics—began testing the waters of the mainstream. Languedoc's numerous Jews, who had lived in the region since the time of the Romans, were among the prime beneficiaries of the culture of clemency that arose out of the crossfire of southern noble, cleric, and townsman. An Easter tradition called "strike the Jew," whereby members of the Toulouse Jewish community would be batted around a public square by Christians, was ended in the middle of the twelfth century, after hefty payments had been made to count and capitouls. The clergy protested, but the ban held. The Church, which had evolved a policy of clearly delineated ostracism of the Jews, howled even louder when non-Christians were allowed to own property and, in some instances, hold office. In Béziers in 1203, the chief magistrate in the Trencavel lord's absence—or *bayle*—was a Jew named Simon. In Narbonne, which supported a Talmudic school and several synagogues, some Jewish merchants possessed vineyards in the surrounding countryside and employed Christian peasants to work the land, an open flouting of the Church's prohibition on Jews having any kind of authority over Christians. Whereas these changes were usually effected through the greasing of palms or the paying of steep taxes, they nonetheless signaled the dawning of a freer, or at least more freewheeling, society.

From the perspective of a newly invigorated Rome, all of this took on the appearance of an infernal downward spiral, a slippery slope of moral and spiritual degeneracy. While hardly a multicultural Camelot, as sometimes suggested by its twentieth-century boosters, medieval Languedoc was exceptional enough to be viewed as objectionable. Innocent III would write frequently to Count Raymond and implore the scion of crusaders to act. One letter seethes, "So think, stupid man, think!"; another calls him a "creature both pestilent and insane." It is not clear, however, whether Raymond could act, given the fetters on his power, the autonomy of the towns, and the subversive spiritual tolerance that now existed between Languedoc's Catholics, Cathars, and Jews.

As it turned out, Raymond did nothing. The count of Toulouse would not persecute his own people. Innocent and his advisers, at a loss without a noble ally in Languedoc to suppress dissent, had to work a revolution of their own. As the new century dawned, the men of the Church set out to convince Raymond's people of the error of their ways. They met the heretics face-to-face.

4.

The Conversation

THE CATHARS AND THE CATHOLICS argued. On points of doctrine and Latin, on the role of the Church and the devil, on the nature and meaning of humanity's existence, on the beginning and the end of the cosmos. In the first years of the 1200s, Languedoc became a land of loud disputation, a medieval Chautauqua held by competing speakers with souls to save and demons to vanquish. The churchmen sought out the heretics and challenged them to debate. Local lords guaranteed safe-conduct for the participants and made their great halls and castle courtyards, ordinarily the haunt of troubadours and jongleurs, available to the robed holy men. Priest and Perfect squared off in blazing sunshine and guttering torchlight as the laity came in from the fields and out of the taverns to listen and to learn.

The Cathars fell back on the New Testament, which they knew in both its Latin and Occitan translations, and on the stellar example of their own lives of poverty and self-denial. According to their lights, Catharism was the true faith, the one descended from the simplicity and sanctity of Jesus' apostles. That a beastly Roman cabal had somehow hijacked a straightforward message was proof, if any more were needed, of the workings of Evil.

The churchmen, having forbidden any vernacular version of Christian Scripture to avoid just such twisted intepretations of revealed truth, looked at their interlocutors, quite literally, as demagogues from hell. The champions of orthodoxy relied on centuries of biblical exegesis, on a tradition that stretched back to the days of Jerome, Ambrose, and Augustine, and on an institutional legitimacy that doubled as the wellspring of European culture.

The debates lasted for days, drew thousands of onlookers, appealed to the judgments of the audience. A chronicler lamented: "O dolorous case! To think that among Christians the ordinances of the Church and the Catholic Faith should have fallen into such disregard that secular judges were called in to pronounce upon such blasphemies!" The Cathars no longer needed to conceal their heterodox beliefs, as they had done two generations earlier in Lombers. Their friends in the nobility—Count Raymond VI of Toulouse, Viscount Raymond Roger Trencavel, Count Raymond Roger of Foix, King Pedro II of Aragon—had no intention of lighting any bonfires.

Neither side hid its contempt for the other. In a debate of 1207, when a female Perfect rose to rebut a point of discussion, a monk snapped at her, "Go back to your spinning, Madame, it's not your place to speak to such an assembly." Cathar debaters, smarting from years of incendiary slander in which they had been accused of infanticide and performing the obscene kiss, referred to the Church as "the mother of fornication and abomination."

The impetus behind this flurry of insult was Pope Innocent III. Innocent was willing to try anything to stem the tide of heresy, even if it meant talking to those who should be roasting. Raymond had proved deaf to his entreaties and overtures: One of Innocent's first acts as pope had been to pardon the count, excommunicated by his predecessor in 1195 for bad behavior toward the monastery at St. Gilles, yet the ingrate leader of Languedoc remained unconcerned about heresy in his homeland. The pope's subsequent hectoring had met similar indifference. In 1200, Innocent promulgated a decree that called for asset forfeiture, the medieval template of what modern justice does to drug smugglers. The property of heretics would be turned over to their persecutors, and blameless family members would be disinherited. Not only that, Innocent declared that the property of Catholics who refused to hunt heretics was also liable to seizure. In Languedoc, however, these radical measures amounted to little more than whistling in the wind.

At the same time as he was approving the debates, the pope discreetly tried to interest the powerful in more ambitious schemes. Innocent attempted again and again to organize a punitive campaign against the Cathars. Papal letters in 1204, 1205, and 1207 to King Philip Augustus of France promised the monarch all of Languedoc if he would raise an army and put the land to the sword. The king demurred, out of feudal scruple— Raymond was technically his vassal—and out of his consuming need to fight England's King John. Besides, he did not want the pope telling him what to do.

For all his dislike of heresy and the nobility of the south, Innocent recognized that the Church had to reform in Languedoc. His colorful appraisal of the Narbonne clergy—"dumb dogs who can no longer bark"—extended to other dioceses. A council in Avignon asked bishops, among other things, to refrain from hearing matins in bed, gossiping during mass, and spending enormous sums on lavish hunting livery for themselves and their mounts. The bishop of Toulouse in 1201, Raymond of Rabastens, had mortgaged Church property so that he could hire mercenaries to conduct a protracted personal war against his own vassals. The diocese soon went broke, but the bankrupt bishop retained the warm friendship and support of that inevitable irritant, Count Raymond. The pope replaced Rabastens with Fulk of Marseilles, who spent his early days as bishop beating off creditors; it was said that he didn't dare send his mules to get water at the public well for fear of their being impounded. The ineffectual prelates of Carcassonne, Albi, Béziers, Narbonne, and other Languedoc towns eventually were forced from office, but only after years of arm-twisting.

To do all this talking, preaching, and deposing, Innocent relied heavily on Cistercian monks, whose order had drawn men of exceptional talent to the Church throughout the twelfth century. The decision to bestow the disorganized diocese of Toulouse on Fulk of Marseilles was judicious. A Cistercian cleric who had been a rich merchant before finding his vocation and heading to a monastery, Fulk possessed the worldly expertise needed to bring order to the financial mess left by Rabastens. What's more, Fulk had also been a troubadour; Dante, in his *Divine Comedy*, placed him in Venus's quarter of the heavens. A man of three callings—spiritual, material, artistic—was precisely the type suited to champion the Church in the vibrant and complex city on the Garonne.

As papal plenipotentiaries, or legates, to Languedoc as a whole, Innocent appointed three southerners who had risen far in the Cistercian world. Arnold Amaury was the head of the order, the man in charge of its 600 abbeys and thousands of monks. The other two papal legates, Peter of Castelnau and a certain Brother Raoul, hailed from the monastery of Fontfroide, an exquisite place for prayer and meditation that still stands in the hills above Narbonne. Peter, a lawyer-monk with no patience for disagreement, seems to have been the most overbearing of the three, for his stays in cities and remote parishes occasionally gave rise to death threats. Not that he and his colleagues expected adulation. As regular clergy, the secular priests distrusted them; as emissaries of Rome, the Cathars loathed them; as dispensers of excommunications and interdicts, the nobility and townspeople despised them.

The trio of Cistercians set about their work with determination. They went on elaborate revivalist tours to overawe the populace and bring them back into the fold of Catholicism. City governments and local lords were forced to swear allegiance to the Church, on pain of instant excommunication. The legates offered and accepted invitations to debate the Cathars. At Carcassonne in 1204, at the behest of the young King Pedro of Aragon, Peter and Raoul stood their ground against the Perfect Bernard de Simorre while a jury composed of thirteen Cathars and thirteen Catholics adjudicated the proceedings. As Cistercians trained to obey unquestioningly, they spoke of the beauty of submission and the need for absolute authority. This was not, obviously, a line of reasoning fated to win applause in Languedoc, and the debate ended inconclusively. The legates continued their mission, admonishing lax bishops, bullying petty nobles into teaming up against Count Raymond, crisscrossing the landscape in the hope of working an evangelical miracle. In Montpellier during the spring of 1206, the three tired monks concluded that they had failed. Peter of Castelnau had tried to resign a year earlier, only to be rebuffed by the pope. Now all three wanted to abandon their legatine mission. The number of heretics they had converted was derisively small, and the pleas and threats expressed in their sermons had been whisked away like flies. Worse yet, in many places they had become figures of fun.

Two strangers approached them in Montpellier—Spaniards. The Cathar story was about to take a final twist before the dogs of war were loosed. The younger of the two men, Domingo de Guzmán, the future St. Dominic, would not put an end to the heresy, but the Order of Friars Preachers, or the Dominicans, that he went on to found ten years later would be crucial, and cruel, in eliminating Catharism. As Latin wordplay has it, they were the *domini canes*—the dogs of god.

Saints and heretics have the same problem: Their stories have been so distorted by biased biographers that their lives are obscured by lies. What can be discerned about Dominic, through the thicket of hagiography, is his clear-eyed itinerary of piety and his effect on his contemporaries. Like Innocent III, he was a leader of great faith and adamantine conviction. As a brilliant student in Castile, he impressed the local nobility, of which he was a member, by offering to sell himself into slavery in order to free Christians held captive by the Moors. Noticed by Diego de Azevedo, the bishop of Osma, Dominic accompanied the older man on two diplomatic missions to Denmark before finally heading to Rome in the winter of 1205–6 to meet with the pope. Innocent, ten years Dominic's senior, recognized spiritual power when he saw it. He denied the Spaniards' request that they evangelize the Baltic countries and ordered them to Languedoc instead.

Saint Dominic
(Museo di San Marco, Florence/Art Resource, New York)

In March 1206, according to the saint's many biographers, Dominic and Diego interrupted the commiseration of Arnold Amaury, Peter of Castelnau, and Raoul of Fontfroide in Montpellier. The two newcomers had several suggestions to make. They had passed through Languedoc on their travels and seen the Cathar Perfect at work. What struck them, and what was doubtless a source of the heresy's popularity among the laity, was the sincere, saintlike poverty of the Cathar leaders. They lived as the apostles had, with the utmost simplicity, their only possessions a few sacred books and the garment on their backs. It was no wonder that the legates could make no headway against them. As princes of the Church and envoys of the pope, the Cistercians traveled in great state, a suite of retainers, body-guards, servants, and sycophants always at their beck and call. To the spiritual seekers of Languedoc, the legates appeared as pampered hypocrites, unable to speak to the soul. The times called not for feudal swank but for genuine material destitution.

Dominic and Diego had correctly identified the most winning trait of their opponents: apostolic poverty. Another heterodox Christian sect, the Waldensians, went around as dirt-poor preachers and implored other churchmen to do likewise. (Reformers at heart, the Waldensians had been rashly anathematized as heretics in 1184, thereby radicalizing them only more.) And the lure of the pauper was not limited to Languedoc. In 1210, an unwashed beggar who had been drawing crowds in central Italy was brought for questioning before Innocent III at the Lateran. After telling his visitor to take a bath and then spending a restless night dreaming about what the man had said, the pope astutely gave his approval to the supremely unorthodox Francis of Assisi. On the ceiling of the Assisi basilica honoring the ever-popular saint, Giotto immortalized Innocent's dream, which led to the foundation of the other great order of friars, the Franciscans. Ragamuffin piety hardly matched the pope's ambitions for a revitalized Church, but no one, it seems, could turn down the gentle Francis.

In Montpellier, Dominic and Diego did not trigger any dreams, but they were similarly persuasive. The Cistercian grandees agreed, at least temporarily, to do without the perquisites of their high office. Heretical Languedoc must have looked on in stupefaction as the barefoot legates, led by the saintly Spaniards, stumbled through the summer of 1206, begging alms and preaching tirelessly. Debates were held in Servian, Béziers, Carcassonne, Pamiers, Fanjeaux, Montréal, and Verfeil, the last being the place where an apoplectic Bernard of Clairvaux had been silenced in the mid–twelfth century. The Perfect rose to the challenge, the weeklong conversations punctuated by stinging invective and theological grandstanding. It was an astounding moment in the history of religion.

The champions of Catharism included its preeminent preacher, Guilhabert of Castres; a nobleman-turned-Perfect, Benedict of Termes; a former knight from heretical Verfeil, Pons Jordan; and an acid-tongued ascetic aptly named Arnold Hot. Diego and Dominic, according to the Catholic chroniclers who are our sole historical sources, gave as good as they got. In Fanjeaux and Montréal, Dominic argued before crowds that were blatantly hostile to Catholicism. The grande dame of the area was an admired Perfect, Blanche of Laurac; three of her four daughters had followed her example, and her only son, Aimery of Montréal, made no attempt to disguise his disgust with the papal legates. Later Dominican lore has Dominic inspiring a miracle during one debate. A heretic tossed the saint's notes into a fireplace three times, but they would not burn. The paper then wafted upward, charring a ceiling beam—which now adorns the church in Fanjeaux—before floating back down to an awestruck assembly.

The debates failed to spur massive defection from the Cathar cause. Dominic converted anywhere from a dozen to 150 people in these years, the number varying according to the religious enthusiasms of the historian consulted. His most important spiritual conquests were several impoverished young noblewomen living in a home of a female Perfect. Again, this achievement comes complete with a fiery miracle narrative. As the Spaniard stood on the hilltop of Fanjeaux looking out over the golden farmland stretching to nearby Montréal, three flaming spheres came streaking downward out of the sky. They touched down at tiny Prouille, a lowland hamlet in which, Dominic realized, he had to set up a convent for his girlish Cathar converts. At the prompting of these great balls of fire, the saint had once again put his mimetic finger on another strength of Catharism: its network of havens for surplus women in Languedoc society. On his deathbed in Bologna, according to French Catholic novelist Georges Bernanos, Dominic confessed, "I reproach myself for having always liked the conversation of old ladies less than that of young women."

Dominic's stamina, perhaps even his secret vice, was not shared by his companions. By early 1207, the meager harvest of souls, along with the ardors of life on the road, forced the papal legates to return to their former lives. Arnold traveled to Burgundy to preside over a general meeting of the Cistercian order; Peter, whose overweening nature had bloomed into obnoxiousness, went off to resume hectoring the nobility into arresting all of the people whom he had been recently debating. Brother Raoul of Fontfroide, discreetly encouraged by Dominic and Diego, thought it wiser to keep Peter away from the public discussions so as not to goad already hostile audiences. His debating place was taken by another strong-willed, if less antipathetic Cistercian, Bishop Fulk of Toulouse.

Within a few years, Dominic's perseverance in the ways of poverty had won him a reputation rivaling that of the Perfect. The Spaniard's ceaseless wanderings through the hinterlands of Foix, Toulouse, and Albi brought him deep within dualist country. At one point, according to legend, a group of heretical peasants intercepted him in the middle of a field and asked him what he would do if they attacked him. Dominic's famous reply: "I should beg you not to kill me at one blow, but to tear me limb from limb, that thus my martyrdom might be prolonged; I would like to be a mere limbless trunk, with eyes gouged out, wallowing in my own blood, that I might thereby win a worthier martyr's crown." He was left alone.

It was Peter of Castelnau who brought these years of talking to a close, although not in the manner he intended. In the spring of 1207, he visited the minor nobility of western Provence and ordered them to persecute heretics instead of using mercenaries in private wars that often harmed Church interests. At the time, the Provençals were in revolt against their titular overlord, Raymond of Toulouse. Although they swore to obey Peter on the subject of mercenaries, Count Raymond flatly refused. He could not conduct his business without hired troops, and he was neither inclined nor able to hunt down his people for their religious beliefs. Peter excommunicated him instantly, dissolving all feudal obligations owed to him by his vassals. He did this in front of a large gathering, thundering out the final flourish of his anathema: "He who dispossesses you will be accounted virtuous, he who strikes you dead will earn a blessing." It was, historical consensus holds, an extraordinarily provocative act by Peter, which signaled an impatience with the campaign of preaching and debating.

Backed into a corner, Raymond did what he had always done since becoming count in 1194: He made promises he had no intention of keeping. He agreed to be the scourge of heretics and to drive the mercenaries from his lands. In August of 1207, Raymond was pardoned.

Summer turned to fall, and nothing happened. Dominic

preached at Prouille, Fulk debated at Pamiers, Raymond dallied at St. Gilles, Arnold conferred with Peter, and Innocent wrote again to the king of France. Finally, the churchmen sought to break the impasse.

Raymond was singled out for punishment again. As the most powerful lord of a Languedoc rife with heresy, he was held responsible for the hideous blemish disfiguring the face of Christendom. A list of offenses was drawn up once more: He had stolen Church property, offended bishops, outraged abbots, used mercenaries, given public office to Jews, and supported the Cathars. A new excommunication ensued. All of Europe was invited to disregard him, to take whatever was his with the blessing of the pope.

Raymond tried to negotiate again. He invited Peter of Castelnau for talks that winter in his castle at St. Gilles. According to the correspondence of Innocent III, our principal source for the incidents to follow, the negotiations led nowhere, and Raymond ended up physically threatening the legate in front of witnesses. No doubt the diplomatic count could no longer bear the meddlesome monk, in much the same way that King Henry II of England had lost his patience with Becket.

On January 13, 1208, the talks broke off amid much acrimony. Peter left St. Gilles with his retinue, bound for Rome. Early the next morning, opposite Arles, Peter and his escort rode out to the ferry crossing of the Rhône. As they waited by the riverside, the irreparable occurred. An unknown horseman bore down on them and drove home a sword through Peter's back.

The legate of Pope Innocent III lay dead on the ground. The conversation was over.

5.

Penance and Crusade

BUNDLE OF BIRCH CUTTINGS came whistling through the hush and landed with a crack on pale white flesh. The sharp twigs came down again and again. The crowds surging up the steps of the church at St. Gilles watched in fascination as their lord was scourged like the meanest of villeins. It was always a pleasure in the caste-conscious Middle Ages to watch the high and mighty humbled in public. Stripped to the waist and chafed by a rough cord around his neck, Count Raymond swore over sacred relics his undying obedience to the pope and his legates. The twenty or so bishops in attendance, like the northern chronicler who recorded the episode, must have been pleased to see Raymond so thoroughly humiliated.

Count Raymond, now in his early fifties, had given his consent to this public scourging in his ancestral fief. This day—June 18, 1209—may have been an agony of mortification, but it was also the culmination of eighteen months of frantic diplomacy.

Ever since Peter of Castelnau was felled by an assassin, Raymond had maintained that he was innocent of the crime. For him to have ordered one of his men to kill the legate, he claimed, would have been a blunder of monumental proportions, even if he had had angry words with Peter in that fateful January of the year previous. All his life Raymond had avoided confrontation, preferring to defer promises and drown disagreement in a murky pool of diplomacy. Had he wished to murder Peter, he insisted, he certainly wouldn't have had it done a stone's throw from his own home. Besides, the poisonous monk had made many enemies in Languedoc.

Still, Raymond was the prime suspect in what would remain an unsolved murder mystery. It would have upset the designs of too many people not to have the crime pinned on the count. Furthermore, his pretensions to diplomatic genius were undermined when he sent Raymond of Rabastens as one of his advocates to Rome. Rabastens, the spendthrift who had reduced the diocese of Toulouse to indigence, would have been a noxious presence to Innocent III—the pope had expended five years of effort to oust Rabastens in favor of Fulk.

Not that Rabastens stood much of a chance anyway. From the moment the news of Peter's murder reached Rome, the curia was crying for Count Raymond's hide. On March 10, 1208, Innocent called for a crusade, which was to be preached by the wrathful Arnold Amaury and the eloquent Fulk. The two white-robed furies ranged across Europe, asking for armed support in crushing the Cathars. The kings and emperors of the north equivocated. They were too busy fighting among themselves to accede to this proposed breach of feudal custom. They had no quarrel with their vassals in Languedoc; why should they take up arms against them? But Innocent, Arnold, and Fulk insisted throughout 1208, bombarding the lords with letters and exhortations. Finally, King Philip Augustus of France relented and released his most powerful barons to go and make war on their southern kinsmen. Nobles whose names are unfamiliar now—Eudes, duke of Burgundy; Hervé, count of Nevers; Peter of Courtenay, count of Auxerre—then commanded respect and awe because of their vast estates and the mass of mounted knights they could field. These nobles, accompanied by tens of thousands of footsoldiers, were heading south as Raymond underwent his degrading penance.

Raymond's scourge was Milo, a curial notary who had been named the new papal legate. So great was the crush of onlookers that the two principals, penitent and punisher, had difficulty leaving the square to regain the sanctuary of the church. They elbowed their way past the crowd and squeezed through a portal in the facade. The pairing of the two men owed nothing to chance. It was Raymond who had been instrumental in Milo's promotion—in his rush to come to terms, he wrote to Innocent that he was willing to negotiate with anyone except Arnold Amaury. Even so, the conditions that Raymond accepted at Milo's prompting were unusually harsh: He had to give up all rights over any religious foundation in his domains, hand over seven of his castles, never again use mercenaries, let the legates pass judgment on any complaint filed against him, apologize to all the bishops and abbots he had offended, dismiss all Jews from his service, and treat as heretics all those who were designated as such by the Church.

And he had to submit to this day of disparagement, half-naked before his people, beaten by the clergy, for a crime he continued to deny having ordered and for which he had not been tried, much less convicted. He was indeed being treated as if he were a latter-day Henry Plantagenet atoning for the murder of Thomas Becket, a comparison that escaped no one, least of all Pope Innocent, who remembered his boyhood in the Campagna.

When the service in the church of St. Gilles came to an end, Raymond was at last free to go. Only he could not; the dense throng of curiosity seekers in the nave would have made any attempted departure out the front door a gauntlet of further shame. The count was hustled down a stone stairway leading from the altar to the crypt, out of which there was a subterranean exit. The priests forced Raymond to make one last stop—at the grave of Peter of Castelnau. This was their final reproach to the nobleman whom they had at last bludgeoned into obedience. Raymond stood, in the words of the chronicler, "naked in front of the tomb of the blessed martyr . . . whom he had assassinated. This was God's just judgment. He was forced to pay respect to the body of him he had scorned during life."

Fourteen days later, the count of Toulouse traveled north with his knights to join up with the crusading army as it descended the left bank of the Rhône. He was a Saint Gilles, of the family that stormed Jerusalem in 1099. Raymond had announced after his scourging that he wanted to take up the cross, hound the heretics, punish all those who sheltered the Perfect. He did not say that all he really wanted was to make sure that the crusaders stayed off his lands; they could not very well harm the possessions of one of their own. Events would show that the count of Toulouse had not changed in the slightest and that his aversion to persecution remained strong. Raymond the penitent was, in fact, unrepentant.

Trebuchet, mangonel, chatte, chain mail, destrier, gonfalon, halberd, crossbow, pike, ballista—the old words and weapons of warfare transmit a blunt message of ancestral trauma that neither rarity nor foreign origin can soften. The army that Raymond rode out to meet, at the river town of Valence, bore these awful weapons in its baggage, ready to shout down the debates of Dominic and the Cathars with the unanswerable argument of force. The monstrously large host, which had assembled in Lyons, stretched out for four miles on the march, its supplies bobbing alongside it on a flotilla of barges. There would be few sights more terrifying in all of the thirteenth century.

Like all great feudal armies, the crusading force of 1209 counted among its multitude hundreds of mounted knights, the armor-clad killers at the apex of the belligerent pyramid. Nobles instructed since boyhood in the hack and chop of hard-ridden collision, the knights were the commanders and, paradoxically, the main participants of any pitched battle. Each, according to his means, came with a retinue of grooms, handlers, infantrymen, and archers, whose loyalty to their lord outweighed any other consideration.

Less honor bound were the bands of *routiers* (mercenaries) that accompanied the army. Some of these routiers were mounted brigands, others foot soldiers in the cause of pillage. All were the shock troops of the feudal fighting machine, seconded by the unruly *ribauds* (whence the English word *ribald*), the unwashed mass of ragtag adventure seekers with nothing to lose and nothing to hold sacred. It is commonly thought that medieval society was an unmoving, if unpleasant, pastorale; in fact, the landless, the restless, and the desperate roved the countryside in large numbers. In a tradition rich in irony, the ribauds elected a "king" from their midst at the start of each campaign. This king would negotiate on such matters as who would rob the corpses of the enemy and who would pay the whores. In hiring routiers and accepting ribauds, the crusade displayed a double standard. The use of mercenaries, who tended to wreak freelance havoc with monasteries, had been one of the main complaints brought against the nobility of Languedoc by the Church.

The host of 1209 far surpassed the average medieval army in fervor. There were pilgrims by the thousand, a cross sewn on the shoulder of their rough tunics. Crusaders had been promised a full remission of their sins, a moratorium on their debts, and a transfer of Church funds into their pockets. The expedition had all the advantages of an expedition to Palestine with none of the drawbacks of distance. For the French northerners, the proximity of Languedoc was ideal for doing one's "quarantine"—the forty days of military service necessary to earn a crusader's indulgence—then returning home in time for harvest and hunt, happy in the knowledge that heaven's gate had swung open for one's soul. The warriors did not consider the intended victims of their crusade to be fellow Christians. Heretics were not Christians; they were heretics.

Many of the nobles picking their way down the Rhône had ridden together seven years earlier on the strange Fourth Crusade. Encouraged by Innocent III, a cavalcade of French chivalry had set off to undo the damage wrought by Saladin's reconquest of Jerusalem in 1187. They planned on succeeding where the Third Crusade of Barbarossa and Richard Lionheart had failed. Instead, they ended up being mercenaries for the mariners of Venice, who had demanded such an extortionate fare for passage to Palestine that the knights could afford only to give payment in kind. This they did by spending the winter of 1202–3 besieging and sacking the Christian city of Zara, an Adriatic port that belonged to the Venetians' commercial rival in the area. After Zara, the crusaders were taken by their shippers to Constantinople, which, by no coincidence, was Venice's other principal maritime competitor. The crusaders saw a chance to salvage some respectablility from their sorry meanderings by deposing the Greek Orthodox emperor and installing a Latin puppet in his place. First, however, they had to take the city, which they did in 1204 with vandalous panache, destroying more works of art and cultural treasures during their action than at any other time in the entire millennium of the Middle Ages. The orgy of rapine and robbery lasted three days and nights.

Such bloody sideshows had come to characterize crusades. Whenever a mass of people intent on violence and assured of salvation got together, neutral bystanders knew to get out of the way. European Jewry, in particular, was subject to slaughter at the hands of the exalted en route to fight the infidel. A feudal host was already sinister; one that had God on its side was downright diabolical. The crusade to Languedoc promised to be no different.

On July 2, 1209, Raymond came into the encampment of Arnold Amaury, asking to join the holy cause. Arnold acceded to the count's request, even if he, like the chronicler who recorded the event, suspected that the count was insincere in his militant piety and wished only to spare his lands from invasion. Arnold had received instructions from Innocent, who had appointed him to lead the crusade. The pope's letter took the long view:

You ask us urgently what policy the crusaders should adopt with respect to the count of Toulouse. Follow the advice of the apos-

tle who said: "I was clever, I caught you by tricking you." . . .
Be wise and conceal your intentions; leave him alone at first in
order to attack those who are openly rebellious. It will not be
easy to crush the adherents of Antichrist if we let them unite for
a common defense. On the other hand, nothing will be easier
than to crush them, if the count does not aid them. Perhaps the
sight of their disaster will really reform him. But if he persists in
his evil plans, when he is isolated and supported only by his
own forces, we can defeat him without too much trouble.

The crusade of 1209 did not turn its fury on the count of
Toulouse. He was not the only lord in Languedoc.

6.

Béziers

IN JULY OF 1209, RAYMOND ROGER TRENCAVEL was twenty-four years old, the viscount of Albi, Carcassonne, Béziers, and all the lands that surrounded them. His family was ancient, powerful, one of the two great clans to control the lowland valleys of Languedoc. The news from Provence alarmed him: His mother's brother, Count Raymond of Toulouse, was guiding a mass of armed men through the delta of the Rhône, telling the foreigners where to bivouac, where to find clean water, where to ford the myriad tributaries of the great river. The army would soon march into Trencavel territory.

When Viscount Raymond Roger had first heard of the ominous preparations in the north, it was generally assumed that the crusade's target would be Toulouse. In early 1209, he had rebuffed Count Raymond's proposal of a defensive alliance, presumably on the strength of that assumption. He, like many others, would have believed that it was Count Raymond who, notwithstanding his protests of innocence, had ordered the murder of Peter of Castelnau. In Raymond Roger's view, the boldness of that crime was now surpassed by the sheer gall shown by Raymond in joining forces with the crusade that he, in effect, had conjured into existence. The consequences of the count's latest trick were obvious to Raymond Roger: His lands, not Raymond's, had become the quarry.

The young Trencavel realized the extent of his peril when his spies told him just how large the crusading host appeared to be. In mid-July, the viscount saddled up and galloped east to the Mediterranean, then northward along the coast road, the Via Domitia, laid out a millennium earlier for Roman legionnaires. His destination was Montpellier, a city devoid of tolerance for Catharism and the last stopping-point of the crusaders before they entered his lands. Four years previously, Raymond Roger had wed Agnes of Montpellier, a strategic marriage that ensured a tranquil border to his north and pleased the suzerain overlord of both Carcassonne and Montpellier, King Pedro II of Aragon. None of that web of feudal connections mattered now; the invading northerners were welcomed in Montpellier, which the pope had explicitly instructed them to spare.

Raymond Roger met with Arnold Amaury and the French barons. He announced that the Trencavels were willing to submit to the wishes of the Church. Like the count of Toulouse, he too would hound the heretics from his lands. If some of his vassals had been infected with the Cathar leprosy, they would be punished. Raymond Roger presented himself as a stout Christian who demanded nothing more than to join the holy crusade.

This was a change of heart that was even more preposterous than the one announced a few weeks earlier by Count Raymond

Seal of Raymond Roger Trencavel
(Hôtel de ville, Béziers)

of Toulouse. Arnold Amaury, as a churchman who had spent so much of the last decade in Languedoc, would have known that the young Trencavel was a friend to the Cathars. Upon the death of his father in 1194, Raymond Roger had had as his guardian Bertrand of Saissac, the heretic who violated churches and dug up dead abbots. During the viscount's boyhood, the regent for Trencavel had been the count of Foix, the mountain man with a sister and a wife who had become Cathar Perfect. Arnold Amaury would have seen that as the boy grew older, the indignities to the Church only worsened. The Catholic bishop of Carcassonne had been chased out of the city for daring to preach against heresy. His replacement was popular with the Trencavels, because he was ineffectual and compromised by the astounding fact that his mother, his sister, and three of his brothers had received the consolamentum. Another crime in Arnold's eyes would have been the viscount's willingness to let a Jew be his bayle, or representative, in Béziers. To the monk leading the crusade, the young viscount had violated so many of God's laws that his feigned eleventh-hour orthodoxy could be viewed as yet another insult to the Church.

Arnold dismissed Raymond Roger. It had taken almost ten years for the holy father to bestir the ferocious warriors of France from their torpor. He would not disband the crusade on the eve of its first great action.

Returning to Béziers, Raymond Roger called for an assembly of the townspeople to tell them the bad news. There was to be no truce, no reprieve. The northerners were less than a day's march away, and they would not listen to reason. The people of Béziers—the Biterrois—were fearful but not terrified. Their town stood overlooking the River Orb, its tall fortifications built on an ocher hillside. Although the three pro-crusade chroniclers who are our sources for this episode variously describe the Biterrois as "fools" and "madmen," one of them, William of Tudela, conceded that the townspeople thought they could easily withstand a siege. They had provisions stocked, and the peasants from the countryside crowding the town had brought with them enough food to sustain the Biterrois for weeks. The very size of the besieging host, they believed, could prove its greatest weakness. "They were sure the host could not hold together," William of Tudela stated. "It would disintegrate in less than a fortnight, for it stretched out a full league long." With so many mouths to feed under the pitiless glare of the summer sun, the Biterrois hoped, the attackers would be forced to move on, just to survive. And once their quarantine was up—their forty days of service—most of the soldiery would no doubt head home, their swords rusty from disuse. By this reckoning, Béziers would not collapse; the crusade would.

The bishop of Béziers, who was part of the crusading force,

arrived from Montpellier with a final offer. He had a list of 222 names—the Cathar Perfect of the town. He demanded that they be handed over for immediate punishment or else the crusaders would arrive the next day to lay siege to the city. The impassive burghers of Béziers, as one chronicler put it, "thought no more of his advice than of a peeled apple." Like the city fathers of Toulouse, they had fought hard for their independence from noble and bishop; it was out of the question that they should surrender any of their own townspeople to strangers from the north. In 1167, in the city's Church of St. Mary Magdalene, the burghers of Béziers had murdered Raymond Roger Trencavel's grandfather for interfering with their liberties. His son, the current viscount's father, had retaliated two years later, on the feast day of Mary Magdalene, by perpetrating a massacre. The memory of that slaughter had entered civic culture as a reminder of how dear was the cost of winning their freedoms. The merchants and traders of Béziers would not abandon them now. The Perfect would not be betrayed, by either Catholic or Cathar. A chronicler had the townspeople replying to the bishop, "We would rather drown in a salty sea than change anything in our government." The bishop got on his mule and rode back to the crusader camp; many of his clergy remained behind, out of solidarity with their parishioners.

Viscount Raymond Roger did not stay. Given the Trencavels' bloody legacy in Béziers, he and the townspeople must have harbored ambivalent feelings toward each other. In the face of a common enemy, the young lord and the Biterrois came to an understanding. Instead of manning the battlements, Raymond Roger rushed back to Carcassonne, to the heart of his territory, to raise an army from his vassals in the Corbières and the Montagne Noire. He planned to return to Béziers as soon as was practicable and attack the crusaders. Raymond Roger was escorted to Carcassonne by all of Béziers's Jews. Crusades spelled doom for Jews, even if they were not directly concerned with either the cause or the outcome.

The next day was July 22, 1209, the Feast of St. Mary Magdalene.

The date was not without poignancy. From the eleventh century to the present day, the gypsies living near Béziers and farther up the coast toward the Rhône have had a predilection for Mary Magdalene. They believe that Mary was forced to flee Palestine by boat shortly after the disappearance of her beloved Jesus and that she, Martha, and the raised-from-the-dead Lazarus made landfall near Marseilles, from which they spread the good news about the Nazarene into the pagan countryside of Rome's provincia Narbonnensis. It is this Mary, the flawed penitent, the once fallen woman, the one to whom proof of Jesus' resurrection was first given, who has stoked the fires of popular piety among the common people along the Mediterranean coast.

Mary Magdalene had an even better reputation among the gnostics, the classical ancestors of the Cathars. According to many of these thinkers, Mary was actually the foremost among the apostles, outranking Peter and all his successors in Rome. The gnostic gospels were suppressed in the editing of the collective work that came to be known as the New Testament, but those that survived elsewhere often gave her an exalted, pastoral position. Even the gospel of John—admittedly, the oddity when compared with the synoptic gospels of Matthew, Mark, and Luke—assigns Mary a staggeringly important role, in which she is singled out to pass the first message from the resurrected Christ to the apostles. Orthodoxy subsequently played down her status and threw its weight behind Peter; many heretics were not so sure. Certainly, the implications of her apostolic primacy—women could be leaders, not just breeders—found an echo in the tentative parity between the sexes allowed in some dualist faiths. The Cathars, who prized the Gospel of John for its gnostic elements, would not have found Mary as antipathetical as other figures in orthodoxy's communion of saints.

It was fitting, then, that the most important date in the history of Béziers, an acropolis of Catharism defended by its Catholic majority, should coincide with the feast day of a saint so rich in ambiguity and gnostic significance. Fitting, perhaps, but not particularly auspicious; for all her many attributes, Mary Magdalene was never equated with Lady Luck.

By July 22, the crusade had swarmed all over the flats to the south of Béziers. As the Biterrois on the walls watched, tens of thousands of men pitched tents, watered their horses, and lit campfires. Stretching to the distant horizon was an ocean of changing shape and constant movement, ceaselessly shifting in the summer sunshine. Trees were felled, enclosures built, flagstaffs erected. Hundreds of banners, garishly dyed for the gray monotony of the north, fluttered near the pavilions of the lords. The singing of monks could be heard, as could the braying of beasts of burden. The army prepared for a long stay before Béziers.

Just how long was the question. Arnold Amaury had already summoned the crusading lords to a meeting. During his days alongside Peter of Castelnau and Raoul of Fontfroide, Arnold had stayed in Béziers frequently. On the monthlong march down the Rhône, the leader of the crusade would have told the French barons that the city looked impregnable. Now they could judge for themselves; their siege experts rode out to a respectful distance from the city walls and trotted around the entire circumvallation of the ramparts to look for flaws. In the view of the clergy, these French men of war, feared from Palestine to England for their warrior prowess, would surely find the way to defeat this stubborn, satanic city.

As the meeting convened to discuss what was to be done, the great mass of the army was finishing its tasks. From three chroniclers, William of Tudela, Peter of Vaux de Cernay, and William of Puylaurens, it is possible to piece together what happened on that fateful afternoon.

A handful of the camp followers—kitchen boys, muleteers, varlets, thieves—drifted down to the River Orb, shirts and hats in hand, to find a cool respite from the day. The Orb passed close to the southern fortifications of the city, within shouting distance. Inevitably, insults were exchanged between the men by the riverside and those atop the walls. One of the crusaders rashly walked onto the bridge spanning the Orb, a clear shot for any deadly defensive crossbowman, and loudly taunted the burghers of Béziers. The sight of this half-naked riffraff rankled the proud men behind the walls. A few dozen youths of Béziers decided to teach the scum of the crusade a lesson. They gathered spears, sticks, banners, and a few drums, then swung open a gate and went charging noisily down the slope to the river. The foolhardy loner on the bridge barely had time to choke down his last jeering taunt before they were on him, pummeling and beating him senseless. As his friends scrambled up the bank to help

The massacre at Béziers (from the *Canso*, or *La Chanson de la Croisade*)
(Bibliothèque Nationale, Paris)

him, he was thrown off the bridge and splashed with finality into the muddy Orb. By then the donnybrook was on.

Farther downstream, the "king" of the camp followers—the ribauds—saw the lone heckler go hurtling down into the Orb. He also saw the open gate to the town. In the words of the chronicler: "He called all his lads together and shouted 'Come on, let's attack!' " By twos and threes, then by the hundreds, a throng came racing toward the mayhem, the scent of battle driving them forward. To return to William of Tudela's account, mindful of medieval exaggeration: "Each one got himself a club—they had nothing else, I suppose—and there were more than fifteeen thousand of them, with not a pair of shoes between them." The motley combatants surged toward the bridge.

At the open gate of Béziers, the men and women must have screamed to their brave young roustabouts down below. From their vantage point atop the slope, those inside the city would have seen the thickening crowds converging on the bridge. The brawling Biterrois had made a ghastly mistake. The conventions of medieval warfare held that a besieging army should never be attacked when it is newly arrived and thus still fresh. Sieges were wearying ordeals of attrition for both sides, and risks were best taken when the opponent had grown tired. The crusaders, still well supplied with food and water, were not demoralized. If anything, they were itching for a fight.

The men of Béziers, outnumbered and exposed, fought their way back to the rampart, up the slope they had so playfully descended just a few moments earlier. As far as can be inferred from the chronicle record, the club-wielding crusaders were among them, shoving through the open gate and into the city itself. Proud Béziers was no longer inviolate; the attackers streamed into the town.

The Biterrois on the battlements saw the spreading stain below. They deserted their posts to descend to the streets to join the melee. Outside, crusaders propped long ladders against the walls of Béziers and scampered up to the unguarded heights. The town was wide-open.

The distant shouts reached the noblemen gathered around Arnold Amaury. A chronicle related, "Now the crusading knights were shouting, 'To arms! To arms!'" The great barons and their armored infantry, the most effective killers of any feudal host, prepared to launch the assault.

In all probability, it was at this moment that the famous order was—or was not—given. Professional opinion is divided on whether Arnold Amaury actually said, in the vernacular, "Caedite eos. Novit enim Dominus qui sunt eius" (Kill them all. God will know his own). That lapidary phrase was most likely the invention of a pro-crusade chronicler writing thirty years after the fact. What is certain is that there is no record of anyone, certainly not Arnold Amaury, head of the Cistercian order and the loftiest representative of the vicar of Christ, trying to halt or even hinder the butchery that was about to begin. Not even Count Raymond, who is not thought to have taken part in the sack of the city, is mentioned by the chroniclers as attempting to discourage the crusader bloodlust.

Lord and pilgrim, monk and groom—all now rushed into Béziers. Catholic priests within the city put on vestments for a mass of the dead. Church bells tolled. At the cathedral in which the canons were holding a vigil for the Catholic faithful, the soldiery from the north charged the congregation, broad swords slashing and stabbing until no one within was left standing. The bishop's auxiliaries were all slain.

The attack moved inexorably up the gentle slope of the hillside town, the Biterrois falling back through the narrow streets. The crusaders showed no mercy. Women and children crowded into the Church of St. Mary Magdalene in the upper town. They prayed to the patroness for protection, on her feast day. The chronicler Peter of Vaux de Cernay stated that there were 7,000 of them in all, an impossibility given the size of the sanctuary. They must have numbered about 1,000, an estimate based on the maximum capacity of the church. In any case, the church was full of terrified, weeping Catholics and Cathars when the crusaders broke down the doors and slaughtered everyone inside. A jumble of human bones, the victims of the massacre, was discovered under the floor of the church during renovations in 1840.

The townspeople now all dead, the lords of the crusade turned their attention to the material wealth of the city. The rabble who had stormed the bridge, according to William of

Tudela, had already begun looting: "The servant lads had settled into the houses they had taken, all of them full of riches and treasure, but when the French [the lords] discovered this they went nearly mad with rage and drove the lads out with clubs, like dogs." The knights' fury was understandable. The spoils of war were always apportioned by the leaders of an army, not by its followers. In the view of barons of the crusade, the ribauds and mercenaries were taking what rightly belonged to the conquering nobility.

The elected king of the ribauds, the man who had spotted the open gate beyond the skirmish on the bridge, called on his men to stop their plunder. They could not possibly defend themselves against the armored knights. But there would be a price to pay. "These filthy stinking wretches all shouted out 'Burn it! Burn it!'" a chronicle noted. "[They] fetched huge flaming brands as if for a funeral pyre and set the town alight."

The wooden dwellings in the cramped streets were tinderboxes. The knights watched helplessly as flames engulfed first one, then another quarter of the town. The roof timbers of the great cathedral of St. Nazaire caught fire and collapsed. Soon the entire town was ablaze. The soldiery gradually backed out of the inferno of Béziers. They staggered past the bridge over the Orb and returned to where they had begun this strenuous afternoon of abattoir Christianity. As they watched, the city was consumed in flames, literally a funerary pyre for what scholarly consensus estimates at 15,000–20,000 victims.

Everyone in the town, from graybeard Cathar Perfect to newborn Catholic baby, was put to death in the space of a morning. In the days before gunpowder, to kill that many people in so short a time required a savage single-mindedness that beggars the imagination. To the crusaders bitter about the lost booty of affluent Béziers, there was consolation to be had in knowing that they had done God's work so efficiently. Personal salvation had been ensured by this stunning victory. In his letter to Innocent, Arnold marveled at their success. "Nearly twenty thousand of the citizens were put to the sword, regardless of age and sex," he wrote. "The workings of divine vengeance have been wondrous."

A threshold had been crossed in the ordering of men's minds.

7.

Carcassonne

To approach Carcassonne for the first time is to dream with your eyes open. The turrets and bastions of the old city stand on a deceptive rise in the valley of the River Aude, so that the crenellated citadel appears suddenly, floating in the middle distance, a visitor from another time. The tan stone blocks of the ramparts turn auburn, then mauve in the late afternoon sun. In sight of the Trencavels' restored battlements, long-vanished combatants ride into the periphery of awareness, their clamorous quarrel a faint murmur carried on the wind. For Carcassonne, in the summer of 1209, came after Béziers.

Like any atrocity worthy of the name, the deed done at Béziers spread fear far and near. Following the Feast of St. Mary Magdalene, the crusading army spent three days encamped upwind from the scene of its triumph. One local notable after another rode up to to offer his homage to the new arbiters of legitimacy. Most of these minor lords came from the lowlands

Carcassonne
(Jean Pierre Pétermann)

between Béziers and Carcassonne, through which the northern host would have to march if it were to attack the Trencavel capital. Fright dictated these surrenders, which would later prove as shifting as the grass upon which the crusaders trod.

At Carcassonne, the scarcely believable news from Béziers disabused Raymond Roger of any hope that this was to be a conflict like any other. In an era where populations numbered in the tens of thousands, rather than in the millions of today, the deliberate annihilation of 20,000 lives administered a direct, animal shock to Languedoc, like the amputation of a limb. The viscount took drastic action to make his country inhospitable to the crusade. For miles around Carcassonne, he ordered every windmill destroyed, every crop burned, every animal slaughtered or brought into the embrace of the thick city walls first traced by the Romans, then reinforced by the Visigoths.

In Raymond Roger's castle, built by his great-grandfather and still standing as a stolid mass of hewn stone dominating the medieval city, the viscount welcomed the loyal lords who had heeded his call for help. These men, unlike the lowland nobles exposed to imminent attack, came from the rugged highlands on either side of the Aude valley: to the north, the Montagne Noire and the Minervois, rugged heights cut by waterfalls and shrouded in dense forests; to the south, the Corbières, bald mountains slashed by sudden gullies and guarded by massive castles. It was these hinterland vassals who would be Catharism's stoutest defenders in the early years of the Albigensian Crusade.

The northerners arrived on August 1. Leery of the bolts and quarrels from Carcassonne's crossbows, the crusading nobles ordered their tents and pavilions pitched well out of range. An impulsive Raymond Roger, according to a chronicler, urged an immediate surprise attack. "To horse, my lords!" the viscount shouted. "We'll ride out there, four hundred of us with the best and fastest horses, and before the sun has set, we shall defeat them."

Cooler heads prevailed over this absurd bravado—the defenders were hopelessly outnumbered. The most convincing counsel for caution was voiced by Peter Roger of Cabaret, lord of a gold-mining fief on the Montagne Noire. Béziers had shown that an ill-prepared sortie could finish as a fiasco (the Biterrois had been "stupider than whales," sniffed one chronicler), and the crusaders before Carcassonne were not a tired or disgruntled besieging army, easily surprised and defeated. In any event, the crusader camp was too far away to storm by surprise. The seigneur of Cabaret rightly surmised that the northerners would first assail the two fortified suburbs of Carcassonne that stood outside the city walls. He argued for barreling out of the Trencavel capital once the suburbs came under attack; the crusaders would be closer, and harder-pressed, and the surprise just as total.

The next day, August 2, 1209, was a Sunday, and both sides waited in pious impatience. At dawn on Monday, the northeners struck; they chose Bourg, the weaker of the two suburbs. Battering rams, chanting monks, clambering soldiers on their ladders, charging knights on warhorses—the medieval phantasmagoria came to life in all its brutality. Within two hours the bloodied defenders of Bourg scattered in panic as the flimsy walls of their settlement let in the mob. From atop the rock-solid battlements of Carcassonne, archers and bowmen loosed flight after flight into the crusaders, but the wave of warriors could not be stopped. Neither Raymond Roger nor Peter Roger sallied out to Bourg to counterattack. Curiously, none of the three chroniclers who are our sources for this engagement gives a reason for the abandonment of their plan.

There was no slaughter on this day. Instead, the men of the crusade crashed past the burning houses and down the slopes leading to the River Aude—and its precious wells. The inhabitants of Bourg had time to stumble beyond the barbicans of Carcassonne and to safety behind its fortifications. They would place still more strain on the overcrowded city's resources. The crusaders had captured the northern approach to the Trencavel capital and, more important, commandeered its water supplies. The action at Bourg had been a hard-fought tactical victory, in which one minor noble from the north had distinguished himself for his bravery. Simon de Montfort, until then a respectable if shabby presence in the silken company of his betters, would rise to prominence in the siege of Carcassonne. The crusaders made their plans for the attack on the second suburb, Castellar, to the south of the city.

The unfolding of Simon's destiny was delayed the next day by the unexpected arrival of 100 armored horsemen. The crusaders, who were at table "eating roast meat," William of Tudela helpfully noted, rose to greet the newcomers warmly. Gold-and-red pennants fluttered on the tips of their lances, identifying the splendidly caparisoned warriors as nobles from Aragon and Catalonia. Their leader, King Pedro, a vigorous man in his midthirties, first sought out the tent of his brother-in-law, Count Raymond of Toulouse. (Raymond's fifth wife, Eleanor, was Pedro's sister.) It is reasonable to assume that Raymond was a noncombatant at both Béziers and Carcassonne, given the absence of any mention of him taking part in the actions. In all likelihood, the count had simply stood by and watched as his northern peers behaved as badly as any band of marauding mercenaries. At his tent, pitched on a leafy hill at a distance from the main encampment, he and the few other nobles of Languedoc with the crusade would have told King Pedro what they had witnessed at Béziers.

Pedro then met with the leaders of the crusade. Arnold Amaury, who had begun his rise to power as an abbot in Catalonia, knew that the young king was held in high esteem in Rome. On coming to the throne, the monarch had made over his kingdom to the Holy See. In so doing, he became a direct vassal of Innocent III, who, in his drive to fill Church coffers and enforce

Seal of King Pedro II of Aragon

respect for the papacy, welcomed the spiritual and material obeisance of a great prince. The king's orthodox credentials were impeccable. Even if he did not enforce the antiheresy laws he had drawn up for his kingdom, his belligerence toward the Muslim majority in the Iberian Peninsula had made his a blessed name at the Lateran. Pedro the Catholic could not be ignored.

He had a legitimate grievance. Viscount Raymond Roger of Carcassonne was his vassal and thus part of his extended feudal family. It was true that Pedro's own suzerain, Innocent, had organized this assault on Trencavel, but that did not necessarily mean that the Aragonese was any less distressed by this trampling on his jurisdiction. A great lord, feudal custom held, always had a say in the fate of his vassals. Pedro announced that he had come to see Raymond Roger Trencavel, his embattled young protégé.

The wounded dignity of the Spaniard underscored the misgivings of the northern nobles beholden to King Philip Augustus of France. They might very well have wondered who had the authority to threaten a seigneur like Raymond Roger and deprive him of his birthright. Ever since the pontificate of Pope Gregory VII in the eleventh century, successive popes had argued that the Church could depose any unsatisfactory baron, but the men with the swords had disagreed. Innocent, the ablest man to wear the tiara in two centuries, had launched this crusade partly to put some backbone in the papacy's theocratic posture. That the punitive expedition took so long to organize showed the reluctance of lay rulers, especially Philip Augustus, to cede any ground on the treacherous terrain of sovereignty. At heart, the greatest nobles of the crusade sympathized with the Trencavels and the Saint Gilles, although they may have been puzzled by both clans' tolerance of heresy. Pedro served notice that even the most orthodox of monarchs were ready to show their displeasure with the ambitions of Rome.

Pedro gave up his destrier, or warhorse, for the finer-looking palfrey that his grooms had brought for him. Accompanied only by three men and riding, as William of Tudela reported, "without shields or weapons," he spurred the mount up the slopes to the walled city. The drawbridge came creaking down and the portcullis was raised amid much cheering. When Pedro had stayed there five years earlier, to preside over the debate between Cathar and Catholic, Carcassonne had been a peaceful, prosperous place. As he entered the city now, the stench must have hit him; it is estimated that more than 40,000 people had taken refuge behind its walls.

When Raymond Roger tried to greet his liege lord as his savior, he was soon put back in his place. A chronicler related

Pedro's speech to his vassal, in an admirable passage summing up the younger man's plight. Raymond Roger had just complained of the horrors wrought by the crusaders when Pedro replied:

> In Jesus's name, baron, you cannot blame me for that, since I told you, I ordered you to drive out the heretics, as there are so many people in this town who support this insane belief. . . . Viscount, I am very unhappy for you, because it's nothing but a few fools and their folly that have brought you into such danger and distress. All I can suggest is an agreement, if we can get it, with the French lords, for I am sure, and God himself knows, that no further battle with lance and shield offers you any hope at all, their numbers are so huge. I doubt very much whether you could hold out to the end. You are counting on the strength of your town, but you have got it crammed with people, with women and children; otherwise, yes, I think you could see some hope in that. I am very sorry indeed for you, deeply distressed; for the love I bear you and for our old friendship's sake, there is nothing I will not do to help you, barring great dishonor.

Chastened, Raymond Roger asked the king to intercede on his behalf with the besiegers. The monarch of Aragon and Catalonia rode back to the crusader encampment, confident that the sweet voice of custom would prevail. The negotiations, however, quickly went nowhere. In the end, Arnold Amaury reluctantly consented to allow Raymond Roger, along with eleven companions of his own choosing, to leave Carcassonne with whatever they could carry; what happened to the city and the thousands within it would be left to the discretion of the crusaders. Pedro, disgusted with the demeaning offer, remarked that "donkeys will fly" before the viscount accepted such a deal. When Pedro presented the terms to Raymond Roger the next day, the younger man all but chased his superior from his sight. He declared that it would be better to be flayed alive than to acquiesce in such a base betrayal of his people. Pedro then left Carcassonne and returned to Aragon, grieving for his vassal and angry at the pope's legate.

On August 7, the crusaders attempted to storm Castellar, the southern suburb of Carcassonne. At daybreak they charged across its dry moat in full cry, but this time the stream of rocks and arrows loosed by the defenders left scores of attackers writhing on the ground, crawling back to the safety of the trees. One knight, bleeding from the thigh, lay all alone at the bottom of the moat, helpless and exposed. A crusader dashed back out into the line of fire and slid down the slope to his rescue. He propped the man up and hustled him to shelter, the missiles kicking up the dirt all around them. Both sides witnessed this exceptional act of courage, but only the crusaders, for now, knew the hero's name: Simon de Montfort.

Seeing that Castellar was better defended than Bourg, the northern lords ordered their siege engines brought into play. This was a very wealthy group of barons, so the number and size of these fearsome weapons had to be considerable. First there were the mangonels, small, torque-powered catapults that launched the medieval equivalent of shrapnel. These clouds of rock and pebble swarmed over the walls at great speed, maiming and killing those unfortunate enough to be caught out in the open. Then there were the trebuchets, the "spoon" at the end of their long shaft large enough to accommodate larger rocks and burning brands, which crashed into the wooden galleries atop the walls. Finally, in smaller numbers, there were the compact howitzers of siege warfare since antiquity, the ballistas.

The shouts and grunts of the artillerymen alternated with the whoosh of their airborne missiles. As would become common in the Albigensian Crusade, monks and bishops sang hymns to remind the combatants of the supernatural purpose behind the fracas. A team of laborers started building a makeshift causeway across the moat, using logs and stones and anything else that came to hand. Carpenters away from the fray put the final touches on a chatte (or cat)—a mobile shelter, topped by a platform of planking, beneath which twenty to thirty men could stand. The cat would be wheeled over the rough causeway and up against the fortifications; the men inside the shelter, experienced sappers, would set to work tunneling under the foundations of the walls. To prevent the defenders from setting the cat ablaze as it crossed over no-man's-land, unwanted horses and pack animals were slaughtered and skinned, and their wet, bloody hides draped over the planking. The besiegers might not have tried this tactic against the superior fortifications of Carcassonne itself, but the walls of Castellar were less imposing.

According to the chonicler Peter of Vaux de Cernay, the plan worked, but just barely. As the great, bloodied device got rolling, the crusader catapults lashed the defenders with an unrelenting storm of stone. From behind the narrow slits in the walls of Castellar, crossbowmen and archers took aim at the juddering cat as it came closer. Flaming arrows, quarrels, brands went flashing through space. Those that lodged in the superstructure of the shelter fizzled out in the puddles of fresh blood on the skins. The cat reached the wall. The men inside, who would have been soaked in the gore that had dripped from their animal protection, grabbed pick and spade and set to work. Soon they were digging for their lives. A lucky shot had ignited the cat as it stood against the rampart.

As the cat went up in flames, the sappers furiously carved out a protective niche in the wall so that the men atop the battlements could not take aim at them. Before their wooden shelter collapsed, the siege experts had secured their position and were ready for a long night's work. The defenders would now have to listen helplessly as the sappers dug a mine gallery beneath the fortifications. The classic sabotage scenario of medieval warfare would be played out at Castellar.

From underneath the rampart, in the darkness, the sappers scrabbled away at the loose gravel and packed earth until they reached the first row of heavy stone. This they propped up with beams and braces, until a large segment of the wall was precariously held up over a deep tunnel by a system of wooden stays, groaning under the weight. The makeshift supports were then drenched with olive oil, suet, pig fat, and other inflammable substances. They jammed the tunnel itself with straw, twigs, and branches brought across the moat under cover of darkness.

At dawn on August 8, the signal was given and the kindling lit. Great clouds of black smoke came pouring out of the hole. Within the mine, the flames from the branches and straw licked the wooden stays and braces, until they too caught fire. Burning, they weakened, cracked, and then collapsed. The heavy stone above came tumbling down with them. The wall was breached.

The crusaders were soon up and over the rubble and into Castellar. A vicious fight ensued, in which most of the defenders of the suburb were killed. The lords of the crusade, pleased with the outcome, repaired to their tents. Raymond Roger and his men, seeing their opportunity, came charging out of Carcassonne to counterattack and clear the suburb of the crusaders. Most of the northerners left to garrison Castellar were hacked to pieces. This savage massacre, the revenge of Béziers, subsided only when hundreds of mounted knights came riding back from the crusader encampment, their vigilance reawakened by the screams of the dying. The Carcassonnais could not withstand the shock of superior numbers. They fought their way back to the safety of their city, and a gate was swung smartly shut behind them.

Carcassonne was secure, but the siege had begun in earnest. Each side caught its breath. The crusaders had paid dearly for the prize of Castellar, but it was the defenders who would suffer more. The disaster of the previous week—the fall of Bourg with its irreplaceable sources of fresh water—could not be undone. The cisterns of Carcassonne were befouled, and as August wore on, the torrid heat did its awful work. Infants started dying, then the children, the old, and the infirm. Sickness spread; the animals lay down in misery. Soon there was rotting carrion in the streets. A blanket of flies settled over the city; the ground was alive with maggots. There was no water to be had, anywhere. "Never in all their days," wrote the chronicler who supplied these details, "had they known such suffering."

Toward the middle of August, a horseman approached the walls of Carcassonne and identified himself as a kinsman of Raymond Roger. He wanted a parley with the viscount. Although the chronicles do not give the identity of this crusader emissary, it seems that his claim to kinship was recognized. Raymond Roger, accompanied by dozens of men-at-arms, rode out of the city to hear what the man had to say.

The crusader's tone was sympathetic. "I hope . . . that you

and your people will prosper!" William of Tudela reported him saying. "I certainly advise you to hold out if you are expecting relief to arrive soon. But you must be well aware that nothing of the kind will happen." The anonymous noble, having under-scored Trencavel's isolation, then threatened Carcassonne with the same fate as Béziers. It was time to negotiate a surrender. The viscount was guaranteed safe-conduct to and from the cru-sader encampment if he agreed to meet with the barons of the north.

Reassured by the word of his kinsman, Raymond Roger Trencavel rode alone away from his city and, as his enemies watched, made his way to the tents of the great northern nobles. The viscount was brought to the pavilion of the count of Nevers, Hervé de Donzy. He would never be a free man again.

What precisely transpired inside the tent has been hidden by the discretion of the pro-crusade chroniclers who are the sources for this eventful summer of 1209. What can be conjectured is that the nobles of the crusade arrived to greet this young man with the respect due a valiant foe. No doubt Arnold Amaury was present, careful to prevent some hiccup of chivalrous feeling from interfering with his plan to get rid of the viscount. That, it turned out, was the whole point of this siege. Even if, as some historians conjecture, the entire leadership of the Cathars was sheltering within Carcassonne, the head of the crusade thought it more important to eliminate the viscount than to pursue the heretics, which was, in theory, the stated object of the crusade.

The people of Carcassonne were told that they were free to go. In fact, they had to go; their viscount could not help them now. Catholic, Cathar, and Jew, one at a time out a narrow postern, the Carcassonnais deserted their city, and their fortunes.

If they attempted to leave with anything more than the shirt on their back—jewelry, money, finery—it was confiscated. "Not even the value of a button were they allowed to take with them," a chronicle states. Thousands of barefoot, scarcely clad unfortunates wandered out into the scorching stubble of the black fields, their livelihoods gone and their dignity shattered. They dispersed in all directions, randomly, over hills and along river courses, each to a destiny unknown and unrecorded. Carcassonne was to be resettled.

Raymond Roger was brought back to his empty city in chains and forced down the stone steps of what had been, until two days previously, his castle. The viscount was manacled to the wall of his own dungeon. Whatever deal he had struck in the crusader camp to save his people, it is exceedingly doubtful that he consented to this fate for himself. Three months later, the once healthy Trencavel was found dead in his cell. His successor spoke of dysentery and the mysterious workings of divine agency, but many in a sullen Languedoc suspected foul play.

That successor was Simon de Montfort. He had been given the lands of the Trencavels by a grateful Arnold. The greatest barons of the crusade had first been offered the huge holdings, but all turned down the tempting prize, out of feudal principle and, no doubt, fear of the reaction of their watchful monarch in Paris. But Simon possessed so little land in the north that his windfall threatened no one in the kingdom of France, and his skill as a warrior had been abundantly proved. His was a perfect match of ambition and ability. On August 15, 1209, he was made viscount of Béziers and Carcassonne, and all the Trencavel possessions in between. It was the feast day of the other Mary, the mother of Jesus.

Simon de Montfort (from a stained-glass window in the cathedral at Chartres)
(Mansell Collection/Time, Inc.)

The great army packed up and got ready to go home, its crusading quarantine completed and its sordid place in history assured. Simon had wrung a promise from the northern barons that they would return if he needed them. Count Raymond summoned his twelve-year-old son from Toulouse and cordially presented him to Simon and the assembled nobility at Carcassonne. Since one of the greatest nobles of Languedoc had just been ignominiously dispossessed, it is not unreasonable to assume that Raymond was presenting his son to these northerners as a way of asserting his family's legitimacy. A chronicle relates that the boy met with their approval.

The mass of crusaders left Languedoc for France. Simon settled with forty diehard knights, and their several hundred armed soldiers, in the citadel of Carcassonne. Most of his followers were minor nobles from Picardy and Ile de France; all were in search of adventure and wealth. There was even an Irishman, Hugh de Lacy, a malcontent of Norman lineage expelled from County Meath. Simon promised these men fiefs if they stayed and subdued the lands he had usurped. He would need their help, for beyond the walls of Carcassonne the new viscount was surrounded by people who hated him.

8.

Bad Neighbors

Et ab joi li er mos treus	I go to her with joy
Entre gel e vent e neus.	Through wind and snow and sleet
La Loba ditʒ que seus so,	The She-Wolf says I am hers
Et a.n be dreg e raʒo,	And by God she's right:
Que, per ma fe, melhs sui seus	I belong to her
Que no sui d'autrui ni meus.	More than to any other, even to myself.

S O SANG THE TROUBADOUR PEIRE VIDAL, bound for the castle of Cabaret, of the most beautiful lady of his day, Etiennette de Pennautier, or Loba. Those who traveled to the highland hideaway to woo her included men from the uppermost ranks of society: Bertrand of Saissac, the guardian of the young Trencavel; Aimery of Montréal, a lord of the rural Cathar heartland;

Raymond Roger of Foix, the hotheaded Pyrenean count. In the first decade of the 1200s, Cabaret had become Languedoc's foremost shrine on the pilgrimage of courtly love. In 1210, the crusade would make it synonymous with sorrow.

Cabaret was a rugged estate hugging the forward slope of the Montagne Noire, its wealth attributable to its gold and copper mines. At the time of the crusade, Cabaret had three tawny stone fortresses—Cabaret, Surdespine, Quertinheux—grouped on a height from which the plain around Carcassonne could be glimpsed, ten miles to the south. Loba was married to the brother of the seigneur, Peter Roger, the man who had been at Raymond Roger's side throughout the defense of Carcassonne, and who had implored the impetuous young Trencavel to refrain from rushing out to attack the crusaders on the day of their arrival. It is not recorded whether Peter Roger advised similar caution before the viscount accepted the safe-conduct that was subsequently violated by the crusaders. A measure of satisfaction was won by the imprisoned viscount's allies, when, a few weeks after the fall of Carcassonne, Simon de Montfort and his army were soundly repulsed before Cabaret. The wild terrain gave them no purchase for a long siege, and the attackers abandoned all hope of taking the place.

In the months following this defensive victory, Cabaret became the nerve center of minor rebellion. The occupying French lost control of about forty of the hundreds of castles that had originally submitted to the crusade in the wake of the Béziers massacre. From Cabaret, raiding parties stole through the scrubland by moonlight to lay traps for the new rulers of the Trencavel domains. In one such ambush, Bouchard de Marly, a member of Simon de Montfort's inner coterie, was disarmed and dragged back to captivity at Cabaret. Yet these were minor skirmishes, occurring in the dead of winter; the coming of warm weather would signal a return to more ambitious engagements.

In early April, a stumbling procession of about 100 men in single file arrived at the gates of Cabaret. They had walked across the inhospitable countryside from Bram, twenty-five miles away, a poorly fortified lowland town that had yielded to Simon de Montfort after only three days of siegework. The exhausted, whimpering men were Bram's defeated defenders; each trudged through the dust of the courtyard with face downcast, an arm outstretched to touch the shoulder of the man ahead in line. The people of Cabaret soon saw the reason for their odd parade discipline. The men had been blinded, their eyes gouged out by the wrathful victors. So too had each man's nose and upper lip been sliced off—they were walking skulls, their unnatural, immutable grins a hideous spectacle of mutilation. Their leader, who had been left with one eye so as to guide his companions from Bram to Cabaret, brought the grotesque march to a halt in front of Peter Roger, his knights, and their ladies.

Simon de Montfort, the new master of Carcassonne, had begun the campaign of 1210. The soldiers of Christ were once again on the move.

For the next two decades, the fate of the Cathars became intertwined with a political power struggle between feudal lords. There could be no backing down from the uncompromising precedents set in 1209. Pope Innocent had made it a crime not only to be a heretic but also to tolerate the presence of heretics in the community. Since the highest secular authorities in

Languedoc continued to scoff at such a notion, they could be deposed with the pope's blessing.

What was needed to stake a claim in the resulting Languedoc land rush was ruthlessness, orthodox piety, and a predisposition to conquest stemming, usually, from one's meager inheritance. Many of the settlers in armor were second or third sons from the north, hoping to reverse the bad luck of their tardy births. The southerners whom they dispossessed with the approval of the Church became nobles without land, castle, or income. They were known as *faidits*—fautors—a banditry of angry men looking for revenge. It was these faidits who ferociously defended their pacifist Cathar kin.

Simon de Montfort was the prime creator and crusher of faidits. A second son from an estate near the forest of Rambouillet, a woodland to the southwest of Paris, Simon came from an illustrious but not particularly affluent clan. His Anglo-Norman parents bequeathed to him the county of Leicester, in Britain. It was a bequest as beautiful and useless as the sky, since the Plantagenets on the English throne were loath to recognize the claims of nobles so uncomfortably close to their enemies in Paris. It would be up to Simon's fourth son, another Simon de Montfort, to reclaim his English patrimony and, in the course of an illustrious career, champion the cause of baronial freedoms in the teeth of royal tyranny. The father defended papal bulls; the son, the Magna Carta.

The elder Simon was a deeply devout man, respected for being straightforward in his dealings and for leading men by example. The admiring Catholic chroniclers of the time speak of his winning manner and distinguished appearance. One text lingers lovingly in its description of a tall, handsome aristocrat with a great mane of hair and a muscular build. Simon was, by all accounts, fearless. On several occasions, his comrades-in-arms had to restrain him from single-handedly taking on an opposing army. At the impregnable castle of Foix, a furious Simon rode with just one companion to the main gate and shouted up insults at those who defied his will to conquest. From the rain of missiles that formed the defenders' response, only Simon emerged alive.

In many respects, he was the opposite of Count Raymond of Toulouse, whose religious liberality, sexual profligacy, and elastic word were all traits Simon considered poisonous and immoral. A hardened warrior with an overriding sense of honor, Simon first drew attention to himself during the Fourth Crusade. Encamped with the greatest lords of France outside the Dalmatian port of Zara, he refused on principle to take part in the siege of a Christian city. When the Venetians subsequently persuaded the crusaders to embark for further outrages in Byzantium, Simon led a rump of disgruntled knights out of the Balkans in search of other mariners willing to take them to Palestine. After an inconclusive campaign under a crusader king, he returned home in 1205, his honor safe but his purse depleted.

Another of Simon's distinguishing characteristics was his conspicuous monogamy, which set him apart from most of his peers. His wife, Alice of Montmorency, remained Simon's life-long partner, and the couple had six children together. Alice shared in his battlefield successes and dizzying dash to prominence. She could usually be found at Simon's side, even in the dreariest of army camps. Alice, the first cousin of the captured Bouchard de Marly, arrived in Languedoc in March 1210 at the head of a troop of reinforcements for her husband, the new viscount.

While no army of Simon's would be as immense as the one assembled in 1209, each marching season swelled the number of men under his command, for the pope renewed the call for a crusade every year. From a mere handful of adventurers nervously waiting out the winter, the forces at Simon's disposal mushroomed in the fine weather, only to contract once again as each fresh supply of armed pilgrims completed its quarantine and returned to the north. Among the more vigorous knights beyond the Loire and the Rhine, a trip south to Languedoc during these years was irresistible, even without the crusading indulgence. An absence of two months was too brief for any serious trouble to develop at home, but long enough to hone one's skills in the storming of castles and the shedding of blood. A shrewd strategist and accomplished fighter, Simon de Montfort ran, in effect, a permanent, practical tutorial in warfare for the belligerent nobility of the north. When not bogged down in a siege, Simon ceaselessly galloped the length and breadth of his new domains, stamping out dissent, demanding homage, battling dispossessed nobles intent on revolt. His fair-weather allies had to keep up with him in a zigzagging marathon of intimidation.

The Perfect ran from the contagion of violence. Such horrors as Béziers and Bram strengthened their belief that the Church of Rome was illegitimate. The institution violated its own laws. For simpler souls, a similar damning conclusion could be drawn from what they witnessed in these years: The harmless, holy people within the villages were being forced to flee the foreign warriors without. The crusaders destroyed vineyards, burned crops, took what was not theirs. One of Simon's first measures was to institute an onerous annual poll tax, the proceeds of which went to the pope. It was as if he were encouraging people to side with the Cathars.

Resistance to his authority was widespread. In the countryside around Albi, Simon de Montfort rode triumphantly into villages and towns that paid him elaborate civic homage—then defied his representatives once he had returned to distant Carcassonne. The town of Lombers, where the pioneers of Catharism had faced down an assembly of bishops in 1165, did not even wait for Simon to leave. Their submission came only after a botched assassination attempt.

Other settlements that Simon visited were mysteriously deserted. At Fanjeaux, the hilltop settlement that had witnessed both lively arguments and balls of fire, he found a ghost town. The homes of the female Perfect were empty, their spinning wheels and looms surrendered to the insistent intrusion of the winds. In the valley below, at Prouille, Dominic's young women worked hard in their new convent, but their heretical kin had vanished.

Some of the Perfect went to Montségur, a castle in the Pyrenees. In 1204, the fortress had been rebuilt, at the behest of farsighted dualist leaders, by a wealthy Cathar believer linked to the ruling family of the region. The eagle's nest served as the ultimate bastion of heresy, an unassailable fastness that all turned to in time of need. Mount St. Bartholomew, a green goliath looming over Montségur, could be seen on the southern horizon from almost any point in central Languedoc, a constant reminder of the haven of sanctity nearby. Much of the Cathar leadership, including Guilhabert of Castres and other debaters of Dominic, headed to Montségur to weather the storm of war.

Others moved to the territories belonging to Raymond Roger, the count of Foix. His kinswomen, Esclarmonde and

Philippa, ran Perfect households, and his unofficial tolerance of the dissident creed was a secret to no one. He and Simon had signed, after much skirmishing, a year-long truce. The deal, brokered by Pedro of Aragon, was designed to give the Occitan cause some breathing room after the Trencavel debacle. In Toulouse, yet another destination for the Perfect, Count Raymond continued to show his customary reluctance toward persecuting his subjects.

Many of the Cathars in the old Trencavel lands chose to put their trust in the redoubts of the minor nobility. Hundreds of wandering dissidents heard of the hospitality of Geralda, the lady of Lavaur, a town midway between Albi and Toulouse. The Perfect hurried over the rolling farmland to find safety behind her walls. Although in theory a defenseless widow, Geralda had as a brother the pugnacious Aimery of Montréal. He made a tactical submission to Simon de Montfort in 1210, but everyone in Languedoc knew where his heart lay.

The other destinations for the displaced heretics stood dangerously close to Carcassonne and Béziers but seemed as reassuringly invulnerable as far-off Montségur. At Cabaret, Peter Roger and his people nursed the blinded of Bram. The Cathars were welcome in Cabaret, as were any knights ready to make risky guerrilla sorties into the valley. Some thirty miles to the east, an equally formidable hideout rose on the upland known as the Minervois. The capital of this hardscrabble region, Minerve, became a Cathar citadel. The local lord, William of Minerve, was a professed believer in dualism, and the fugitive Perfect deemed that his town, if attacked, would provide them a secure sanctuary from the fury of the crusade.

Geology appeared to bear them out. Even today clifftop Minerve wavers in the heat as if held aloft by faith alone, its stone mansions clustered over a precipitous drop. On all sides save one are yawning canyons carved out of the bedrock by converging streams. Almost entirely surrounded by cliffs, the town seems to hover in space. Its sole level approach was blocked, at the time of the crusade, by a castle turning its massive windowless back on an arid plateau.

On June 15, 1210, the forces of Simon de Montfort appeared on the clifftops opposite Minerve, the rampant red lion on his personal pennant planted with finality on the heights. On Simon's order the forces of the crusade separated, so as to triangulate better on the defenses of the town. Three catapults were set up, and soon a steady barrage of missiles went whistling straight across the abyss and into the town. Gradually, as the hours and days passed, gaping holes were smashed in the town walls. The crusaders, stuck out in the open on an inhospitable plateau, needed a quick victory before the summer grew hotter.

The crusading camp looked and sounded like a booming shantytown, the men scavenging for wood and hammering together makeshift huts and lean-tos in order to create some precious shade. But the carpentry had not all gone into shelter; after a few days a huge trebuchet, dubbed La Malvoisine (Bad Neighbor) by the crusaders, was rolled into position across from Minerve. Simon and his noble allies had dug deep in their purses to have this awesome Big Bertha of a catapult constructed. Some time in late June, Malvoisine's outsized arm traced its first deadly trajectory toward Minerve. When the arm stopped with a shudder, an enormous boulder sailed in silence through the sunlight for a few instants before landing with a telluric thud—at a place somewhere on the cliff face below the town. Then another boulder hurtled to the same spot, and another. This was not impaired marksmanship; it was inspired artillery work.

A nineteenth-century rendering of a medieval trebuchet
(Roger-Viollet, Paris)

Malvoisine was pounding a walled staircase leading down from the town to the canyon floor, where another wall protected the city's wells. Normally the fortified system was foolproof, affording protection from the keenest-eyed archer. But the sheltered stone stairway could not possibly withstand Malvoisine's incessant bombardment. When access to the well went, so too would all hope of withstanding the siege. Within days, the decision was taken in Minerve: The trebuchet had to be destroyed.

One night at the end of June, a few men of the town slipped stealthily across the canyon floor. The saboteurs carried oily rags, ropes, knives, and some glowing embers. In silence they climbed the opposite cliff face in the blackness, inching their way up to the silhouette of the catapult etched against the stars. Two sentries at the foot of Malvoisine were taken by surprise and slain. The men of Minerve then turned to their tall wooden tormentor, tied rags to it, splashed its legs with oil. The first, timid flame spiraled upward.

Another sentry, who had just come out of the bushes after relieving himself, shouted loudly until a knife was promptly buried in his heart. The alarm had been given, however, and the flames had just begun. The chronicler Peter of Vaux de Cernay did not say whether the saboteurs had time to clamber back down the cliff face to safety or were killed by the crusaders rushing to put out the blaze. Simon's men beat the flames with coats, shirts, and bedding until Malvoisine was saved.

Slightly charred, the trebuchet resumed its work at daybreak. The staircase was promptly rendered unusable. Now, in concert with the three lesser catapults, Malvoisine started lobbing its enormous payload into the center of Minerve. Walls collapsed, killing those huddled behind them. The now waterless town, built on a layer of impenetrable granite, could not afford to let the rotting remains of the unlucky imperil the health of the living. Each night, the day's dead were dumped into the canyon far below. The month of July wore on; the pitiless bombardment continued. Every evening brought with it the same ghastly chore; every morning, a parched despair. Like Carcasssonne, the town would be bested by thirst. William of Minerve knew at last that he had to surrender.

After much haggling, William offered all his lands and castles to Simon de Montfort. The northerner, impressed by his opponent's candor in defeat, magnanimously gave William a minor valley fief in exchange for Minerve and the country that surrounded it. To William's relief, Simon also agreed to spare the town's defiant inhabitants. A weird zephyr of mercy briefly danced through the canyon.

The agreement, worthy of thirteenth-century gentlemen, was about to be concluded when Arnold Amaury asked to speak. By chance, he had arrived at Minerve on the eve of William's submission, just in time to influence the terms of capitulation. Simon had been made a great viscount through Arnold's agency, so he could not overrule the legate's wishes. And they seemed, on the surface, to be entirely reasonable. Everyone found in the town had to swear allegiance to the Church and abjure any other belief. Some of the more zealous northern pilgrims complained that these conditions displayed far too much leniency. They had come to Languedoc to wipe out heretics, but Arnold and Simon were giving these cat-buggering vermin a chance to lie their way out of danger. A chronicler had Arnold respond knowingly, "Don't worry. I fancy that very few of them will be converted."

William of Minerve returned to his people. Although credentes like himself would gladly swear the oath, the Perfect were immune from such base instincts as self-preservation. True, they had come to Minerve to avoid certain death, but only as a means of continuing their work as exemplars of otherworldly purity. Deliberate suicide, when other options were available, was a form of material vanity. But now they were faced with a choice between dying and renouncing the consolamentum, which was really no choice at all.

There were approximately 140 Perfect in Minerve, separated into two houses for men and women. None of the bearded, black-robed male Perfect agreed to take the oath. A priest was rebuffed by a Cathar who said, "Neither death nor life can tear us from the faith to which we are joined." Three of the women, however, abjured the dualist faith and thereby chose to live. To their Perfect sisters, these three were to be mourned, for they had relinquished their chance to commune with the Good for all time.

The 140 Cathar Perfect of Minerve were led down the ruined staircase to the canyon floor and tied to stakes planted in great piles of wood and kindling. The fire was lit. Peter of Vaux de Cernay, a chronicler and crusader fierce in his hatred of the heresy, claimed that the Cathars jumped joyfully into the flames, so perverse and life denying was their faith. The other chronicles omitted this detail. William of Tudela added only that "afterwards their bodies were thrown out and mud shovelled over them so that no stench from these foul things should annoy our foreign forces." The first mass execution by fire of the Albigensian Crusade had taken place.

It was July 22, 1210, once again the Feast of St. Mary Magdalene.

9.

The Conflict Widens

THE TRIUMPHS OF SIMON DE MONTFORT coincided with a diplomatic offensive by Raymond of Toulouse. Ever since August 1209, when he presented his twelve-year-old son to Simon and the great barons of France in Carcassonne, the fortunes of Raymond had waned. It took no great strategist to see that the crusade, once done with the Trencavel territory, might vent its violent piety on the rest of Languedoc. Despite Raymond's elaborate penance in June and his passive presence in the camp of the crusaders at Béziers and Carcassonne in July and August of 1209, signs of ecclesiastical hostility toward him were not long in returning.

In September, he was excommunicated again. The charge—not having lived up to the promises he had made at his public humiliation at St. Gilles—was partially true but verged on the vindictive, given the short amount of time that had elapsed between promise and nonfulfillment. Arnold Amaury raised the stakes by excommunicating the civic government of Toulouse as well and placing the city under interdict—that is, in a state of spiritual limbo during which no Catholic services, not even baptism and burial of the dead, could be legitimately performed. The accusation dealt with sheltering heretics, which the Toulousains disingenuously denied.

In attacking such a powerful force as the consuls of a rich and independent city, the papal legate was showing that the Church in Languedoc had been emboldened by the military success of the crusade. The count and his consuls, alarmed at this turn of events, decided to take their case directly to the pope. Fearing that he might be overruled, Arnold implored the excommunicates to stay in Languedoc and negotiate with him. His entreaties were ignored, and the Toulousains left for Rome in late 1209.

Innocent III must have awaited the aggrieved Occitans serenely. No pope in memory had been as powerful as Innocent was in the eleventh year of his pontificate. He ruled turbulent Rome with undisputed authority. He had consolidated his holdings, brought distant kingdoms to their knees, become the lawgiver of Europe, and purged the ranks of the clergy of undesirable loafers. His brother Riccardo had long ago finished constructing the Torre dei Conti, the brick fortress towering over the city as proof of the family's might. It had taken Innocent and his kinsmen only a few years to coerce the great clans of the city into obedience; the Frangipani, Colonna, and others of their ilk had been bought or outmaneuvered and were forced to sit out his pontificate in tight-lipped silence. The so-called Patrimony of Peter, the swath of central Italy coveted by German emperors, was now firmly back in the camp of the papacy, its fertile estates and trading cities handing over a rich tribute to

Innocent every year. No one had paid much attention to the indigent popes of the twelfth century; now all of Europe sat up when Innocent rose to speak. Thundering anathemae had variously fallen on the monarchs of France, Germany, and Britain, and intractable disputes between laymen were regularly referred to the pope in his role as ultimate arbiter. A zealous bureaucracy dedicated to elaborating canon law had expanded, for Rome's aim was nothing less than to codify, and thereby control, the affairs of a continent. Even the disgraceful Fourth Crusade had been turned to Innocent's advantage. The sack of Constantinople led to the installation of a Latin patriarch in the episcopal palace of Byzantium. For the first time in centuries, all of Christendom genuflected toward Rome.

Yet there remained, as Innocent put it, "foxes in the vineyards of the Lord," and the vineyard most at risk belonged to the men who had traveled to see him. The meetings between Innocent and the men of Toulouse seem to have been cordial, perhaps even warm. The chronicler who was the most antipathetic to the Occitan cause, Peter of Vaux de Cernay, claimed that the pope harangued Count Raymond repeatedly during his month-long sojourn in Rome. Another contemporary source, William of Tudela, gave an entirely different cast to the proceedings and itemized as proof of good feelings the gifts offered to Raymond by the pope: a gold ring, a "princely cloak," and a fine palfrey. It is reasonable to speculate, given Innocent's subsequent instructions to his legates, that the pope may have felt an affinity for Raymond, notwithstanding the invective that had peppered the pontiff's letters to the count prior to the crusade. Raymond was an elder statesman, a representative of an ancient family with blood ties to England, France, Aragon, and other, smaller principalities. As a nobleman, Innocent may have had second thoughts about dispossessing such an important figure. Squashing the Trencavels was one thing; getting rid of the great Saint Gilles, another. As a lawyer, the pope would have been fully aware that the march of canon law sometimes stepped on the toes of feudal practice. The presence of the consuls alongside Raymond showed that henceforth Church courts would have to take into account emerging civic customs. But as the supreme pontiff, Innocent knew that neither class sentiment nor legal scruple should prevail over questions of faith. In his view, Raymond was a protector of heretics and always had been.

In the wake of the Occitan embassy's extended visit, Innocent lifted the interdict hanging over Toulouse. In January of 1210, he wrote to his legates with instructions. The count was not to be restored to the state of grace he had enjoyed following his scourging at St. Gilles, but neither was he to be cast out of the Christian community. A special ecclesiastical tribunal was to be convened in Languedoc in the spring to give Raymond his day in court. If, on that occasion, he could clear himself of the charges of murdering Peter of Castelnau and of reneging on the promises undertaken during his penance at St. Gilles, then he was to be left alone. The excommunication would be lifted and the count given all the help possible in chasing the heretics from his lands. If, on the other hand, Raymond refused to exculpate himself, or failed to do so, his case was to be referred directly to the pope. On matters of such gravity, only Innocent could arbitrate.

While Raymond pleaded in Rome, Toulouse was in an uproar, its reputation as a city of tolerance and intelligent self-interest shattered, thanks to the eloquence and agitation of the man with a miter. Fulk, the merchant-turned-troubadour-turned-monk-turned-bishop, no longer needed to have his mules clop softly past his creditors. The debts of his diocese were paid in full, and the first successes of the crusade had spurred him to action.

For Fulk, the time had come to put an end to what he viewed as the scandalous acceptance of Jews and heretics in his city. Even as their brothers in sin burned at Béziers, the bishop knew that the black-robed weavers strolled openly through the streets of Toulouse, spreading their malignant dualism. A chronicle spoke of knights dismounting in front of Cathar holy men to perform the melioramentum, the ritual exchange of greeting and blessing between believer and Perfect, without the slightest attempt at discretion. Worse yet, in Fulk's eyes, the Catholics of Toulouse took such displays for granted, as if their fellow citizens' damnable practices were as normal as making the sign of the cross.

Fulk embarked on a campaign of preaching to instill the fear of hellfire in the faithful. The former troubadour crafted his homiletics carefully—and almost lost his audience as a result. The bishop fulminated on the evil of usury and charging interest on loans, which was forbidden to Christians in early medieval society. Yet brandishing the bogey of interest, often a prelude to persecuting Jews in medieval revivalist tours, failed to impress the sophisticated Toulousains. Commercial loans in the city had become commonplace, and the sale of shares—as was done to raise capital to rebuild flood-damaged Garonne textile mills—had been reinvented in the Toulouse of these years. The Jews, excluded from most professions except moneylending, were seen as respectable civic partners, as were their Christian rivals in banking, some of them Cathar credentes.

The normally astute Fulk, who had also been a businessman,

Bishop Fulk of Toulouse depicted guiding Dante and Beatrice in the *Paradiso* (The British Library)

may have underestimated the appeal of the heresy to the traders of Toulouse. Catharism, not Catholicism, spoke to the protocapitalists of the city, because its all-or-nothing approach to the material world allowed credentes to do whatever they wanted with their money. The bishop in his silks denounced cash; the Perfect in his simple robe conceded its necessity. The Church's position—calling money sinful while practicing rapacious tax collection—was hard to defend, even for someone with Fulk's gifts of oratory. In their countersermons, the Cathars would have driven home their advantage. Fulk's talk of virtue and vice about things mired in matter was, to the Perfect, yet another example of the pettifoggery that the Church passed off as moral teaching. If dubious distinctions had to be drawn, trading in money could, in fact, be considered a worthier occupation than bartering crops or livestock. Money and interest were abstractions, thus less tainted with the tangible evil of the material.

The bishop then opted for the argument of force. Fulk's medieval city was not a monolith of anticlerical consuls and striving artisans. Deep rivalries existed among districts, guilds, even families; inevitably, some people had been left behind, bankrupted, badly used by banker and merchant. In the neighborhood near Fulk's cathedral of St. Stephen, the strength of episcopal patronage could be marshaled and put to good use working God's mischief.

From his pulpit, Fulk sharpened his attacks on the profiteers, the godless, the landless, and the usurers, this time calling for reprisals. Among the ranks of the disgruntled, he formed a religious militia, called the White Brotherhood. They wore a large white cross emblazoned on dark robes and marched in torchlight procession through the streets of their enemies. Heavily armed, they launched nighttime attacks on the houses of prominent Jews and Cathars. Arson became respectable, almost sacramental.

Out of self-defense, the embattled opponents of the bishop responded by founding the Black Brotherhood. Its task was to confront the chanting vigilantes and make sure they did no harm. Like an Italian Renaissance city two centuries before its time, Toulouse in 1210 was wracked by gang warfare, in which scuffles and ambushes left dozens killed or wounded. The Blacks and the Whites terrorized a populace accustomed to civic peace. Bishop Fulk, revolted by the workaday amity between different creeds, had accomplished his goal.

Although Fulk succeeded in making an unholy mess of their city, the returning Raymond and his consuls knew that the supreme menace to Toulouse came from without. Not that the devout hooligans of the White Brotherhood failed to qualify as a serious vexation, or the bishop as a monumental pest. Relations between bishop and count, in fact, could hardly have been more acrimonious. Fulk treated Raymond somewhat like a stinking fish, at one time demanding that the count take a walk outside the city walls so that priests could be ordained in an odor of sanctity unpolluted by the fulsome proximity of an excommunicate. The threat of a renewed interdict was waved repeatedly in the face of Raymond's allies.

Yet as bothersome as Fulk and his Whites were, their campaign of troublemaking was a pallid reflection of the darker force abroad in Languedoc. If Toulouse was to retain its independence, it had to come to terms with Simon de Montfort's army as quickly as possible, before the marauding French finished picking over the carcass of the Trencavel domains. To spare Toulouse and its dependencies from being next in line, Raymond had to muster arguments and allies in his campaign for rehabilitation. The softening of Innocent, which had been the purpose of his trip to Rome, was having its desired effect: The legates were organizing, albeit in a dilatory fashion, a council to hear the count defend himself against the charges that had led to his excommunication. During the spring and early summer of 1210, the same season that Simon was mutilating at Bram and building Malvoisine at Minerve, Raymond raced throughout Languedoc and Provence, settling disputes with local monasteries, pulling down offensive castles, making payments of reparation. His intent was to live up to all the promises made at his public humiliation.

In July 1210, three months past the pope's deadline, the special conclave convened in St. Gilles, the same Rhône town where a year earlier Raymond had allowed himself to be scourged by Milo. The people of Béziers were now all dead, as was Raymond's nephew, the Trencavel viscount of Carcassonne. So too was Milo, who died unexpectedly in the spring of 1210. Toulouse, Raymond's capital, was on the brink of civil war, and Simon had just burned the Cathars at Minerve. Only the greatest nobles of the south, Raymond Roger of Foix and Pedro of Aragon, stood by the count in his effort to keep the plague of crusade away from his lands.

Raymond came to plead his defense in the murder of Peter of Castelnau. The churchmen of the south, even if they despised Raymond, would have to listen to what he had to say. Innocent's instructions had been explicit.

Yet the pope underestimated the animus harbored against Raymond by the Catholic hierarchy of Languedoc. Arnold Amaury still headed the anti-Toulouse drive, but he was now ably seconded by a certain Thedisius, Milo's replacement. Peter of Vaux de Cernay, the most pro-Catholic of the three chroniclers to report on the council, candidly admitted to the schemings that had preceded the meeting: "[Thedisius] desired most passionately to find some lawful means by which the Count could be prevented from demonstrating his innocence. For he saw very well that if the Count were given authority to exonerate himself—an end which he might achieve by means of fraud or false allegations—the whole work of the Church in this country would be ruined."

At the conclave Arnold Amaury asked to speak before Raymond. His line of argument was simple: When the churchmen had met in Avignon the previous September, Count Raymond had not carried out the terms of his penance and, as a result, had been excommunicated. Not all of those terms were carried out even now, particularly those that concerned illegally levying tolls on Church lands. Therefore Raymond had been, and still was, a perjurer. If he could not be trusted on such minor matters, he should not be listened to on far graver affairs. The Cathar heresy, which he had also sworn to eliminate, flourished in his lands. There could be no pleading if the accused was already without a trace of credibility. He had lied once; he should not be allowed to lie again.

The assembled bishops and abbots, coached beforehand in the springing of this perjury trap, agreed that the word of a forsworn nobleman was worthless. Raymond of Toulouse would not be allowed to speak. Even the chroniclers who detested him noted that tears welled up in the count's eyes as the decision was handed down. The count had been gagged on a technicality that even the punctilious pope had not foreseen.

Innocent's instructions had given the council the power to absolve Raymond but not to condemn him. If he could not speak, absolution was impossible. The tonsured heads at St. Gilles voted to extend indefinitely the excommunication decreed in September 1209. In so doing, they were not taking any initiative that could be construed as disobeying the pope; they were merely upholding the status quo. The perjury argument was an ingenious tactic, a great moment, one could say, in the annals of lawyering. Innocent went along with the decision, although he may not have been convinced of its justice. In a letter to King Philip Augustus of France shortly thereafter, he allowed, "We know that the Count has not justified his actions yet; but whether this omission is his fault or not we cannot tell."

Raymond would spend the next six months trying to get the prelates to change their minds. An absurdist round of conferences and conclaves enlivened the major cities of Languedoc, as Raymond went knocking on doors that would not open because he was an excommunicate. His promises of greater concessions to the Church were automatically invalid unless accompanied by a sworn oath; yet he could not swear to anything until his excommunication had been lifted. And the count could not request a hearing, since, as a perjurer, he could not speak.

Time pressed in the latter half of 1210, for Simon de Montfort's unbroken string of victories brought him closer and closer to Saint Gilles territory. Victory at Minerve was followed by the taking of Termes, a hilltop castle in the Corbières that was thought unassailable by anything less than mountain goats. As Simon and his cadre of grizzled knights and crusaders from Germany and Flanders clung to the steep slope, a Paris priest and siege engineer named William directed the fire of the catapults and Simon's ever-faithful Alice of Montmorency hustled reinforcements through the dangerous defiles to her husband's exposed position. After four months, Termes surrendered and its lord was sent to a Carcassonne dungeon.

Termes and a succession of hangings and burnings called forth a new wave of capitulation. Even Peter Roger of Cabaret dropped his defiance, by announcing to his prisoner, Bouchard de Marly, that he would hand over to him all his lands, castles, and titles in exchange for lenient treatment from the new viscount of Carcassonne. Bouchard went free, and the rebel base on the Montagne Noire shut down. By the new year, the great majority of the old Trencavel possessions had been taken.

King Pedro of Aragon tried to prevent the war from engulfing the rest of Languedoc. In January of 1211, he made a generous overture to the Church: Pedro recognized Simon de Montfort as his vassal, thereby giving a sworn seal of approval to the new viscount among the nobility on both sides of the Pyrenees. The bond of vassalage, a complex link of subservience for the vassal and obligation for the liege lord, was above all else a contract that established legitimacy. In recognizing Simon, Pedro was consigning the infant son of the late Raymond Roger Trencavel to feudal irrelevance and, in the process, acknowledging the Church's right to depose his vassals without his permission. It was an important concession for which Pedro sought something in return: the restitution of his brother-in-law, Raymond VI, to his rightful place as the most important lord of Languedoc. Pedro might well have added that Raymond de Saint Gilles, count of Toulouse, Quercy, and Agen, duke of Narbonne, marquis of Provence, viscount of the Gévaudan, was no mere serf to be trampled underfoot.

Arnold Amaury promised to end the charade of Raymond's ostracism the following month at a council in Montpellier. On February 4, 1211, Pedro and Raymond were told to wait in the cold outside a church while the Church's proposal was dictated to a scribe by the legates. Given Arnold's record as a merciless negotiator, the two men standing in the chill February wind must have braced themselves for a stern document.

Arnold did not disappoint. Raymond had the offer read to him by a literate member of his entourage. The legate enjoined the count to forsake the use of mercenaries, to pay the clergy their due, to levy no illegal tolls, to stop employing Jews, and to deliver all heretics in his lands to the crusaders within one year. It was the second part of the document that innovated: All of the castles and fortresses of Languedoc had to be demolished; Raymond and his subjects were forbidden to eat meat more than twice a week; henceforth all were required to wear only coarse brown robes; the nobles were forced to move out to the countryside and live "like villeins," and all of their property, goods, and earthly possessions were placed at the disposal of the crusaders. Furthermore, Raymond was required to go to Palestine and stay there until permitted to return by the Church.

This was not an olive branch; it was a club. Raymond seethed in silence, then, according to a chonicler, gestured to Pedro: " 'Come here, my lord king,' he said with a smile. 'Listen to this document and the strange orders the legates say I must obey.' The king had it read out again and when he had heard it, he said in a quiet voice, 'Almighty God in heaven, this must be changed!' "

The Church was asking nothing less than for the entire nobility of Languedoc to vanish and leave the way open for others to fill the vacuum. Raymond galloped off without even deigning to reply; he would never again even consider joining a crusade. For this and his previous acts of brazen impiety, he was solemnly excommunicated once again, and all of his territories were placed under interdict. Innocent chose to confirm the sentence.

The holy war finally approached the lands of Toulouse in April of 1211, when Simon de Montfort brought his crusaders to the town of Lavaur. Among their number were Enguerrand of Coucy, a wealthy noble from Picardy, and Peter of Nemours, the bishop of Paris. Peter had come to Languedoc to join his brother William, the priest of the Paris cathedral chapter whose expertise as a siege engineer had helped reduce Termes to submission. Many historians believe that Dominic, a good friend to Simon de Montfort, was also in attendance at Lavaur. To complete the crusader panoply, several hundred men of the White

Brotherhood took their places on the hillside opposite the town to chant out hymns under the direction of Bishop Fulk of Toulouse.

The siege of Lavaur lasted longer than expected because Simon lacked sufficient forces to smother the town, his reinforcements having been annihilated by Count Raymond Roger of Foix. In a surprise attack, Raymond Roger and his wild-eyed mountain knights fell upon a large column of crusaders who had made the long march from Germany to join up with Simon. Less than a day away from Lavaur, they were ambushed at Montgey, a hill near St. Félix en Lauragais, the village where the Cathars had met in 1167. The Pyrenean knights plowed into the thousands of hapless foot soldiers and killed as many as possible before the crusaders at Lavaur could ride to the rescue. When Simon arrived, Raymond Roger and his men had already taken flight. The leader of the crusade found only crowds of peasants from nearby villages, knives and clubs in hand, finishing off what the count of Foix had started.

The following month came Simon's response. On May 3, 1211, the walls of Lavaur were breached by Father William and his sappers, and the crusaders successfully stormed the town. The eighty Occitan knights who had commanded the defense of Lavaur were all hanged, in an egregious flouting of the rules of warfare. Captured noblemen were usually imprisoned or ransomed off to their families; in killing all of the nobles, the crusaders were showing that the legitimate rulers of Languedoc were just as much the enemy as the heretics. The leader of the defeated defenders was Aimery of Montréal, the lord who had hosted Cathar-Catholic debates and, in 1210, sworn allegiance to Simon de Montfort. He paid a steep price for double-crossing the northerner; the weight of Aimery's large and lifeless body was said to have snapped the crossbeam of the gallows.

Aimery had broken his word to Simon in order to come to the aid of his sister, Geralda, the lady of Lavaur's castle. Their mother was Catharism's grande dame, Blanche of Laurac, whose three other children had become Perfect. Although neither Aimery nor Geralda had received the consolamentum, both were known to be credentes, and Geralda, a widow, gained a certain fame for her generosity to the indigent. She was, according to the sources of the time, the most beloved noblewoman of Languedoc. After hanging her brother, Simon de Montfort had Geralda thrown down a well, then stoned to death. Even by the standards of the day, the act was shocking.

Yet the fate of Geralda, Aimery, and his knights was just a prelude on that May day of 1211. The lady's reputation for hospitality, especially after the terrible summer of Béziers, had spread throughout the south —Simon de Montfort and Arnold Amaury found 400 Perfect in Lavaur. As Fulk's White Brotherhood sang a Te Deum, the Cathars were marched to the riverside and burned, in the largest bonfire of humanity of the Middle Ages.

10.

A Time of Surprises

I N THE CENTER OF THE IBERIAN PENINSULA, the blazing plain
of La Mancha once stretched out as a no-man's-land between
Christian and Muslim. Beyond the abrupt mountains of the Sierra Morena, in the parched river valley of the Guadalquivir,
rose the rich mosques and minarets of Al-Andalus, the most
accomplished Islamic civilization ever to have gained a lasting
bridgehead in western Europe. North of the Morena's rocky divide stood the forlorn forward position of medieval Christendom, the brooding line of castle after castle that gave Castile
its name.

In the year 1212, a host of 70,000 crusaders, led by four
Christian kings, trudged across the dusty expanse of La Mancha
to fight against the Almohad armies under the command of their
new caliph, Muhammad al-Nasír. The Muslim forces fanned out
over the jagged mountains until they thought all the passes
through the Sierra Morena had been blocked or primed for sud-

den ambush. A local shepherd knew otherwise and guided the Christian hordes safely through a defile hitherto unsuspected by either side. Thus it was in Andalusia, not Castile, that on July 16, 1212, the two great armies met on a plain to join battle. Nearby was the village of Las Navas de Tolosa. The elite defenders of the caliph chained themselves to the tent poles of their monarch's red silk pavilion, so that flight would be impossible if the day went against them. The Christians won a crushing, total victory. There would henceforth be no stopping the inexorable spread of the Reconquista, the Christian reconquest of Spain.

The tidings from Las Navas de Tolosa set bells pealing across a continent. For Innocent, here at last was a crusade that had scored an unambiguous, untainted triumph. No sack of Constantinople, no holocaust at Béziers—just a clear-cut massacre of the heathen Moor. Even more gratifying was the news that the hero of the hour was King Pedro II of Aragon, whose inspired leadership of the army's left wing proved decisive in winning the day. Pedro had brought thousands of his vassals to the fight, including some from his turbulent possessions in Languedoc. Simon de Montfort, as viscount of Carcassonne, had sent fifty knights to join forces with their Aragonese suzerain. Arnold Amaury, recently named archbishop of Narbonne, had once again shouldered his armor and ridden out to combat. He had shown the king that he, too, was now a worthy vassal of Aragon.

In victory Pedro became a secular saint, an untouchable paladin of the Church. His faithful annual payment to Rome, his respect for ecclesiastical rights, his warrior valor placed in the service of a holy cause—no cleric could now even try to tarnish the glittering reputation of the thirty-eight-year-old monarch of Aragon. Troubadours sang of his gallantry, monks of his piety, and ladies bestowed their favors on this most Christian of heroes.

It came as a surprise, then, when the golden boy of orthodoxy demanded that another crusade, the one in Languedoc, be suspended immediately.

The king made the pope a proposition. He, Pedro, would act as a ward over all the lands of Toulouse for a few years. His brother-in-law, Count Raymond VI, would relinquish his territories in favor of his adolescent son, who would be educated in the court of Aragon in the ways of devout governance. When he attained manhood, Raymond VII could come into his inheritance, which would by then be cleansed of Catharism by the Aragonese king. The son should not pay for his father's shortcomings.

Moreover, Pedro demanded that his vassals north of the Pyrenees—the counts of Foix and the neighboring mountain domains of Béarn, Comminges, and Couserans—be left in peace by the Church and its sanguinary servants. In Pedro's view, Simon de Montfort had overstepped himself; having begun his career as an enemy of the Cathars and a spiritual athlete, he had become an outlaw. Simon had, in 1211 and 1212, attacked lands over which Pedro was suzerain, territories that had never been infected by heresy. Worse yet, according to the Aragonese's reading of the recent past, Simon had taken advantage of Pedro's absence in Andalusia on God's business to launch his assault.

The crusader against the Moors was picking a fight with the crusader against the Cathars. At the Lateran Palace the 28 steps of the Scala Santa awaited Innocent's troubled footfalls, for the pope now needed divine guidance.

Pedro's support was manna to the Toulousains. Simon had outsmarted and outfought them for more than two years. Even with the awkward nature of his army, which bloated, then shrank as forty-day crusader tours of duty were undertaken and completed, Simon had smashed and burned his way across all of Languedoc. As far north as Cahors, as far west as Agen, as far south as the Pyrenees, the tireless successor to the Trencavels had stretched his grasp over most of the lands of the Saint Gilles and the lower-lying fiefs of King Pedro's mountain vassals.

Simon may have been a gifted strategist, but his opponents helped him by their bumbling. What had been a peacetime boon—truculent independence—turned into a wartime albatross. Occitan lords, faidits, and citizen armies seldom acted in concert, even when the weight of their numbers would normally have beaten the often depleted ranks of the crusaders. In the autumn of 1211 at Castelnaudary, a town midway between Toulouse and Carcassonne, a small garrison under Simon held out for days in the face of a massed army of Languedoc knights and foot soldiers. When Bouchard de Marly and Alice of Montmorency, Simon's wife, rumbled into the plain from Carcassonne at the head of a column of reinforcements and wagon loads of supplies, the knights of Raymond Roger of Foix immediately charged down to attack. Thousands upon thousands of their fellows watched the ensuing combat from a hilltop, waiting for the order to join the battle. It never came. Count Raymond of Toulouse, as wretched a general as can be imagined, dithered ineffectually in the Occitan camp. Seizing the moment, Simon made a daring dash out to rescue his would-be saviors, thereby changing certain defeat into victorious stalemate.

Not all of the south courted debacle so assiduously. The family of Foix, the crusade's most feared foe, consistently acted with the belligerence it had shown at Castelnaudary and Montgey. When Simon, in his sole mistake of these years, attempted

in June 1211 to besiege Toulouse with a force too small to encircle the city, Raymond Roger ignored Count Raymond's pleas
for caution and repeatedly rushed out of the ramparts to kill as
many of the besiegers as possible. Simon, seeing his losses
mount, lifted the siege within a fortnight. Roger Bernard of Foix,
Raymond Roger's son, then ventured into Simon's territory on
missions of mayhem. Near Béziers, well within the countryside
pacified by the terror of 1209, Roger Bernard met up with a
group of crusaders bound for Carcassonne, who naturally
thought that any cavalcade of knights so deep in God's country
had to be supporters of orthodoxy. The subsequent attack came
as an utter surprise, and the unfortunate northerners were
dragged back to the castle at Foix, where they were tortured and
torn to pieces.

Still, such reverses were the exception. In 1211 and 1212,
Simon was free to cut a swath all around Toulouse. He gave the
defiant, if disorganized, city a wide berth, but nonetheless penned
off its access to the hinterland. He picked off one castle after the
next, and his conquest soon came accompanied by further outrage. In the town of Pamiers, the new master of Languedoc
drew up decrees in December of 1212 that effectively abolished
southern law in favor of northern feudal practice. In many ways
this was the unkindest cut of all, for time-honored systems of
inheritance, justice, and civil procedure formed the touchstone of
medieval identity. Simon's statutes, among other things, forbade
southern noblewomen from marrying suitors from Languedoc;
henceforth, brides with fetching dowries would be compelled to
wed only northerners. The desire to destroy, then colonize, became manifest.

The shifting nature of the conflict made the crusade stray
from its original purpose. As Simon used his talents to carve out

a kingdom for himself, fewer bonfires were lit. He had no time to winkle out the heretic hidden in the sheepfold when there were nobles in a nearby castle refusing to pay him homage. In any event, the devastating flames of Lavaur, Minerve, and other towns had shown that there was no safety in numbers. The surviving Perfect heard the word from Montségur: It was wiser to wait out the storm in the house of one's family, or in a cave in the Corbières, than to gather in a castle or city that the invincible Simon de Montfort would eventually get around to storming. For those imperiled few still living in the midst of orthodox spies, a trek over the Pyrenees to the discretion of Aragon and Catalonia was always an option. For all his talk, Pedro the Catholic ignored the Cathars in his domains. No more than the counts of Toulouse and Foix, the king of Aragon was loath to persecute his own people.

As the year 1213 dawned, Innocent grappled with the contradictions of the holy war he had launched four years earlier. Simon's forays into the lands held by Pedro's vassals smacked more of temporal ambition than of spiritual devotion. A genie had been unbottled at Carcassonne when Simon was allowed to usurp Trencavel. Innocent sympathized with King Pedro, his vassal and his champion, qualifying his ambassador to Rome as an "extremely cultivated" man. Moreover, now that the Moors were on the run and the Cathars weakened, Innocent wanted to turn the attention of Christendom eastward, to the reconquest of Jerusalem. In a letter to Arnold Amaury, the pope claimed that a new crusade to Palestine must take precedence over any further action in Languedoc. Accordingly, Innocent prepared a surprise of his own: In stern letters sent out in January of 1213, the pope announced that the Albigensian Crusade was over, effective immediately.

Before this stupefying news arrived from Rome, the situation in Languedoc had worsened. In a tense meeting at Lavaur, Pedro and Arnold Amaury brought their irreconcilable views out into the open. One wanted the preservation of the southern nobility; the other, its destruction. Since Pedro's failed intercession at Carcassonne to save the young Trencavel, Arnold had never once backed down in the face of pressure from the Aragonese king. If anything, Arnold had always upped the ante, changing unacceptable offers into insulting ones. The novelty this time came from Pedro, who no longer meekly walked away from Arnold's provocations. The victory at Las Navas de Tolosa had made of him an equal, if not a superior, to the legates in the construction of Christendom's future. He could now show his hand, and, like Arnold, Pedro did not disappoint.

In February 1213, he convoked the quarrelsome lords of the south and had them swear to let him govern their possessions during these times of emergency. Languedoc was now his protectorate. With his brother, Sancho, who was the count of Provence, Pedro created in one fell swoop a vast new entity, the makings of a protostate that, had it survived, would have dramatically changed the course of European history. From Saragossa in Aragon and Barcelona in Catalonia, their holdings now stretched in a great unbroken arc around the Mediterranean almost as far east as Nice, encompassing Toulouse, Montpellier, and Marseilles. Pedro aimed for nothing less than the unification of the Occitan- and Catalan-speaking peoples under one monarch.

The pope's men, reeling from such audacity, then received Innocent's letter. The pope had written Arnold, "Foxes were destroying the vineyard of the Lord . . . they have been captured." To Simon de Montfort, he was more explicit: "The illus-

Territory controlled
by Simon de Montfort

Territory King Pedro
proposed to govern

Le Puy

Valence

Bordeaux

Garonne

Rodez

Millau

Rhône

Albi

Avignon

Auch

Toulouse

Montpellier

Arles

Bayonne

Muret

Béziers

Marseilles

Carcassonne

Narbonne

Pamplona

Foix

Perpignan

Gerona

Saragossa

Barcelona

Tarragona

0   Miles   200

0   Kilometers   200

Mediterranean Sea

© 2000 *Jeffrey L. Ward*

trious king of Aragon complains that, not content with opposing heretics, you have led crusaders against Catholics, that you have shed the blood of innocent men and have wrongfully invaded the lands of his vassals, the counts of Foix and Comminges, Gaston of Béarn, while the king was making war on the Saracens." Both letters ordered an end to the crusade.

Arnold Amaury rebelled. A decade's worth of preaching, scheming, prosecuting, burning, hanging, and warring was in danger of being undone. He rode across Languedoc, rallying the bishops of the south to mutiny and dictating their letters of dismay to Innocent. A frantic embassy left for Rome. Preachers who had gone north to whip up enthusiasm for the crusading season of 1213 were instructed to continue their work, regardless of what the pope had said. Simon de Montfort, the jigsaw of his conquests the missing piece in Pedro's master plan, brusquely renounced his bond of vassalage to Aragon. By doing this unilaterally, he was once again breaking the feudal rules. Understandably, the man intent on establishing French dominion of the south would not be at home in some sort of Greater Occitania.

Arnold assembled his arguments. Unlike his gagging of Raymond, a decision that dangled by the thread of technicality, an honest point could be made this time: that King Pedro had been disingenuous in his representations to the pope. His Pyrenean vassals, contrary to his claims, had tolerated heresy in their domains for more than fifty years. Thus, argued Arnold, it was a Christian's duty to bludgeon them into obedience, which was precisely what Simon de Montfort had been doing. The crusade could not be finished, for the very simple reason that the Cathar enemy was still standing, not least of all in the largest city of the land. The abbot of the monastery at St. Gilles, never a friend of Count Raymond's, wrote to the pope of "the most putrid city of Toulouse, its viper's bloated belly stuffed with rotting and disgusting refuse."

Innocent spent the spring listening and reading. Pedro argued from feudal custom; Arnold, from canon law. Both men were right. Innocent III was many things—noble, lawyer, priest—but above all else he was the one and only supreme pontiff of Christendom. The choice before the vicar of Christ was clear: secular order or spiritual uniformity, the law of the land or the law of the Church, tolerance or bloodshed, peace or war, Pedro or Simon. The old house of the empress Fausta at the Lateran waited for its occupant to exercise his free will.

On May 21, 1213, a papal letter informed the world at large that the crusade against the heretics of Languedoc had been reinstated. Innocent had made his historic flip-flop.

In the early evening of September 11, 1213, Simon de Montfort and his men reached the bank of the Garonne opposite the town of Muret. The sky, chroniclers related, was clear, after a torrential rainstorm had nearly swamped the crusaders in a gulley the night before. Muret, its 200-foot-tall castle keep visible from Toulouse, twelve miles to the north, would be the site of the fateful encounter. Simon, who had made his last will and testament that morning, led his army across a bridge and into the eastern gate of the city. There was no resistance, for Muret, like so many other settlements on the periphery of Raymond's capital, had been cowed into submission by the crusade. Its location was ideal because the small group of loyal northerners garrisoned there could easily disrupt communications between Toulouse and Foix.

In Simon's forced march from Carcassonne, he had summoned every knight available to him, stripping his other fortresses of all but a skeleton force. He was faced with a great menace, and, ever the warrior, he was riding out to give battle. The off-again, on-again nature of this crusading year had not supplied him with a steady stream of manpower from the north, but he had still managed to assemble a fighting host: 800 heavily armed horsemen and 1,200 foot soldiers and archers. From the

castle where Simon was housed that night, there was an unob-
structed view to the west. Immediately outside the city walls
were the masses of common soldiers from Toulouse who had
been laying siege to Muret since August 30. Two miles away,
farther off to the northwest, began a waving expanse of gold
and blue and red—the banners of the Catalan, Basque, Gascon,
Occitan, and Aragonese nobility. All the lords on both sides of
the Pyrenees had rallied to the call of King Pedro. The south
had finally united against the north. The crusaders were outnumbered, it is estimated, twenty to one. Pedro, who had insisted
that the soldiery of Toulouse desist from storming Muret earlier
in the day, wanted Simon to fall into a trap.

As night fell, the churchmen with the crusaders engaged in
last-minute diplomacy between the two camps. Bishop Fulk and
the legates had long lobbied for a definitive confrontation; now
that it seemed inevitable, they did not like the odds. The
mounted clerics galloped back and forth in the gathering gloom,
before finally admitting to themselves that the time for talking
was over. Simon spent the night with his confessor; Pedro, according to a memoir written years later by his son, relaxed with
his mistress. Pedro had let Simon enter Muret unmolested so that
the crusader would be faced with a stark choice: venture out to
attack against overwhelming odds, or remain behind the ramparts and face inevitable defeat in a long and painful siege.
Simon, whose skill as a general had been proved in Languedoc,
had accepted Pedro's terms.

In the morning of September 12, Pedro summoned a war
council. He exhorted his fellow Aragonese to show the same
courage that had earned them glory at Las Navas de Tolosa a
year earlier. Each knight was invited to distinguish himself for
his valor on the field of battle. Count Raymond, the oldest man

present, begged to differ, suggesting that it would be more prudent to fortify their camp and wait for Simon to attack. The quarrels of the crossbowmen, Raymond argued, would soften the crusader charge, and then the southerners could use their superior numbers in a counterattack.

For voicing this proposal, the count of Toulouse was ridiculed. Victory had to be won with panache or not at all. The chronicler who recorded the conference had a Catalan grandee remark woundingly, "It is a great pity that you who have lands to live on should have been such cowards as to lose them." Raymond left the meeting to confer with his closest vassals. He and his men would form the reserve, or third corps of cavalry, whose job it was to stay in camp until an emergency arose.

In Muret at the same time, Simon de Montfort ordered his knights to burnish their armor and get ready for battle. At a meeting with his lieutenants, Simon's assessment of the situation agreed with Raymond's in the other camp. The crusaders had to risk a pitched battle in the open countryside, or they were lost. A chronicler reported Simon saying, "If we cannot draw them a very long way from their tents, then there's nothing we can do but run." The northern nobles prepared themselves for almost certain death. Masses were said, confessions heard. According to Peter of Vaux de Cernay, who was an intimate of the crusader leader, Simon headed to the terrace of the castle to arm himself, in view of the thousands of Toulousain militiamen encamped outside the town in expectation of plunder. Had his piety been tinged with superstition, he might not have ridden out to battle, for bad omens came in quick succession. First, he genuflected at a chapel door and broke the belt holding up the chain-mail chausses on his legs. A new belt was found. When his squires helped him atop his massive destrier, the girth securing the armored saddle snapped and he was forced to dismount. As a new one was being cinched into place, the horse reared up in alarm, delivering a blow directly to Simon's head. He staggered backward, stunned. A wave of laughter wafted up from the watching soldiery of Toulouse.

Simon ignored the worried looks from his entourage and rode with recovered dignity to the hundreds of knights waiting in the lower town. Bishop Fulk appeared with a relic, a chunk of wood from the True Cross, and implored the soldiers of Christ to kneel and kiss it. As each man took his turn awkwardly dismounting and clanking over in full armor to the prelate, it became obvious that the ceremony would take too much time. Horses and men grew impatient. A bishop from the Pyrenees grabbed the relic from Fulk's hands and gave a collective blessing to the assembly, assuring that those who died in battle would go directly to heaven.

Simon's cavalry filed out a gate and picked its way along a towpath between the bank of the Garonne and the walls of Muret. The militia and the southern nobles were on the other side of town, to the west. Once beyond the fortifications, the crusaders headed northward, hugging the riverside's west bank, as if slinking off to safety. They formed their three corps as they rode: the first, under William of Contres; the second, under Bouchard de Marly; the third, under Simon.

A long way off to the left, a mile or so distant in the west, the knights of the Occitan coalition cantered out into the plain. In the first corps of the southern cavalry were Raymond Roger of Foix and his fellow highland counts, as well as a large contingent of Catalans and Basques determined to show their individual prowess. We do not know if there was a leader to this large group. Behind them was a smaller corps, made up of the Aragonese under the command of their king. Pedro had switched armor with another knight so that he would not be singled out and taken hostage during any fighting. And back at camp, in reserve, were the forces of Count Raymond. The 30,000 auxiliaries—the militia in front of Muret, the archers, the crossbowmen, the infantry—were not involved. Out in the field, then, the numerical superiority of the southern cavalry was slightly less than two to one.

The crusaders wheeled left and charged. If siege warfare in this era was a science, pitched battle had all the finesse of a freight train. William's heavy cavalry rumbled across the wet grass, slowly picking up speed, followed by the squadrons of Bouchard and Simon. Soon the French knights were in full cry, bellowing out the name of their patrons. "Montfort!" "Auxerre!" "Saint Denis!" A chronicler relates: "Across the marshes and straight for the tents they rode, banners displayed and pennons flying. Beaten gold glittered on shields and helmets, on swords and hauberks, so that the whole place shone."

Seeing the flashing phalanx coming closer in the sunlight, the southern knights in the first corps spurred their mounts forward, heads bowed in anticipation of the nearing collision. William's wall of men and metal grew ever larger, their massive warhorses covering ground at full tilt. The shock of impact was tremendous. Count Raymond's son, then sixteen years old and safe in the Occitan camp, would later liken the sound of the crash to "a whole forest going down under the axe." The compact core of William's crusaders hurtled through the southerners like a cannonball. Men and horses went down, screaming. Swords swung, maces flailed, as the warriors from the north pressed the advantage gained by their punishing charge. The melee was well under way when Bouchard de Marly's hundreds

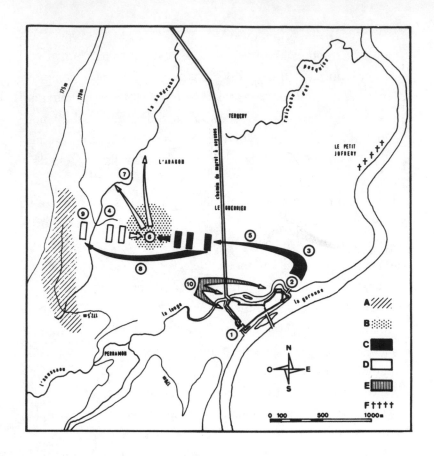

The battle of Muret

A: Camp of Pedro II and his allies; B: probable location of the cavalry combat;
C: crusaders' cavalry; D: allied cavalry; E: militia of Toulouse; F: graveyard.
The crusaders left Muret (1) and rode along the river, out of sight of the besiegers
(10). Once on the plain, they wheeled left (3) and drove straight toward the allied
tents (4). The first two crusader corps crashed into the allied corps (6).
While the allies fled toward a small river (7), the third crusader corps
charged the allied reserve (8,9).

of knights smashed into the pack, dealing a second, decisive
hammer blow to the disorganized southerners.

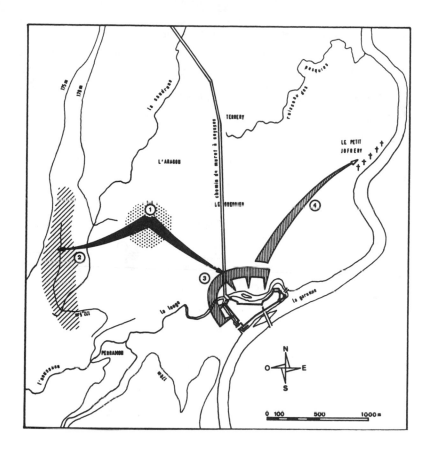

After the cavalry combat (1), the crusaders fell on the allied camp (2) and doubled
back on the militia besieging Muret (3), which fled in disorder (4).

The crusaders were trampling and dispersing the foe when
the banners of the king of Aragon were seen fluttering over a
second corps of southern cavalry. Bouchard and William must
have hollered over the tumult, for soon the disciplined crusaders
regrouped for another charge. They galloped over a meadow
toward the approaching Aragonese. Another sickening concus-
sion ensued, and a clanging, clamorous fight began. The crusaders, according to the chronicles, hacked their way to the man

wearing Pedro's armor; somewhere in the confusion, unheard by the northerners, the real monarch had revealed himself and shouted, "I am the king!" Whether it was a cry of defiance or an admission of defeat has never been known. A sword cut through the air, and King Pedro of Aragon fell to the ground, dead.

At the camp, Raymond's reserve had not budged, and the disaster was total. Bloodied survivors of the battlefield fell back, spreading the incredible news of Pedro's death. The army started to disintegrate, as men packed up hurriedly for a dash to safety.

Then Simon de Montfort and his knights, the third corps of the crusading cavalry, barreled into view and pounded headlong toward the demoralized southerners. The panic was general: Those who could, rode or ran away; those who couldn't, died.

The citizen soldiery from Toulouse before the walls of Muret heard a fatally false rumor: Simon's men had been routed by the brave king Pedro. Heartened, the thousands of lightly armed besiegers continued to harass the defenders on Muret's ramparts, believing that the town would soon fall. From the west came the thunder of hooves. The Toulousains turned and looked. It was the crusaders, bearing down on them in the full feral majesty of warriors who had fought their way out of the shadow of the valley of death. The Toulousain militia scattered in abject terror, the majority racing northeast toward the Garonne, where their barges were moored.

There was great sport for the crusader cavalry as the men of Toulouse sprinted across the open countryside. They were ridden down like wild animals, pursued and skewered during one long afternoon spent in the madness of a manhunt. The town of Muret emptied as Simon's soldiers charged out to kill the wounded. Hundreds of the desperate threw themselves into the river, drowning their floundering comrades in the struggle to stay afloat. It was an epic butchery, unseen since Béziers. The low estimate is 7,000 killed outright—a mass grave would be unearthed in the nineteenth century—in this postscript to the main encounter. Toulouse, the great city on the Garonne, went into mourning.

The horror of the battle's closing stages did not overshadow Simon de Montfort's achievement. He had won a miraculous victory yet again. The surprise was total. Count Raymond and his son fled to London, to the protection of their kinsman, King John. Pedro of Aragon, the one man who could resist the ambitions of Simon and the legates, of France and the French, was gone. The death knell of Muret sounded on both sides of the Pyrenees.

11.

The Verdict

"ILENCE!" INNOCENT STOOD IN HIS SLIPPERS in front of the
high altar at the Lateran and yelled at an unruly crowd of
priests, "Silence!!"

An eyewitness wrote that the hubbub only worsened, as
members of the congregation gave up on insults for fists. Miters
were dislodged, tonsures ruffled, crosiers swung. The second
plenary session of the Lateran Council degenerated into an undignified tussle between bishops who supported different pre-
tenders to the German throne. The pope vainly hollered for
order, this time in the vernacular, but no one in the riotous
conclave paid him any heed. Disgusted, the vicar of Christ
stalked out of his cathedral, followed by the cardinals of the
curia. The afternoon of November 20, 1215, would not be remembered for its episcopal decorum.

The council itself was another matter. A month-long conclave three years in the planning, the meeting brought together

the largest assembly of churchmen in a millennium—61 archbishops, 412 bishops, 800 abbots and priors—as well as representatives from every kingdom, duchy, and county in Christendom, 2,283 dignitaries in all. The Fourth Lateran Council (it had smaller predecessors in the twelfth century) was a lavish, polyglot, oversized spectacle stage-managed by Innocent III as the showcase of his pontificate. Marking the apogee of the medieval papacy as a power broker, the council filled the streets of Rome with haughty lords and proud prelates, bickering fanatics and barefoot friars, boyish princes and litigious dowagers. Not since antiquity were so many important doctrinal decisions made by the Church. The crush of ecclesiastical finery was so great that at the opening ceremony the bishop of Amalfi dropped dead from suffocation.

Given the pope's theocratic bent, the assembly not only defined dogma but also legislated on the secular affairs of Europe. So many political and legal fiats flew out of the Lateran that the hundreds of lay ambassadors summoned by Innocent could only stand by and watch the awesome papal machinery in action. Trial by ordeal, the hoary Germanic custom of tying people to logs or making them walk through fire, was supplanted by Roman law, administered by the curia. The barons of Britain, who had rammed the Magna Carta down their king's throat earlier in the year, were anathematized. The Jews of Europe were required to wear a distinctive yellow circle on their clothing, so that they would no longer be mistaken for first-class citizens of the medieval polity. No person great or small was exempt from the call to recapture Jerusalem, lost to the Muslims in 1187. The list of decrees and exhortations lengthened as the month progressed. The Fourth Lateran Council was the clearest expression of Innocent's quest to be the shepherd of European destiny. Naturally,

The Fourth Lateran Council (from the *Canso,* or *La Chanson de la Croisade*)
(Bibliothèque Nationale, Paris)

the continent's most notorious black sheep—Languedoc—
received special attention.

The protagonists in the Albigensian Crusade were all in
Rome, with the notable exception of the Cathar Perfect and a
confident Simon de Montfort. The southerners had come to
argue over who would get what. Since Muret and a subsequent
year of further brutality, Simon had exercised de facto sovereignty over all of Languedoc. It was up to the pope, however,
to make the final settlement. The southern clergy, led by Fulk
and Arnold, wanted to ensure that the partisans of the Saint
Gilles did not chisel away at the gains won on the battlefield.
Indeed, Count Raymond VI of Toulouse, his fifth and last wife
(a sister of the late Pedro), and his nineteen-year-old son had
come to Rome for the momentous meeting. They would have
formed a bathetic trio in the banqueting halls of the city, their
plight as highborn homeless capable of wringing sympathy from
their fellow nobles.

Accompanying the count of Toulouse was a large delegation

of lords from Languedoc, led by an indignant Raymond Roger of Foix, who had been forced the year before to place his castles in escrow to the Church. There was even a nobleman of dubious Cathar lineage with the southern embassy, Arnold of Villemur. It is impossible to conceive of a worse place for a suspected heretic to linger than in the biggest convention of churchmen of the Middle Ages.

The pope invited all the concerned parties in the Cathar wars, lay and religious, to a special audience, a caucus of sorts, away from the larger deliberative body of the Lateran. The men of Languedoc were given permission to speak their minds freely before the referee of Christendom. Given the strife and bloodshed of the past six years, Innocent's hope for dispassionate discussion was, at best, pious. Too many deaths separated the two camps; too much horror had scarred the face of Languedoc. A chronicler told of how the session immediately turned nasty.

It was Fulk, the bishop of Toulouse, who opened the hostilities. The eloquent prelate launched an attack on Raymond Roger, claiming that the advocate for the southern cause should not be allowed to speak, much less to regain his castles. The count of Foix, Fulk pointed out, had long had heretics in his family and had permitted Montségur to be rebuilt as a citadel of sedition. Raymond Roger retorted, disingenuously, that he was not responsible for the actions of his Perfect sister Esclarmonde and that he was not the suzerain lord of the country over which Montségur stood guard. Undeterred, Fulk reminded everyone of the count's role in the infamous massacre of the crusaders at Montgey. The bishop addressed the pope directly:

And your pilgrims, who were serving God by driving out the heretics, mercenaries and dispossessed men, he has killed so many of them, slashed and broken and hacked them in two, that their bodies lie thick on the field of Montgey, the French still weep for them, and it is upon you that the dishonor falls! Out there at the gateway rise the moans and cries of blinded men, of the wounded, of men who have lost their limbs or cannot walk unless someone leads them! He who broke those men, maimed and tortured them, does not deserve ever to hold land again!

Raymond Roger held a radically different opinion of the crusaders in question. He wasted no time in diplomatic circumlocution:

Those robbers, those traitors and oath-breakers adorned with the cross who have destroyed me, neither I nor mine have laid hold on one of them who has not lost his eyes, his feet, his fingers and his hands! And I rejoice to think of those I have killed and regret the escape of those who got away.

After making this terrible admission, he turned his ire on Fulk. Innocent listened as Raymond Roger thundered out his indictment of the bishop of Toulouse:

And I tell you that the bishop, who is so violent that in all he does he is a traitor to God and to ourselves, has gained by means of lying songs and beguiling phrases which kill the very soul of any who sing them, by means of those verbal quips he polishes and sharpens, by means too of our own gifts through which he first became an entertainer, and through his evil teaching, this bishop has gained such power, such riches, that no one dares breathe a word to challenge his lies. . . . Once he was elected bishop of Toulouse, a fire has raged throughout the land that no water anywhere can quench, for he has destroyed the souls and bodies of more than five hundred people, great and small. In his deeds, his words and his whole conduct, I promise you he is more like Antichrist than a messenger from Rome.

The venomous debate was adjourned by the pontiff. He had at last seen for himself what his zeal for crusade had wrought. The Christians of Languedoc hated each other and were unafraid to shout out their hatred in the holiest halls of Christendom. Upset and angry, the pope rushed out of the meeting room and headed toward his private quarters. "There now," a chronicler has one of Raymond Roger's nephews remarking, "haven't we done well? We can all go home, for we have driven the pope indoors."

In his search for quieter surroundings, Innocent retreated to the gardens of the Lateran. The calm was temporary—a number of southern clergy invested the cloistered quadrangle and demanded to hear the pope's judgment. Innocent, in an effort to set an example of Christian mercy, suggested that only the lands and goods of proven heretics be ceded to Simon de Montfort and the rest of Languedoc be returned to the various highland counts and to the young Raymond of Toulouse. He spoke at length of the noble and Christian demeanor of the youthful Raymond, echoing the arguments made by the ill-fated Pedro three years earlier: The son should not suffer for the sins of the father.

The southern clergy howled in protest. Fulk, once again, stepped forward, his language of dissent veering toward disrespect:

My lord, true pope, dear Father Innocent, how can you covertly disinherit the count de Montfort, a truly obedient son of holy Church, one who supports yourself, who is enduring such wearisome strife and conflict and is driving out heresy, mercenaries and men of war? Yet you take from him the fief, its lands and castles, which he has won by the cross and his own bright sword, you take away Montauban and Toulouse if you separate the lands of heretics from those of true believers . . . and that is not the smaller share. Never have such cruel sophisms or such obscure pronouncements been declared, nor such absolute nonsense!

Others followed Fulk's lead. The pope was beseeched to give Simon the entire prize. Even if Catholics were dispossessed, the churchmen argued, the stain of heresy had splattered everyone in Languedoc. Innocent, although the pontiff, could not defy the wishes of an entire province of his clergy. A Cistercian from Southampton reminded the pope that the younger Raymond's mother had been Joan of England, whose dowry had included several inalienable territories in Provence. Innocent seized on this information to deliver his verdict: Simon retained all the lands of the Trencavels and the Saint Gilles, save the scattered possessions in Provence which went to the young Raymond. His father received a handsome pension from Simon. Innocent demanded, as ever, that the hunt for the Cathars be intensified.

The victory of Muret was thus writ large, affixed with a leaden papal seal. Amid much solemnity, the decision was promulgated in mid-December 1215. Simon de Montfort was now, legally, the lord of Languedoc. He held more land than the king of France.

The defeated embassy of Occitan nobles left Rome just before Christmas. The merchant ships docking in the ports of Languedoc brought the news of Innocent's decision. Everywhere in the south, from the Garonne to the Rhône, partisans of Raymond and protectors of the Cathars had to decide whether to shed tears or to sharpen swords.

12.

Toulouse

I N JUNE OF 1218, a full two and a half years after the Lateran
had handed him Languedoc, Simon de Montfort was still in
his armor. For the past nine months he had been waging a sta-
tionary war, thundering out orders, leading charges, fighting off
counterattacks, laying siege to his perennial enemy: the city of
Toulouse. The property transfer Innocent decreed in 1215 had
made Toulouse the capital of Simon's territory, the crown jewel
of his conquest, the ruby metropolis that would make him rich.
Such was the intent of the Lateran verdict; its consequence was
wholly different, for Toulouse had rejected the lease granted by
the pope. The staunch followers of the Saint Gilles, the outraged
vassals of the Trencavels, the fierce warriors of Foix, the dispossessed nobles of the Corbières and the Montagne Noire, the
friends of the Cathars—all had gathered in the proud city on the
Garonne to thwart their new, papally approved, French overlord.

The siege of Toulouse was a long, ugly engagement, truly medieval in its cruelty. Both sides knew that this time they were locked in a fight to the death. Any unlucky besieger captured by the defenders, according to a chronicler, had his eyes gouged out and tongue cut off before being dragged half-dead through the streets tied to a horse's tail. Dogs and crows finished him off, after which his severed hands and feet would be placed in the spoon of a trebuchet and sent whistling back to his comrades.

Simon de Montfort, no stranger to such tactics, had plans to obliterate the city. The tents and workshops of his army were deployed in a settlement dubbed "New Toulouse," the area where the wrathful northerner promised to build a new capital once he had killed all of his subjects and burned their houses to the ground.

How Simon's triumph in Rome in 1215 became a test before Toulouse in 1218 had nothing of the inevitable about it. Count Raymond's son, the youth who had so impressed the pope with his Christian piety and noble bearing, turned out to be startlingly unlike his father. Raymond the younger was a born warrior, and it was in his birthplace that he first showed his belligerent talent. On returning from the Lateran Council to Avignon in the winter of 1216, he rallied hitherto apathetic Provençal nobles to his cause and boldly captured the crusader-held city of Beaucaire, the Rhône river citadel where his mother, Joan of England, had been delivered of him nineteen years earlier. In storming the town, the young Raymond announced that the Church had no business depriving him of his birthright.

When Simon arrived at Beaucaire to punish the upstart, he was repulsed, repeatedly, by a foe who did not flinch at riding out to clash with the fearsome northerner in open country. The south had lost a hero at Muret but found a new one at Beaucaire.

Throughout the summer of 1216, Raymond the younger held Simon at bay, humiliating the man who had just been made lord of all of Languedoc. On the heels of crusader frustration came calamity. On July 16, 1216—the fourth anniversary of King Pedro's decisive victory at Las Navas de Tolosa—Innocent III died, carried off by a sudden fever in Perugia.

The news of victory in Beaucaire and death in Perugia caused stirrings of revolt, which Simon only exacerbated by reverting to his tactics of quick strike and sudden atrocity. Whereas the task of managing his enormous Lateran windfall cried out for shrewd diplomacy, Simon blithely trod on the toes of potential allies. Even Arnold Amaury, the legate turned archbishop, came out against his onetime crusader partner, excommunicating Simon for pressing his prerogatives too hard in the see of Narbonne. Arnold had wrested the wealthy bishopric from a corrupt prelate, the man once denounced by Innocent as a "dumb dog," only to watch in alarm as Simon, the new count, demanded a share of the power and revenue never claimed by his predecessor. Arnold Amaury, of all people, gradually became a partisan of Raymond the younger.

Yet Toulouse, not Narbonne, was the key to Simon's legitimacy, and it was there that his failings as a statesman became most evident. In August 1216, Simon reluctantly raised the siege of Beaucaire, then raced cross-country—200 miles in three days—to stifle Toulouse's growing restiveness. The Toulousains had not forgiven the crazed manhunt and needless butchery of their citizen militia at Muret, yet they were unwilling to risk defying Simon openly. If anything, their hardheaded merchants were amenable to suggestion as to how their tolerant, prosperous burg might fit into his dominion. Simon had other plans. He approached the town in battle array and sent word that only money and hostages could deter him from attacking. Within hours, barricades sprang up throughout an indignant Toulouse, and furious street fights began. Following a night of violence, Bishop Fulk persuaded an assembly of notables to negotiate with their new count in a meadow far beyond the turmoil of the city. Such an act, the bishop suavely argued, would dramatically demonstrate their trust in Simon's sense of equity.

Even given past crusader actions, the depth of Fulk's treachery impresses. Several hundred emissaries, the richest and most influential men of Toulouse, duly marched out of the protective embrace of their city—and were immediately clapped in irons by the gleeful French. Simon and Fulk had effortlessly made a rich harvest of hostages. To regain its leading citizens, Toulouse was ordered to tear down its remaining defensive walls, demolish its fortified mansions, and scrape together enormous ransom payments. When rebellion broke out anew at these terms, Simon ordered his troops to sack the city. Everything—money, arms, goods, food—was taken in a monthlong rape of Toulouse. Scores of great houses were picked clean, then smashed to their foundations. And the hostages were not handed back to their families; they were loosed in the countryside and instructed never to return.

There was, significantly, no wholesale slaughter. By late October of 1216, Simon's designs had become clear: The capital was to be allowed to survive as a milch-cow, financing his campaigns of pacification and bowing to his absolute authority. He abolished the institution of the capitouls, the city's hallowed system of self-governance, and imposed crippling taxes on an already beggared populace. When he departed in November, leaving behind a garrison, the city was prostrate, in need of time to heal. There were no longer any Black and White Brotherhoods—Bishop Fulk and Count Simon were now universally, infinitely loathed.

Simon's tyranny might have taken root had he not elected to spend most of the following year bringing war to far-off Provence. He tried to expand his holdings, to go beyond the already generous terms of Innocent's decree. As Simon battled in the shadow of the Alps, Toulouse recovered. Grain-bearing barges on the Garonne smuggled weapons into the city, deposed consuls crept secretly into welcoming cellars, tradesmen hoarded supplies in back rooms, and servants and whores spied on the French garrison. Throughout Languedoc the network of Cathar believers, a grapevine untainted by orthodoxy, spread the word about the gathering storm.

On September 13, 1217, a small party of horsemen took advantage of a murky dawn fog to splash across the Garonne at a ford downstream from the sleeping city. They had ridden stealthily northward from the Pyrenees, past Foix and Muret, successfully avoiding detection by the occupying French. Before the mists had lifted, they were in the streets of Toulouse, and the pages of the foremost rider had unfurled scarlet pennons emblazoned with a twelve-point gold cross, the symbol of Count Raymond VI. An eyewitness wrote:

> When the count entered through the arched gateway all the people flocked to him. Great and small, lords and ladies, wives and husbands, they knelt before him and kissed his clothing, his feet and legs, his arms and fingers. With tears of delight and in joy they welcomed him, for joy regained bears both flower and fruit.

"Now we have Jesus Christ," they said to each other, "now we have the morning star risen and shining upon us! This is our lord who was lost!"

A few unfortunate French soldiers caught out in the streets by surprise were summarily cut down. Others managed to fight their way back through the clamor to the castle on the outskirts of the city, where Alice of Montmorency lived with Simon's younger children. The fortress, once the residence of the Saint Gilles, was a high-security enclave, safe from the passions and politics of the town. The Toulousains did not give chase, for almost immediately Raymond and the consuls issued orders. The townspeople were to drop their peacetime occupations at once and rebuild the walls and dig the moats of the defenseless city. When Simon got wind of the uprising, everyone knew, he and his barons would come roaring back through the valleys of Languedoc, intent on mass murder.

September of the year 1217 was the city's finest, most terrified hour. A chronicler told of the frenzy of united action:

> Never in any town have I seen such magnificent laborers, for the counts were hard at work there, with all the knights, the citizens and their wives and valiant merchants, men, women and courteous money-changers, small children, boys and girls, servants, running messengers, every one had a pick, a shovel or a garden fork, every one of them joined eagerly in the work. And at night they all kept watch together, lights and candlesticks were placed along the streets, drums and tabors sounded and bugles played. In heartfelt joy, women and girls sang and danced to merry tunes.

On October 8, the banner with the dreaded red lion fluttered in the fields to the north of the city. Simon de Montfort decided to attack immediately, before moats deepened and walls thickened. The senior churchman in Simon's company, remembering Béziers, exhorted the northerners to "let neither man nor woman escape alive."

The ensuing savagery, like the half-dozen battles in the months to follow, failed to breach the defenses. As the French armored horsemen and infantry hurtled past an obstacle course of sharpened stakes and treacherous ditches in their headlong rush to the gates, the Toulousains— men, women, girls, and boys—let fly with everything they had. "Sharp fly the javelins, the lances and feathered quarrels," an eyewitness wrote, ". . . fast the inlaid spears, the rocks, shafts, arrows, squared staves, spearhafts, and sling-stones, dense as fine rain, darkening the clear skies." From out of a gate burst the Occitan defenders, led by Roger Bernard of Foix, as much a warrior as his father, the man who had told the pope to his face that he regretted not having mutilated more crusaders at Montgey. Thanks to the gruesome heroics of the besieged, Toulouse fought Simon's experienced attackers to a standstill. The eyewitness described the scene with medieval relish:

> How many armed knights you'd have seen there, how many good shields cleft, what ribs laid bare, legs smashed and arms cut off, chests torn apart, helmets cracked open, flesh hacked, heads cut in two, what blood spilled, what severed fists, how many men fighting and others struggling to carry away one they'd seen fall! Such wounds, such injuries they suffered, that they strewed the battlefield with white and red.

Throughout the winter and spring, the same terrible scenario was reenacted—the French charged through a blizzard of missiles until hand-to-hand carnage checked their progress in the lists outside the city walls. Simon attacked from the east, the west, the river, the bridges. His horse drowned in the Garonne, almost taking him with it. He sent his wife and Fulk to France, to convince the warrior nobility that one final crusading quarantine should be undertaken. The call was heeded. From Picardy, Normandy, Ile de France, and England, thousands hurried south to take up their places outside the city. Yet even with superior numbers, Simon could make no headway. Toulouse was no Carcassonne or Minerve; the broad Garonne kept it supplied with water, and its size ruled out a suffocating encirclement. Fresh men and supplies easily slipped through the crusader lines. When Raymond the younger, the hero of Beaucaire, stole past the besiegers and entered Toulouse, the city went into raptures. "Not a girl stayed at home upstairs or downstairs," a chronicler remarked, "but every soul in the town, great and small, ran to gaze at him as at a flowering rose."

By June 1218, nine months into the siege, Simon's prospects looked bleak. His massed crusaders, having completed their forty days of service, were getting ready to go home, as were his many mercenaries, weary of being told that the depleted Montfort treasury would honor its debts once the city was taken. A dangerous defeat stared Simon in the face, one that would dwarf the embarrassment of Beaucaire. In the north, he would be seen as a lord who could not even hold his own capital and who was thus undeserving of further help; in the south, he would seem diminished and deflated, easy prey for rebellion. Simon had to subdue Toulouse immediately, before his army deserted him, or else his nine years of fighting in Languedoc would come to nothing.

Simon, mindful of the success of Malvoisine at Minerve, opted for an all-or-nothing tactic. He had a huge siege engine constructed at great expense. An enormous cat, the likes of which had never been seen in Languedoc, was rolled toward the northern walls of Toulouse in late June. Beneath its bleeding animal hides toiled scores of groaning laborers, inching the pharaonic structure ever closer to the city. On the cat's uppermost platform—which towered over the tallest parapets of the defenses—stood dozens of archers, prepared to rain death down into the streets once they neared the walls. The Toulousains trained their catapults at the tower and, by late afternoon on June 24, had scored enough hits to halt its progress at a safe distance from the city.

Both sides knew that if the cat came any closer, the defense of Toulouse would be imperiled. The crusaders could have brought their superior firepower to bear and punched a fatal hole in the ranks of citizens atop the walls. The Toulousains decided that early the next morning they would charge across no-man's-land and try to burn down the infernal machine. The ferocious Roger Bernard of Foix is reported to have said of the plan, "How we shall fight them! With swords and maces and cutting steel we'll glove our hands in brains and blood!"

Simon de Montfort was hearing dawn mass when the attack came. Messengers arrived three times during the service, imploring the count to ride to the rescue of the cat's embattled defenders. The men of Toulouse were clambering down ladders, rushing across the moats, slashing their way ever closer to the tower. The last of the messengers cried out to his lord, exasperated, "This piety is disastrous!" Unflappable, Simon waited for the consecration, the moment of the mass when the host is elevated, then crossed himself, snapped on his helmet, and said, "Jesus Christ the righteous, now give me death on the field or victory!"

Simon and his knights mounted their destriers and galloped

directly into the melee at the foot of the cat, swords and axes swinging. Within minutes, the tide had turned, and the warriors of Toulouse were staggering backward, badly bloodied, scrambling for the safety of the town. On the walls, the dismayed defenders loaded catapults and drew bowstrings to cover the retreat. An arrow tore through the head of the horse of Guy de Montfort, Simon's brother and comrade-in-arms since their campaign in Palestine. The animal reared up, dying, then a bolt from a crossbow caught Guy in the groin. Their screams of pain carried over the tumult. Simon saw his brother down. He scrambled to dismount when, as the chronicle relates, a mangonel atop the parapet let fly:

> This was worked by noblewomen, by little girls and men's wives, and now a stone arrived just where it was needed and struck Count Simon on his steel helmet, shattering his eyes, brains, back teeth, forehead and jaw. Bleeding and black, the count dropped dead on the ground.

Two crusaders rushed over and draped a blue cape over the body.

Word of Simon's death spread in all directions. Men stepped back, thunderstruck, lowering swords and shields. There was a stunned silence, which was soon broken by a great cheer, swelling louder and louder as the news swept through Toulouse. *Lo lop es mòrt!* (The wolf is dead!) Bells, drums, chimes, tabors, clarions sounded—the noise lasted all day and night.

Simon's eldest son, Amaury, gathered up the corpse and carted it out of sight of the revelers.

For Toulouse, the memory of Muret had been avenged and the devil defeated. For the crusaders, the disaster was total. Within a month the siege was lifted. The giant cat had been

Drawing from thirteenth-century bas-relief in St. Nazaire church, Carcassonne,
showing a scene from the siege of Toulouse and believed to depict the death of
Simon de Montfort
(Mansell Collection/Time, Inc.)

burned by the defenders and one last desperate assault, on July
1, firmly repulsed. The man who had trounced Languedoc, befriended Dominic, burned the Cathars, bullied the greatest
medieval pope, was dead at fifty-three.

As was the custom, his body was boiled until the flesh and
organs fell off the bone, and his remains were placed in an oxhide
pouch. This was interred at St. Nazaire Cathedral in Carcassonne, amid the requisite ecclesiastical pomp. It was his enemy,
the anonymous chronicler of the Cathar wars, who penned a
devastating obituary that, even today, some Toulousains can re-
cite from memory:

The epitaph says, for those who can read it, that he is a saint and martyr who shall breathe again and shall in wondrous joy inherit and flourish, shall wear a crown and be seated in the kingdom. And I have heard it said that this must be so—if by killing men and shedding blood, by damning souls and causing deaths, by trusting evil counsels, by setting fires, . . . seizing lands and encouraging pride, by kindling evil and quenching good, by killing women and slaughtering children, a man can in this world win Jesus Christ, certainly Count Simon wears a crown and shines in heaven above.

13.

The Return to Tolerance

WAR DID NOT CEASE IN LANGUEDOC, but victory changed camps. The Occitan nobles, inspired by the successful defense of Toulouse, at last united to press their advantage against the French. A large punitive expedition organized in 1219 could not check the rebellion. Preached by the new pope—Honorius III—and led by Philip Augustus's son Louis, the crown prince of France, the crusade fell victim to its participants' punctilious observance of the quarantine. Louis and his men returned to Paris after forty days of campaigning, their only accomplishment of note a cold-blooded massacre that mystified even their supporters. Every man, woman, and child in Marmande, an inoffensive market center of about 7,000 inhabitants in western Languedoc, was methodically put to the sword. Having thus doffed his cap to the precedent of Béziers, the future king then spent a few dilatory weeks outside the walls of Toulouse before torching his siege engines and riding home. Amaury

Thirteenth-century troubadour
(Bibliothèque Nationale, Paris)

de Montfort, Simon's son, was left on his own to quell the rebellion as best he could.

But Amaury was not the man his father had been. He did not inherit Simon's steely decisiveness or any of his father's talent for tactical atrocity. In the six years of battle, siege, and skirmish following Simon's death, Amaury was consistently bested by Raymond the younger and Roger Bernard of Foix. The huge Lateran land grant to the Montforts steadily shrank with every castle lost and garrison evicted. The major towns refused to open their gates to the French—and to their allies in the upper ranks of the clergy. The displaced leaders of the Church in Languedoc, including Fulk of Toulouse, had to go into exile in Montpellier.

The worst insult to the Catholic bishops came not from the battlefield, nor even from places that reverted to conspicuous Catharism, like the castles of Cabaret or the workshops of Fanjeaux. The bad news for the hierarchy came from Catholic believers. Many of them now viewed the leaders of the Church as a noxious, national enemy, to be denied the estates and benefices from which they had drawn their income. In the Occitan mind,

Innocent's reasoning about heretics had been stood on its head: It was the higher clergy, rather than the heretics, who should be charged with treason. The bishops were seen as accomplices of the hated French. The troubadours, already ill disposed toward killjoy prelates and papal legates, composed scathing *sirventes* about the warlords with the crosiers. The troubadour Guilhem Figueira began one song:

Roma trichairitz—cobeitat vos engana	Deceitful Rome, your greed leads you astray
C'a vostras berbitz—tondetz trop de la lana	You shear too much off your flock,
Le Sainz Esperitz—que receup carn humana	May the Holy Spirit who took on human form
Entende mos precs	Hear my prayer
E franha tos becs	And smash your beak!
Roma, ses razon—avetz mainta gen mòrta	Rome, you have killed many people without reason
E jes non-m sab bon—car tenètz via torta	And I hate to see you take so bad a path
Qu'a salvacion—Roma, serratz la porta	For in this way you are shutting the door to salvation.
Per qu'a mal govern	Ill-advised the man,
D'estiu a d'invern	Summer and winter,
Si sèc vòstre estern—car Diables l'emporta	Who walks in your steps— The Devil carries him off to the
Int el fuoc d'infern.	fires of hell.

A discouraged Fulk, who had not been allowed to return to his city since he had taken part in the siege of Lavaur in 1211, tried unsuccessfully to have the pope relieve him of his post as bishop of Toulouse.

If such bad feelings had sparked a massive defection from the Church, the bishops could have thrown up their hands and, as is still the custom in some quarters, blamed the Antichrist. But there was no great defection. As if to compound the insult to episcopal dignity, Catholic piety in Languedoc remained strong. Throughout the 1220s, bequests to monasteries continued to be made by burgher and knight, secular priests celebrated mass for devout congregations, and the fledgling Dominican order found ready audiences for its preaching. Even during the darkest hours of crusader sieges, the local clergy within the towns of Languedoc had suffered no manhandling from the laity. Moreover, many in the lower orders of the Church had taken up the Occitan cause. On the death of Simon de Montfort, for example, it was the priests of Toulouse who rang the bells and lit the votive candles. Resentment was directed squarely at the bishops who had brought ruin to a formerly rich land. It was they, not the Perfect, who were shunned by the people.

Yet Languedoc was a pauper, its bustling cities reduced to penury by the exactions of constant warfare. Its merchants were not welcome at the great fairs on the Rhône and in Champagne, the legates of Rome threatening interdict and excommunication to all who traded with the outcasts of Christendom. And even as Raymond the younger vanquished Amaury's loyalists in the field and many of the dispossessed nobles finally returned to their usurped castles, courtly life in Languedoc did not resume in the playful, spendthrift fashion that had once supported scores of performers and poets. The lovely successors of Loba went unsung as their menfolk scrambled for survival in a blighted land-scape. The newly delivered Languedoc of the early 1220s was a fragile creature, isolated and friendless, an all too easy victim should the armies of the north return in force.

During these years, the Cathars ventured out once again into the bright light of day. Inquisition interrogations conducted years later reveal that shortly after the death of Simon, the sur-viving Perfect climbed down from their eyrie at Montségur and sought out the credentes of the lowlands. Guilhabert of Castres, the Cathar "bishop" who had debated Dominic fifteen years ear-lier, reappeared in the Lauragais in the 1220s, preaching the gos-pel of darkness and light and administering the consolamentum to a new generation of novices. He and his fellow heresiarchs padded softly past the ruins of a decade of war. Guilhabert trav-eled to Fanjeaux, Laurac, Castelnaudary, Mirepoix, and Tou-louse, meeting with the decimated families of the dualist faith and testing the waters of tolerance among the Catholic majority. Despite the hardships suffered—or perhaps because of them—Languedoc had not turned against its holy men and women.

In 1226, in the small town of Pieusse south of Carcassonne, more than 100 Perfect met in a council to create a new Cathar diocese. By then, scores of Cathar homes had reopened. At Fan-jeaux, the hilltop village where Dominic and Simon had often met to break bread and discuss the progress of God's work, the harvests of hemp and flax once again found their way to the spindles of Cathar women. An informal network of female dis-sent was woven anew, the daughters and widows of a wounded people drawing strength and status from a life of self-denial. The martyrs of Lavaur, Minerve, and dozens of other burning grounds went unmourned; the thousands who had perished were now in the embrace of the Good, angels forever, their pilgrimages through the sordid world of matter concluded. Their fate inspired envy, not pity. As for the "unconsoled" among the maimed and murdered, the simple, sinful credentes fed to the flames of Rome or cut down by the steel of France, they had attained the status of Perfect in their next life. In the meantime, the church of the "good Christians" looked to resume its discreet place in Occitan life, as in the days before the devastation of the crusade.

The years around 1220 also marked the disappearance of the men who had shaped Languedoc's destiny. Following the deaths of Innocent III, in 1216, and Simon de Montfort two years later, Domingo de Guzmán died in 1221, his passing in Bologna soon shrouded by tales of last-minute miracles. The redoubtable Spaniard was fifty-one at the time of his death, his years of punishing poverty on the road having taken their toll on what must have been an amazingly robust constitution. Dominic had converted few Cathars—the Church was understandably short on moral authority as the crusade raged—and even those he coaxed back into the fold were suspect. It was difficult to punish these champions of asceticism, for the usual regime of self-denial imposed on the repentant resembled in its particulars the way of life of a Perfect. There is a record of one of Dominic's converts being ordered to consume red meat.

However much he failed to bring the dualists back into the fold of orthodoxy, Dominic nonetheless succeeded in firing the imaginations of some of the finest minds of his day. The Dominicans—the Order of Friars Preachers—mushroomed from 60 houses at the time of Dominic's death to 600 just fifteen years later. They, along with the Franciscans, would staff the nascent universities of Europe and crack the theological whip until the time of the Reformation. In Toulouse, the proving ground of the Dominicans, the first tentative bequests of lodgings grew into a citywide empire, until, at midcentury, the mendicant friars had enough muscle and means to break ground for a soaring red-brick Gothic sanctuary—later called the "church of the Jacobins." In the center of its nave now stands the casket of the most influential of thirteenth-century Dominicans, Thomas Aquinas.

In the year after Dominic's demise came the turn of Raymond VI, the admired but flawed old count of Toulouse. One day in early August of 1222, the sixty-six-year-old perpetual excommunicate spent the morning on the threshold of a church beside the Garonne, listening as sympathetic priests within raised their voices so that the aged nobleman could hear their celebration of the mass. At about noon, Raymond fainted from the heat. His escorts helped him to the courtyard of a merchant's house and laid him out under the shade of a fig tree. A stroke soon followed, leaving him speechless. The clergy came running. The prior of St. Sernin, the grandest Romanesque church of Toulouse and the burial ground of the Saint Gilles family since the turn of the millennium, refused to lift Raymond's excommunication but tried to take possession of the dying count anyway. The count's companions, suspecting that the prior was in league with the exiled Fulk and would thus waste no time in throwing Raymond atop a bonfire, bundled up their master in a blanket and took him to safety. Raymond died later in the day, and in spite of repeated requests in the ensuing decades, his body was denied a public Christian burial. On his father's death, Raymond the younger became Raymond VII. The elder man's unforgivable sin had not been cowardice in battle or lechery in bed; he had

earned the hatred of the orthodox for his dogged refusal to persecute the Cathars.

Less poignant, but more emblematic of epochal change, was
the death of Raymond Roger of Foix, in March of 1223. The old
mountain man was engaged in one of his favorite pastimes—
besieging a stronghold of the Montfort clan—when he passed
away in his base camp. He had been the model of the obstreperous Occitan noble that would soon be extinct: He had patronized
troubadours, wooed and won Loba of Cabaret, encouraged his
sister Esclarmonde and wife Philippa to become Cathar Perfect,
told Pope Innocent that he regretted not having killed more
crusaders, and fought the invasive Montforts to his very last
breath. Throughout, he had remained on uneasy terms with the
Church, although he proved a generous benefactor to those clerics willing to condone his excesses. Ironically, it was the Cistercians, the order that had guided the crusade, who gave the
deceased warrior a final resting place in their monastery near
Foix.

These years also saw the passing of Arnold Amaury, the
monk with the stain of Béziers forever soiling his name. In the
twilight of his life, as a mellowed—and much wealthier—
archbishop of Narbonne, Arnold turned against the Montforts
and sought to reconcile Raymond VII to the Church and the
French nobility. Despite the youthful count's convincing protes-
tations of orthodoxy and obedience, consecutive Church councils
in Montpellier and Bourges denied Raymond a voice in their
deliberations. Arnold's change of heart had come too late; he
died in 1225, unable to persuade his clerical colleagues to drop
the pious stonewalling that he himself had perfected.

Yet the death with the most far-reaching consequences during this period occurred in Mantes, France. On July 14, 1223,

fifty-eight-year-old King Philip Augustus succumbed to a fever. He had been the epitome of shrewd leadership, one of the supremely able monarchs that the Capet family of France would have the good fortune to produce every few generations, thereby ensuring the survival of their dynasty and the preeminence of their kingdom in Europe. At the beginning of Philip's reign, the Capets of France had been hemmed in by the Plantagenets of England and the Hohenstaufens of Germany; through diplomacy, guile, and feats of arms, he had subdued his enemies and firmly set France on the pedestal of power that it would occupy, more or less continuously, for five centuries.

Philip Augustus had been single-minded in making his kingdom secure. When Innocent pleaded with him to conquer Languedoc, the French king told the pope that he had, in effect, more important things to do. He had let some of his barons go to the aid of the Montforts, on strictly personal pilgrimages of violence, but in no way had he formally engaged the constellation of northern feudatories that made France the most feared nation of its time. Philip twice permitted his headstrong son, Louis, to swoop down on Languedoc, if only to show the colors: in 1219, notoriously, to order the Marmande massacre; and four years earlier, in the summer before the Fourth Lateran Council, to make a tour of Simon's winnings after Muret. (On that occasion, Louis left early, his only prize the jawbone of St. Vincent, a relic extorted from a southern monastery.) Now Philip Augustus was gone, and with him the restraint that had governed the behemoth of the north.

Six months after the king's death, in January, 1224, Amaury de Montfort admitted that he was beaten. He dug up the oxhide pouch containing his father's remains and led his diminished retinue back to the Montforts' small woodland estate outside of

Paris. The rebels of Languedoc had made a harmless fiction of the Lateran decree. Legally the lord from the Rhône to the Garonne, Amaury had, in fact, lost everything given to his family nine years earlier in Rome. Raymond Trencavel, the son of the man that Simon de Montfort had thrown into a dungeon, returned from Aragon, where he had been raised, and recovered his birthright as viscount of Carcassonne. In Toulouse, Raymond VII and his consuls tried to pick up the pieces of a shattered prosperity. And in the Ile de France, an embittered Amaury and his kinsmen played their last card.

In February 1224, Amaury de Montfort renounced all claims to Languedoc in favor of the king of France. The south now belonged to the French royal family—all they had to do was go and claim it.

14.

The End of the Crusade

SHORTLY AFTER THE DEATH OF KING PHILIP AUGUSTUS, Cardinal Romano di San Angelo became the papal legate to France and to Languedoc. Romano, a scion of the patrician Frangipani family of Rome, was a master diplomat, determined to bring the Albigensian matter to a satisfactory conclusion. For the Church, that meant having a free hand to repress Catharism over generations, with the full cooperation of the secular lords of Languedoc. With the Montforts chased from the province, achieving that goal became ever more complex.

In Languedoc, Romano had to contend with Raymond VII, who wanted to keep the spoils of his conquests and be recognized by the Church and the French Crown as the legitimate ruler of his ancestral domains. Yet no matter how skillfully the young count maneuvered in his quest for a negotiated settlement, the cardinal-legate stalled the coming of peace until he could dictate its terms. In 1224 and 1225, Raymond VII, backed by an infirm

Seal of Raymond VII of Toulouse
(Archives Nationales, Paris)

Arnold Amaury, repeated a set of proposals that both men believed would bring a much-needed reprieve to a war-weary Languedoc. Raymond promised to make a hefty payment of reparations to the Montforts, swear allegiance to the Capets of France, and hunt the Cathars from his lands. At a series of conclaves in these years that were reminiscent of the charade at St. Gilles where Raymond VI had been forbidden to speak, Romano smothered Raymond VII's overtures in procedural delay. In 1226, the cardinal dropped all pretenses and excommunicated the young count, thereby setting the stage for a new crusade.

While fending off peace initiatives in Languedoc during these years, Romano had been engaged in talks in Paris, with the aim of bringing the full might of France to bear on Languedoc. The new king, Louis VIII, had twice been to Languedoc as crown prince; he would have realized that the upheaval of crusade had created a power vacuum that might sooner or later arouse the cupidity of France's two rivals in the southwest, England and Aragon. At the moment, fortunately for the French, neither power threatened to interfere with any belligerent initiative in the south.

The English realm, recovering from the disastrous reign of King John, was in the throes of baronial revolt. (Indeed, in 1216, Louis had briefly accepted the crown of England at the invitation of the barons, until the pope stepped in and excommunicated him.) England's fief holders in Aquitaine were enjoined to remain neutral in the event of a new war in Languedoc. South of the Pyrenees, the merchants of Barcelona had used the disappearance of Pedro at Muret to turn their nation's attention seaward. Throughout the thirteenth century, the kingdom of Aragon would direct its energies to conquering the Muslim-held Balearic Islands, as part of a larger and eventually successful effort to establish a maritime empire to rival that of Genoa and Venice. Languedoc was receding from the horizon of Spain just as Amaury de Montfort was handing it over to France.

These political and dynastic considerations would have weighed heavily at the royal residence at the Louvre in favor of a decision to march south. Yet the first family of France wanted not only land but also money. The document record gives an impression of undignified horse trading, as both Romano and Louis jockeyed for advantage in their proposed joint enterprise. In the end, Romano promised to give the Capets a tenth of all French Church incomes for five years to pay for the cost of crushing Languedoc. And the cardinal delivered—by prying open the coffers of such wealthy sees as Chartres, Rheims, Rouen, Sens, and Amiens. It was a risky stratagem, with enormous consequences—later French monarchs would view the Church, and treat it, as a cash cow.

The royal crusade got under way in the spring of 1226, the mailed chivalry of medieval France once again jangling down the Rhône Valley, this time under the fleur-de-lis banner of King Louis VIII. The army dwarfed its predecessors in numbers and outmatched them in organization and unity of command. For all that, the great force conquered more by intimidation than by battle—and sometimes its powers of intimidation backfired. At the walled town of Avignon, King Louis's crusade came to an unscheduled halt when the frightened city fathers slammed shut their drawbridges on seeing the gargantuan size of the French army. They had originally promised the French free passage through the city and the use of their stone bridge to cross the Rhône—the same bridge of the nursery rhyme "Sur le pont d'Avignon, on y danse"—but once the huge host appeared outside their town, they wanted nothing to do with it. Well protected by their fortifications and well supplied by their river fleet, the Avignonnais held off the infuriated French king for three long months. Stuck out in the marshy flats to the north of the city as the heat and the flies grew unbearable, the army suffered terrible casualties from dysentery. His men, Louis realized, were dying in their own excrement. By the time Avignon finally capitulated, more than 3,000 had perished and tens of thousands more had been weakened by the ordeal. One lord to die from this outbreak of dysentery was an elderly Bouchard de Marly, the faithful friend of Simon de Montfort

Still, the city had surrendered. The fall of supposedly impregnable Avignon impressed the coalition of Languedoc nobles under the command of Raymond VII. So too had a band of preachers sent out ahead of the army by Cardinal Romano, Bishop Fulk, and Arnold Amaury's successor as archbishop of Narbonne, Peter Amiel. The preachers' task was to hammer home the lessons of the recent past by evoking such appalling memories as Béziers and Marmande. For the inhabitants of a weakened, wounded land like Languedoc, the thought of renewed tribulations could have only inspired terror. The propagandists of fear would also have emphasized that this crusade was unlike any other to have descended on the south. Its resources were as limitless as the wealth of the Church; its leader was no mere baron or monk, but the king of France himself. Historian Michel Roquebert has argued convincingly that the French monarchy, although it had been only a formal overlord of much of Languedoc during the twelfth century, held a place of primacy in the collective imagination of the Occitans. The king of France, alone among monarchs, represented the sacred legitimacy of the feudal order—even the independent burghers of Toulouse dated their documents according to the years of a French reign. The Cathars, of course, would have been immune to such thinking, but their compatriots must have quailed at the thought of the king of France coming to punish them. Louis had previously been to Languedoc only as a crown prince; now he was the person of the king, the repository of almost sacramental power. To defy him and his powerful army was to be both doomed and damned.

Faced with such physical and imaginative intimidation, many in the south raised the white flag. As Louis laid siege to Avignon, the once-proud towns of Languedoc sent him embassies to swear their fidelity and to beg for kind treatment. Béziers, understandably, was first in line, followed by Nîmes, Albi, St. Gilles, Marseilles, Beaucaire, Narbonne, Termes, and Arles. At

Carcassonne, the citizenry chased Raymond Trencavel from the city and sent ambassadors to capitulate before the king. As the French poured over the borders of Languedoc, Louis received fawning letters of obeisance from many local nobles. "It has come to our knowledge that our lord cardinal has decreed that all the land of the count of Toulouse shall be annexed to your domain," one letter stated. "We rejoice from the bottom of our hearts . . . and we are impatient to be in the shadow of your wings and under your wise dominion." The author of this missive was Bernard-Otto of Niort, a noble who had been raised by his Perfect grandmother, Blanche of Laurac, and had an uncle, Aimery, and an aunt, Geralda, brutally murdered at Lavaur. If men like him were running like rabbits for cover, the cause of Languedoc was lost.

Raymond VII and the Toulousains resisted the wave of panic, as did Count Roger Bernard of Foix. In the autumn, as the French army marched from town to castle accepting capitulations, the men of Foix and Toulouse harassed and ambushed the northerners in small guerrillalike actions. Some of the more independent French barons headed home with their men. Although the royal crusaders had brought much of Languedoc to its knees through intimidation, the army had not recovered from its disastrous summer before Avignon. King Louis, unwell since the squalor of that siege, suddenly grew feverish and weak. His entourage, seeing his condition worsen, tried to rush him homeward to the comforts of France. At Montpensier, a village in the mountainous Auvergne region, the cavalcade came to a halt; the king was too ill to be moved any farther. Louis took to bed and, according to a pious chronicler, refused the ministrations of a virgin girl who had been slipped between his sheets to rouse his kingly vigor. It was too late, anyway; Louis VIII died in

Blanche of Castile and Louis IX of France
(The Pierpont Morgan Library/Art Resource, New York)

Montpensier on November 8, 1226. He was thirty-nine—and, more important, his eldest son was only twelve. France no longer had a king.

The untimely demise might have turned the tide in favor of Languedoc had the powers in Paris not been steadfast. The hot Spanish heartland that had given the Cathars their holiest foe, Dominic, would now supply yet another devoutly orthodox enemy, Blanche of Castile. The widow of the king and the regent for their eldest son, Blanche brought to the cause of conquest a fiery piety that had been lacking among her Capet in-laws. To her, exterminating the heretics was as important as extending French domains.

As her principal adviser for affairs of state, she took Cardinal Romano, the papal legate. In Rome, the pope gave his blessing to this double duty; in Paris, tongues wagged about Romano and Blanche sharing more than just prayers. Whatever their true relationship, the cardinal and the queen agreed that the royal crusade in Languedoc did not need a king. Over the protests of wealthy French bishops, Romano kept the money flowing while Blanche ordered her army to stay in the south until all resistance was crushed. When the great barons of the north became restive under the rule of a woman, Blanche raised another army to combat them even as she kept a force down in Languedoc. With the encouragement of a new pope, Gregory IX, a nephew of Innocent III, the formidable lady regent pursued the crusade.

It was, in fact, a crusade in name only. The French troops conducted an ugly war of attrition for two years against the forces of Toulouse and Foix. Inconclusive battles were fought, atrocities exchanged—in response to a savage French reprisal at one town, the Occitans cut the hands off the French defenders at another—and fortresses taken and lost. By 1228, the circle of destruction had contracted to the immediate hinterland of Toulouse. Although not big enough to lay siege to the exhausted city, the French army, under the intelligent generalship of Humbert de Beaujeau, could not be chased from Languedoc. Safe behind the walls of Carcassonne, the fortress city they had taken great care to garrison, the northerners eventually hit upon the tactic that would extinguish the last flame of resistance.

In 1228, the royal crusade systematically turned the fertile expanse of the Toulousain into a desert. The French did not seek out battle—indeed, they ran from it. Instead they waged war on the countryside itself. Simon de Montfort had just burned crops; the French army, bankrolled by the Church and blessed by the queen, chopped down orchards and olive groves, uprooted vineyards, poisoned wells, set fires, and razed villages. Applauded by a vengeful Fulk, the men of the north proceeded meadow by meadow, manor by manor, valley by valley, in a medieval Sherman's March of deliberate, thoroughgoing vandalism. The land and its people, extenuated after two decades of savage bloodletting, could stand no more. In the end, isolated and beleaguered, unbeaten yet unable to check the progress of this awful juggernaut, Count Raymond VII sued for peace.

A bundle of birch cuttings came whistling through the hush and landed with a crack on pale white flesh. The sharp twigs came down again and again. Twenty years earlier, Count Raymond VI of Toulouse had staggered up the steps of the church at St. Gilles, his public penance coinciding with the start of the Albigensian Crusade. Now, on April 12, 1229, it was the turn of his son, Raymond VII, to receive the same humiliating treatment, this time to mark the end of the crusade. Just as before, a papal legate handled the switch, bringing the twigs down on the mortified flesh of the nobleman. Just as before, throngs of thrill seekers jammed the stoops, windows, and rooftops of houses for a glimpse of the exalted brought low. And, just as before, the penitent promised to help in stamping out the Cathar faith. For the counts of Toulouse, public obloquy had become a family tradition.

Yet the ceremony was not an exact duplicate of the scourging at St. Gilles. This time the onlookers whispered to each other in French, not Occitan, for the solemnities took place in the heart of Paris, on the Ile de la Cité. On this Thursday before Easter, Raymond and Romano performed their dark duet before the facade of the city's new cathedral, Notre Dame. Rising high over the warren of half-timbered dwellings reflected in the gray wa-

The scourging of Raymond VII of Toulouse in Paris
(Bibliothèque Nationale, Paris)

ters of the Seine, the elegant stone structure, its statuary and vaulting painted every color of the rainbow, stood as a spectacular symbol of cultural exuberance. Unlike the land of the Cathars, France was entering its springtime.

The two men went into the crowded church, past the nobility of the north, and walked down the nave to the high altar. "It was a great shame," wrote a chronicler, "to see so noble a prince, who had long held his own against powers both mighty and many, thus haled to the altar bare-footed, clad only in shirt and breeches." Raymond had agreed to undergo this degrading day for the sake of a lasting peace. His once huge domains were reduced to a truncated, landlocked principality encompassing Toulouse and a few minor cities to the north and west. The French Crown took what had belonged to the Trencavel family, as well as all of Raymond's possessions on the west bank of the Rhône.

A triumphant Te Deum resounded in the stone vault of the cathedral as the canons of Notre Dame were directed to give voice to their joy. It had been almost twenty years since one of their number, William of Paris, weighted trebuchets and adjusted mangonels for the greater glory of God and his servant Simon de Montfort.

From her place of honor, Blanche of Castile surveyed the instructive tableau of count and cardinal standing before her. She had done not man's work but Christ's. Beside her on this memorable Holy Thursday stood her eldest son, Louis. Once grown to manhood, the boy, as King Louis IX, would become the most devout monarch of Europe, eventually earning sainthood for his death on crusade near Tunis. A persecutor of heathen and heretic, Muslim and Jew, St. Louis inherited his mother's extravagant Iberian faith. Across the island from Notre Dame, he would erect the Gothic masterpiece of the Sainte Chapelle, an exquisite stone reliquary for the treasures he had bought from wily traders: a vial of the Virgin's milk, the crown of thorns, and dozens of other costly frauds peddled to the credulous crusader king. In watching the spectacle of Raymond VII's humiliation, the twelve-year-old future saint may have acquired his taste for devotional brio.

To receive the blessing of the cardinal, Raymond sank to his knees. The pose was apt, for the count had acceded to crippling demands in order to wring peace from the Church and the Crown. Not only were his lands cut in half, but his treasury was to be badly bled for the rest of his life. His sole child, a daughter aged nine, was forced into a marriage with one of Louis's many siblings; when they died childless forty-two years later, the county of Toulouse automatically became a part of France. Romano and Blanche also made sure that Raymond subsidized the hunt for heresy. A university was to be established later in the year in Toulouse, its four doctors of theology paid by the count to train future generations of Occitan clerics in the intricacies of orthodox belief. A posse of scholars would henceforth seek out and destroy the remnants of Catharism.

When Raymond, tall and handsome at thirty-one, emerged from the portals of Notre Dame, he was once again a legitimate Christian lord in good standing with both Paris and Rome. His enemies thought him lucky to have been granted even a pittance. Thanks to the usual tangle of noble bloodlines, Raymond of Toulouse and Blanche of Castile had a grandmother in common, the great twelfth-century queen of both France and England, Eleanor of Aquitaine. Were it not for that sentimental connection, Blanche might not have yielded an acre of land to the count.

The bonds of cousinhood stretched only so far. Immediately after the crowds had dispersed on the Ile de la Cité, Raymond and his entourage were carted across the river to the Right Bank and led into the brooding stone fortress of the medieval Louvre. They were held hostage there for six weeks, while the armies of the north tore down the fortifications of Toulouse, reduced dozens of castles to rubble, installed a royal seneschal in Carcassonne, and brought about all the other changes spelled out in the draconian treaty. The ceremony at Notre Dame may have had a touch of déjà vu, but in Languedoc nothing would be as it was before.

15.

Inquisition

O N August 5, 1234, a wealthy old lady of Toulouse said on her deathbed that she wanted to make a good end.

Her servants scuttled down the stairs and out into the street. They had to find a Perfect, hidden somewhere in the attics and cellars of the city. If they were lucky, perhaps the revered Guilhabert of Castres, the Cathar bishop of Toulouse, had come down from the safety of Montségur on a discreet visit to a believer in town. The servants made cautious inquiries at the houses of those who quietly shared the old lady's faith. In time, they returned with what they were seeking—a Perfect, who administered the consolamentum to the ailing woman, then left as stealthily as he had come.

One member of the household had not returned. He had dashed across town to the Dominican monastery, then ducked into its chapel. He made his way round the darkened ambulatory and knocked on the sacristy door.

William Pelhisson, a Dominican inquisitor whose memoir of Languedoc immediately after the end of the Albigensian Crusade gives a vivid glimpse of the altered circumstances of life in Toulouse, was most probably in the sacristy that day. With Pelhisson and his fellow friars was Raymond du Fauga, the bishop of Toulouse, also a Dominican. The bishop was changing out of the vestments in which he had just said mass in honor of the newly canonized Dominic. August 5, 1234, marked the very first time that St. Dominic had his feast day celebrated.

Raymond, William, and the other friars in the sacristy listened to their visitor's tale: A Cathar believer, in the delirium of death throes, lay helpless in her bed just a few doors down from the cathedral. The bishop sent a servant out to fetch the prior of the Dominicans back from his midday meal. Bishop Raymond was always given to the grand gesture; his inaugural act on taking over from the deceased Fulk in 1232 had been to bully Raymond VII of Toulouse into hunting down and executing nineteen Perfects on the Montagne Noire. There was a chance to put on a similarly instructive show for the populace of Toulouse.

According to Pelhisson, the traitorous servant led the bishop, the prior, and the other Dominicans into the woman's house. They climbed the narrow stairs and entered her room. Her relatives shrank back into the shadows on seeing the friars arrive. The dying woman's in-laws, the Borsier family, had long ago fallen under suspicion of heresy. One of them whispered a warning to the sickbed, telling the dying woman that the "Lord Bishop" had arrived.

She apparently misunderstood, for she addressed Raymond du Fauga, the Catholic bishop, as if he were Guilhabert of Castres, the Cathar Perfect.

Bishop Raymond did not correct her mistake. Instead, he

pretended to be the Cathar holy man, so that the woman would damn herself all the more thoroughly. As the others in the room watched, Raymond questioned her at length, eliciting from her a full profession of her heretical faith. He stood over the bed and, according to Pelhisson, exhorted the woman to remain true to her beliefs. "The fear of death should not make you confess anything other than that which you hold firmly and with your whole heart," the bishop advised with mock concern for her soul. When the woman agreed, he revealed his true identity and pronounced her an unrepentant heretic subject to immediate execution.

Since she was too feeble to move on her own, the woman was lashed to her bed. It was carried downstairs and into the street. Raymond led the curious procession past his cathedral and into a field beyond the city gates. A bonfire had been lit in expectation of their arrival. News of the spectacle spread throughout Toulouse. A large crowd assembled, then watched, openmouthed, as a barely conscious woman, with just hours left in her natural life, was thrown into the flames.

"This done," the Dominican eyewitness noted, "the bishop, together with the monks and their attendants, returned to the refectory and, after giving thanks to God and St. Dominic, fell cheerfully upon the food set before them."

The papacy of Gregory IX, begun in 1227, marked a fevered new departure in the race to silence dissent. The notion of a permanent papal, as opposed to an episcopal, heresy tribunal began to gain ground. Prior to Gregory's ascension to power in Rome, the task of ferreting out freethinkers had been left to

Pope Gregory IX appointing the Dominican to lead the Inquisition
(Biblioteca Marciana, Venice)

the bishops. For the preceding fifty years, successive popes had repeatedly exhorted their spiritual viceroys to arrest and try heretics in specially constituted courts. After conviction, the condemned would then be, as clerical euphemism had it, "relaxed to the secular arm"—that is, they were turned over to the local nobility for speedy incineration. The only problem with these diocesan courts was that they were exceptional. Most bishops lacked the intellectual stamina, and perhaps the stomach, to launch a sustained slaughter of the strayed sheep of their flock. Despite the great doctrinal housekeeping at the Lateran in 1215, many bishops and priests were still unsure of what exactly constituted heresy; others were compromised or complaisant because of their ties of kinship to the leading families of their diocese; and others were simply corrupt. Innocent had spelled out his frustrations in his opening sermon at the Fourth Lateran Council: "It often happens that bishops, by reason of their manifold pre-occupations, fleshly pleasures and bellicose leanings, and from other causes, not least the poverty of their spiritual training and lack of pastoral zeal, are unfitted to proclaim the word of God and govern the people." There could be no effective policing of souls as long as the bishops were left in charge.

Like his late kinsman Innocent, Gregory IX wanted results, and on a continent-wide scale. Special papal legates were granted wide prosecutorial power and sent out all over Europe to put down heresy. Some of the men chosen for these posts, unfortunately, soon proved themselves to be overzealous sociopaths. Robert le Bougre (the "bugger"—an epithet that suggests conversion from Catharism) sowed terror in hitherto peaceable northern France. In the Rhineland, the job was given to the sinister Conrad of Marburg. Everywhere Conrad turned, it seemed, hordes of unsuspected heretics lay hidden—in church and castle, commune and manor, convent and city. Hundreds, perhaps thousands, were sent to the stake, often on the same day that they were first accused. As if consciously playing the role of malignant madman, Conrad rode his mule about the Rhineland with a retinue of two: a dour fanatic named Dorso, and a one-handed, one-eyed layman called John. The threesome's appearance only added to their capacity to appall. On July 30, 1233, an exasperated Franciscan friar intercepted the grim trio and murdered Conrad. Instead of provoking a crusade, as was the case for Peter of Castelnau in 1208, this killing of a pope's man merely elicited a disingenuous letter from Gregory to the archbishops of Trier and Cologne on the excesses of his special envoy: "We marvel that you allowed legal proceedings of this unprecedented nature to continue for so long among you without acquainting us of what was happening. It is our wish that such things should no longer be tolerated, and we declare these proceedings null and void. We cannot permit such misery as you have described."

In Languedoc, where there were, indeed, heretics by the hundreds, Gregory showed fewer scruples. He and Cardinal Romano had been careful to staff the episcopal palaces of the south with such heartless prelates as Bishop Raymond du Fauga. A cash bounty was offered to anyone who betrayed a heretic, to be paid from the already overtaxed treasury of Count Raymond. Confiscated property was divided among the informer, the Church, and the Crown. The lure of blood money might have induced the servant of the dying woman in Toulouse to turn his mistress over to her wretched end.

Yet the Church could not count solely on the spontaneous baseness of human nature to finish the job the crusade had begun. An activist pope, Gregory did not wait for a trickle of betrayals to become a torrent. He envisioned a well-organized administration, answerable only to the pope and rigorous in the execution of its investigative tasks. For that, men of unreproachable probity and devotion were needed. A generation earlier, Innocent had looked at Languedoc and called on the Cistercians. His nephew, judging the monks of Cîteaux a spent force, turned to the Dominicans. Innocent's men went to debate and to convert; Gregory's, to prosecute and punish. In the spring of 1233, papal inquisitors were appointed in Toulouse, Albi, and Carcassonne. They would have successors in different parts of Europe and Latin America for more than 600 years.

The accused shall be asked if he has anywhere seen or been acquainted with one or more heretics, knowing or believing them to be such by name or repute: where he has seen them, on how many occasions, with whom, and when . . . whether he has had any familiar intercourse with them, when and how, and by whom introduced . . . whether he has received in his own home one or more heretics; if so, who and what they were; who brought them; how many times they stayed with the accused; what visitors they had; who escorted them thence; and where they went . . . whether he did adoration before them, or saw other persons adore them or do them reverence after the heretical manner . . . whether he greeted them, or saw any other person greet them, after the heretical fashion . . . whether he was present at the initiation of any amongst them; if so, what was the manner of the initiation; what was the name of the heretic or heretics; who were present at the ceremony, and where was the house in which the sick person lay . . . whether the person initiated made any bequest to the heretics, and if so what and how much, and who drew up the deed; whether adoration was done before the heretic who performed the intitiation; whether the person succumbed to his illness, and if so where he was buried; who brought the heretic or heretics thither, and conducted them thence.

The excerpt above, from a much lengthier interrogation checklist, attests to the numbing thoroughness of the Inquisition established expressly to destroy the Cathars. Scores, then hundreds of people were summoned to testify before inquisitors and their clerks. The questions were repetitive, designed to plant doubt in the mind of the person being interrogated as to what exactly the inquisitor knew, and who had told him. A person suspected of Cathar sympathies was not always informed of the charges hanging over his head; if apprised of the danger, he had no right to know who his accusers were; and if he dared seek outside legal help, his unfortunate lawyer was then charged with abetting heresy. Whatever the verdict of the inquisitor—who combined the functions of prosecutor, judge, and jury—no appeal was allowed. Even before judgment was handed down, anyone could be held indefinitely in prison for further questioning, without explanation. It was not so much a court system as a machine to create anxiety.

The *inquisitor hereticae pravitatis* (inquisitor of heretical depravity) tore apart the bonds of trust that hold civil society together. Informing on one's neighbor became not only a duty but also a survival strategy. For 100 years beginning in 1233, the inquisitor was a dreadful fact of Languedoc life, his arrival in the villages and towns the occasion for demeaning displays of moral collapse. In theory, no one could be punished if no one talked— the inquisitor was powerless to act without denunciations. In practice, no community, especially not a rivalry-ridden medieval town, possessed the seamless cohesion needed to combat the power of a secretive tribunal.

The inquisitor arrived in town and consulted with the local clergy. All males over the age of fourteen and females over twelve were required to give a profession of orthodox faith; those who didn't would be the first to be questioned. In his keynote sermon, the inquisitor invited the people of the area to think hard about their activities past and present and to come forward in the following week to give confidential depositions.

After this seven-day period of grace, those sinners who hadn't denounced themselves would be issued summons. The reticent ran the risk of grave punishment, from the loss of property to the loss of life. Aside from the immediate capital crime of being one of the Perfect, offenses included sheltering the Perfect, "adoring" them (performing the melioramentum greeting), witnessing a "heretication" (the consolamentum), and simply failing to report instances of heresy to the Church. Proof of genuine abjuration of error lay in the number of people the repentant sinner was willing to betray. The Inquisition was interested in names—in compiling an inventory of the network of Catharism that had survived the crusade.

Naturally, the unscrupulous immediately came forward to inform against their personal enemies, whether they were credentes or not. This initial list, if nothing else, served the inquisitor with a basis for installing a climate of fear. The denounced were called, sometimes imprisoned, always bullied into giving more names. The inquiry widened, pulling in Cathar and Catholic alike—and only the inquisitor knew which charges had any corroboration. To convict an individual who denied any affiliation with heresy, the inquisitor needed the testimony of at least two witnesses.

Often, people threw themselves on the mercy of the court, admitting to minor transgressions—for example, giving a Perfect a loaf of bread—in a distant past, in the hope that more recent heretical acts would somehow be obscured. When pressed, as ever, to name names, the craftier credentes gave a long list of the deceased, thereby fulfilling their obligation to finger as many people as possible while sparing the living the perils of punishment.

The inquisitors had an answer to this tactic. They dug up

and burned the dead. To the stupefaction of friends and family, cemeteries were turned upside down and decomposing corpses carted through the streets to the burning ground as priests cried, "Qui aytal fara, aytal pendra" (Whoso does the like, will suffer a like fate). These macabre bonfires were just the beginning. If the flaming cadaver had been notorious for lodging a Perfect, his house was razed, regardless of who happened to be occupying it. Depending on the gravity of the postmortem sentence, some descendants of the condemned were disinherited, their property and chattels confiscated by the inquisitor to fund his investigations. Others were imprisoned, or made to sew large yellow crosses on their clothing, as a sign of their familial infamy, or forced to undertake grueling penances. And some talked, although still grieving over the indignities visited on the bodies and souls of their late relatives. The names of the living began filling the Inquisition registers.

The Dominicans were hated. In Albi, the inquisitor Arnold Cathala was beaten to within an inch of his life when he began disinterring bodies. The bishop's armed men had to step in to prevent the burghers from tossing him unconscious into the River Tarn. In nearby Cordes, a fortified settlement founded by Raymond VII in 1222, the enraged villagers threw two agents of the inquisitor to their deaths down a well. At Moissac, a pilgrimage center on the Garonne, where the inquisitors Peter Seila and William Arnald nonetheless managed to burn 210 of the living, heretics were hidden by compassionate Cistercian monks. Even though these papal courts adhered to the merciless legal practices of their day, they were viewed as something new and malevolent, something that aimed at transforming a weary Languedoc into a land of turncoats and quislings. No one was safe unless he did harm to his neighbors.

16.

Backlash

ONE DAY IN 1233, a working man named John Textor, according to the chronicle of William Pelhisson, yelled out into a street of Toulouse as he was being questioned by the Inquisition: "Gentlemen, listen to me! I am not a heretic, for I have a wife and sleep with her. I have sons, I eat meat, I lie and swear, and I am a faithful Christian. So don't let them say these things about me, for I truly believe in God. They can accuse you as well as me. Look out for yourselves, for these wicked men want to ruin the town and honest men and take the town away from its lord."

People stopped to listen, laughed, then applauded. The foolhardy laborer was braying aloud what most of the city was whispering privately. Brothers Peter Seila and William Arnald failed to see the humor. They called their men-at-arms, and soon John Textor lay in chains in their prison.

Not that anyone expected the chief inquisitors of Toulouse

to show mercy to a critic, no matter how humble. Seila, before becoming one of the first companions of Dominic, had been a rich burgher and a supporter of the detested Fulk. In 1215, the Seila family had given the very first bequest to the dirt-poor Dominicans: a large townhouse in the heart of Toulouse. Seila's younger colleague, William Arnald, was a zealous brother from the city of Montpellier. When the Inquisition eventually got around to that stronghold of Catholic orthodoxy in 1234, one of its first acts concerned neither Cathars nor other heretics. At the behest of the city's conservative Jews, the Dominicans threw the works of the great Sevillan thinker Moses Maimonides onto a large bonfire of proscribed books.

Seila and Arnald wasted no time in making enemies. On receiving their papal commission in 1233, they had immediately targeted one of the most prominent Perfect in Toulouse, Vigoros of Bacone. Before his many allies and friends could rally to his defense, Vigoros was tried, convicted, and burned. There followed an unseemly two-year binge of body exhuming, coupled with sweeping imprisonments. To do the actual physical work of arresting, jailing, and executing, the two friars had to force the secular authority of Toulouse to do their bidding, by threatening prosecution of all who dared defy them. Refusing to obey the Inquisition was, according to Rome, as much a spiritual crime as heresy. Therefore it fell within the jurisdiction of Church, not secular, courts. The successful inquisitor used the full panoply of clerical intimidation—threat of excommunication, interdict, dispossession—to obtain the armed men necessary to do his job.

Count Raymond VII and his consuls, wary of bringing war back down on their heads, reluctantly went along with the Dominicans, until their dragnet grew too large to be tolerated. Raymond wrote to Pope Gregory IX that the inquisitors were so noxious that they seemed "to be toiling to lead men into error rather than towards the truth." He complained as well to Paris, so convincingly that Blanche of Castile, the regent who had vanquished the south, sent off her own letter to Rome. The inquisitors of Languedoc, Raymond and Blanche told the pope, had gone beyond the bounds of Christian decency.

Although supportive of his Dominican firebrands, Gregory found himself in a precarious position to impose his will. Politics intervened, in the form of a struggle with the German emperor over the papacy's temporal possessions. Ironically, Gregory's troubles were caused by the man who, as a toddler, had become a ward of Innocent after Emperor Henry VI had been felled by a mosquito in 1197. In a disastrous reversal for the Church, Frederick II, now emperor and in the prime of life, stood as a towering threat to Rome. Known as Stupor Mundi (the marvel of the world), Frederick was a polyglot, eccentric, and energetic monarch, who, from his multicultural court in Sicily, sought to expand his influence throughout Europe. He locked horns with the papacy repeatedly over control of cities around the Mediterranean. Faced with this charismatic foe, Gregory sought help wherever he could find it—including heretical Languedoc. Seeing his chance, Count Raymond declared himself willing to thwart Frederick's designs in Provence, if the pope called off his inquisitorial dogs.

Thus the mid-1230s saw a strange three-way tug-of-war between Rome, Toulouse, and the Inquisition. The pope occasionally admonished his inquisitors in Toulouse to exercise more leniency, even to travel into the remoter parts of Languedoc to avoid creating friction in the cities. The count and his followers, encouraged by the citizenry, stiffened their resistance to the Dominicans. The luckier heretics—many in Raymond's entourage had Cathar sympathies—were spirited out of town by the civic sergeants sent to arrest them. But such trickery only served to enrage and embolden the inquisitors. In the fall of 1235, the year after Bishop Raymond du Fauga's incineration of the old woman on her deathbed, the Dominicans took aim at several consuls of the city. The riposte was quick in coming. In October, the inquisitors were thrown out of Toulouse; the following month, the rest of the Dominicans—including the bishop—had to flee the city under a pelting rain of stones hurled by a jeering mob. The shaken friars, once in the safety of royal Carcassonne, duly excommunicated their enemies and placed Toulouse under interdict.

The pope, after sending a blistering letter to Raymond, lifted the interdict and ordered the inquisitors back to Toulouse. Whereas Raymond's long-suffering father would have been pilloried for condoning such behavior, the count was spared papal thunderbolts because he was needed as an ally. As a sop to public feeling, a Franciscan, Stephen of St. Thibéry, was named inquisitor in Toulouse to work with Seila and Arnald. The Franciscans were reputed to be more humane than the Dominicans, but Brother Stephen soon dispelled this belief, for he proved himself the equal of his Dominican colleagues in prosecutorial ardor.

Despite pressures from the count, the inquisitors persevered. At times they reaped a windfall from convenient conversions to Catholicism: Two ex-Perfect, Raymond Gros and William of Soler, gave the Inquisition reams of names and information about their coreligionists. These prized informers, who had to be protected from the wrath of their former flock, confirmed the friars' suspicions about Catharism—that it was becoming resourceful in the face of persecution. To avoid detection, many of the Perfect had shed their simple robes and would, if neces-

Inquisitors as depicted in *The Men of the Holy Office* by Jean-Paul Laurens
(Musée des Beaux Arts, Moulins)

sary, eat meat in public. The strict separation of the sexes had
even broken down. Some male and female Perfect now traveled
in pairs, pretending to be married couples. The Cathar homes
and workshops had closed, and many of the Perfect had moved
to the safety of Montségur. Only the initiates knew when there
was a holy Cathar on a pastoral visit.

The increased dissimulation proved to the inquisitors that
Catharism was dishonest. In a neat chicken-or-the-egg pirouette
of reasoning, deceit came to be seen as one of the principal hall-
marks of heresy—despite the Inquisition's having made such deceit necessary. In Albi and Carcassonne, after the initial
outbreaks of hostility toward the Dominicans, the French royal
authorities in place—the king's seneschals—helped the work of

the four inquisitors named to root out heresy in the old Trencavel domains. Often, they were supplied with men-at-arms to protect them. In the areas under the control of an independent
Toulouse, Brothers William, Peter, and Stephen were on their
own, traveling with a small retinue of scribes and clerks and
relying on their powers of intimidation alone to bend the local
nobility to their will. When not allowed in Toulouse, the friars
combed the countryside, taking depositions and imposing hundreds of penances and prison sentences. They were methodical,
merciless, and fearless, crisscrossing a hostile landscape as the
resentment of the ordinary people of Languedoc grew.

Raymond Trencavel tried to take advantage of the ground
swell of ill will. The son of Raymond Roger, the viscount vanquished by Simon de Montfort, he had temporarily returned to
Carcassonne in the 1220s, only to be chased out again by a citizenry terrified at the approach of the royal crusade. In 1240, he
assembled an army of exiles in Aragon and marched across the
Pyrenees to lay siege to his capital. It was 1209 all over again,
except that the roles were reversed: Now the French were within
Carcassonne and the Occitans without. As in 1209, the besiegers
first concentrated on Bourg and Castellar, the suburbs outside
the walls. Their inhabitants opened their doors without a
fight—French overlordship and the Inquisition had few local
supporters.

This time, however, Carcassonne held. After a clamorous
thirty-four-day siege during which Trencavel launched eight
separate assaults from the suburbs, the Occitans withdrew as a
French army from the north hurried into Languedoc to attack
them. The dispossessed viscount then retreated to nearby Montréal, which was besieged in its turn by the French. The fighting
was so ferocious that both sides agreed to a truce, and Trencavel

eventually renounced his claim to Carcassonne. He ended up a minor landowner near Béziers and, oddly enough, a crusader in Egypt alongside the king of France.

Raymond VII of Toulouse had not helped Trencavel in his revolt, primarily because he could not risk angering Blanche of Castile and Pope Gregory. Two years later, the situation was changed, and he had nothing left to lose. The pope had died, and with him went any chance of getting Raymond's marriage annulled. The count was desperate for a male heir. The succession clause contained in his penance at Notre Dame in 1229 stipulated that the county of Toulouse would, at his death, be passed on to his daughter and her Capet husband, Alphonse of Poitiers, even if Raymond had produced male offspring. This unusual clause, designed to ensure French dominion over Toulouse, might come to seem unfair and, eventually, untenable if there actually were a boy to lay a claim to the Saint Gilles patrimony. Hence Raymond's desire for a new, young wife who could bear him the sons that his current spouse, Sancha of Aragon, was past the age of producing.

The passing of Pope Gregory set back indefinitely his attempts to change his mate. Emperor Frederick had thrown the papacy into such disarray that there was, temporarily, no one on the throne of Peter to grant any favors whatsoever, whether it was in curbing the Inquisition or releasing him from his marriage vows. The time for diplomacy had passed; his only chance to become master in his own house and the lord of a Languedoc free from the French and their clerical terror lay through resorting to force. By the spring of 1242, the count of Toulouse had assembled his conspirators. They included his first cousin, King Henry III of England, and Hugh de Lusignan, the most prominent baron of Aquitaine. They, along with scores of Languedoc nobles itching for a showdown with the French, planned to put an end to the occupation of the south. The signal for revolt came on the Feast of the Ascension.

On May 28, 1242, Stephen of St. Thibéry and William Arnald stopped in Avignonet, a fortified town in the region between Toulouse and Carcassonne. In this, the heartland of Languedoc Catharism, the two inquisitors had picked their way through the villages of St. Félix en Lauragais, Laurac, Saissac, and Mas-Saintes-Puelles, compiling confessions that the eight scribes who traveled with them faithfully committed to Inquisition registers. The Franciscan and the Dominican moved through the country-side without the benefit of bodyguards. The many credentes of the area must have viewed this small troupe of Catholic clergy-men with dread, since the inquisitors often exercised their power to send Cathar sympathizers to the so-called wall, the dungeon of Carcassonne where prisoners were held in a cramped, clammy space and kept barely alive on a diet of bread and water. In a land where the Perfect had preached for generations—the great Cathar meeting of 1167 had taken place in St. Félix—the guilty numbered in the thousands.

The inquisitors' host on this eve of the Feast of the Ascen-sion was Raymond d'Alfaro, the bailiff of the count of Toulouse in Avignonet. D'Alfaro, wed to the bastard half sister of Ray-mond VII, was an important personage in Languedoc and a con-fidant of his brother-in-law. Although there is no document attesting to the collusion of Raymond in the events at Avignonet, it is highly improbable that his bailiff would have undertaken any action without the count's foreknowledge and approval.

D'Alfaro lodged his visitors in the central chamber of the castle keep, away from the houses of the townspeople. As night fell, one of his men, William-Raymond Golairan, paid a visit to the friars and saw that they were at their evening meal. A few hours later, Golairan returned to the keep and determined that the inquisitors and their aides had bedded down for the night.

In between these two instances of seemingly solicitous hospitality, Golairan had ridden out of town to a spinney of trees known as Antioch Wood. There, as arranged, he met up with a war party from Montségur, several score of heavily armed men who normally guarded the refuge of the Perfect in the shadow of the Pyrenees. Their leader, Peter Roger of Mirepoix, walked among his warriors, choosing which ones would accompany Golairan back to Avignonet. He stayed behind in the shadows of Antioch Wood, lying in wait lest a party of French knights unexpectedly rode past on their way to town.

A few dozen men set off in the dusk behind their guide. They could have been mistaken for laborers coming in late from the fields, were it not for the battle-axes hanging from their belts and the horsemen that brought up the rear. By the time they reached Avignonet, the blackness of night had swallowed them. The knights dismounted, and a groom led the horses to a meadow at a safe distance from the fortifications. The men of Montségur hid behind a slaughterhouse outside the city walls.

Golairan, after making his second visit to the castle keep, returned to the ramparts and opened the gate to Avignonet. The armed men stole through it and into the streets of town. They trod quickly over the cobbles, leaving a man in each alleyway to cover their retreat. At the main entrance to the castle, waiting to join them, stood a group of thirty townsmen, armed with clubs and cleavers.

Commanded by William of Lahille, William de Balaguier, and Bernard de St. Martin, the Cathar credentes from Montségur and Avignonet spilled into the courtyard of the castle and headed for the keep. Softly up the stairs and down the winding stone corridors, their guide led them to the massive oak door of the inquisitors' quarters. Bernard de St. Martin, who had been condemned to the stake in absentia, hefted a two-headed battle-ax and swung it mightily.

A deafening boom echoed within. Pious legend holds that Brother Stephen fell to his knees and began chanting in a trembling voice, "Salve Regina . . ."

The door burst open. Dozens of men streamed inward, their axes slicing through the blackness. Knives slashed, cudgels came down again and again, until the last dull groan had subsided. By torchlight, the murderers grabbed candlesticks, money, a box of ginger, then stripped the dead of their few belongings. Feverish hands rifled through a wooden chest, found an Inquisition register, and ripped it to pieces; a flaming brand was lowered to set the pile of names alight. By the time the ash from hundreds of fearful confessions had risen to the ceiling, then settled back down on the bloodred flagstones, the men with the axes had gone.

In Antioch Wood later that night, Peter Roger of Mirepoix gave a great bear hug to a returning friend. An eyewitness would tell the Inquisition years afterward that he then exclaimed, "Where is my cup?"

The man replied, "It is broken."

The lord of Montségur laughed and said, "Traitor! I would have bound it together with a circlet of gold and drunk from it all my days!"

The cup the two men were talking about was William Arnald's skull, which had been shattered at Avignonet.

17.

The Synagogue of Satan

NEWS OF THE MASSACRE spread quickly, its perpetrators
cheered on their ride home to Montségur. Few in the
south grieved for the murdered inquisitors; there is even a documentary record of a country curé ringing the bell of his church.

Within days, the allies of Raymond VII moved on bishops'
palaces, Dominican houses, and French-held castles, forcing
their occupants to flee for their lives. The brutal crime had
roused thousands from a torpor of fear and inaction. From Toulouse east through the Lauragais and the Minervois, all the way
to Narbonne and Béziers, villages and towns rose in revolt
against the custodians of the shameful treaty of 1229. Languedoc
fought to restore its flouted dignity and traditions, and, for a
time, it succeeded. By the late summer of 1242, Count Raymond
could claim to have recovered his patrimony, and the insistent
interrogations of the Inquisition had been silenced.

It was in the west that Raymond's schemes went awry. Henry

III of England planned to land in Aquitaine, then march north to harass the French and recapture the territory of Poitou, to which his brother Richard of Cornwall had a legitimate claim. The French-speaking Plantagenets of England believed that what is now western France was rightfully theirs. (The Hundred Years' War of 1337–1453 would finally decide the issue in favor of the kings of France.) Unfortunately for the cause of Languedoc's independence, not only did King Henry's campaign fail to defeat the French, it scarcely distracted their attention from Count Raymond's revolt. Unable to convince his truculent barons of the soundness of the enterprise, Henry had made landfall in the southwest with a derisively small force of knights—and was promptly trounced by a large royal French army at Taillebourg, near Bordeaux. Further setbacks throughout the summer induced the other principal conspirator, Hugh de Lusignan, to switch his allegiance and turn against Toulouse. Count Raymond, isolated once again, prepared for yet another long war of attrition as a French army made its way from Aquitaine to the borders of Languedoc.

Not everyone was ready for another decade of ruin. Roger Bernard of Foix judged that the mad revolt was doomed. In a move that stunned his neighbors, the count of Foix negotiated a separate peace with the French in the fall of 1242. No one expected this from the most bellicose family of Languedoc; old Raymond Roger had fought the crusade all his life, and his son Roger Bernard had distinguished himself at the siege of Toulouse in 1217–18. Now that same Roger Bernard, whose mother and aunt had been Cathar Perfect, stabbed the rest of Languedoc in the back by allying himself with the despised Capets. The man who grew up eviscerating the French had become their comrade-in-arms. There could have been no more devastating betrayal to the city and friends of Toulouse than the defection of Foix.

Raymond VII realized that there was no point in bleeding his people white in a conflict they could not possibly win. With Foix opposing him, he was well and truly beaten, and his cause now and in the years to come utterly without hope. He would be the last in his line. In January 1243, Raymond and Louis signed a treaty reestablishing the status quo ante. The relative leniency of its terms—the treaty amounted to a slap on the wrist—made clear that all parties knew this defeat was final and that the once powerful Saint Gilles family had been neutered by Church and Crown. This time, there was no need for a scourging at Notre Dame or any other allegory of abjectness.

The revolt had been a comprehensive failure. The hot gale of revenge that had howled across Languedoc after the murders at Avignonet ended up a mere summer squall. The rebels returned to their previous occupations, heads down and ears cocked for the footfalls of the friars in their villages and towns. The alarums of 1242 were all but forgotten.

The Church, however, remembered its dead. Even if it could never find all of the outlaws responsible for the crime at Avignonet, it had to make sure that such a crime could not be repeated, that its inquisitors could conduct their task without fearing for their lives. There was only one place left in all of Languedoc that openly defied the Church. The clergy habitually referred to it as "the synagogue of Satan." At a conclave held in Béziers in the spring of 1243, it was decided that Montségur had to be destroyed.

Ever since 1204, when Raymond of Pereille had rebuilt the castle atop the height of Montségur, the isolated eyrie had served time and again as a refuge for the Perfect. Raymond, a local lord with several Cathar ascetics in his family, had witnessed the population of his village swell and contract with every vicissitude of war in the lowlands. From its 3,000-foot height, he watched the Perfect scurrying through the wooded valleys to his haven of safety, then leaving again several months or years later, to head north and spread their quiet message of peace. South of Montségur, there stood the great stone wall of the Pyrenees, where the shadows of clouds raced over the tortured slopes of Mount St. Bartholomew.

The coming of the Inquisition brought Montségur scores of new inhabitants. Sometime in the early 1230s, Guilhabert of Castres, the respected Cathar bishop of Toulouse, formally asked Raymond of Pereille if his fortified village could become the center of the dualist faith. By the end of the decade, when Guilhabert died of old age and was succeeded as spiritual leader by Bertrand Marty, there were more than 200 Perfect living in huts and caves around the castle. They were the heart, head, and soul of Catharism in Languedoc. Winter and summer, the days passed in a tireless round of prayer, fasting, and hard work, for the male and female Perfect were not only contemplative ascetics but also artisans turning out such wares as blankets, saddles, horseshoes, and candles to support their settlement. Some were herbalists and doctors, tending to the sick in the surrounding area. Fittingly, the commerce with the farms and villages in the valleys below went beyond the mere material: Montségur also became a site for retreats, the credentes of distant towns making secretive pilgrimages to a community lodged midway between heaven and Earth.

The 200 Perfect were not alone on their mountaintop. Alongside them, in slightly fewer numbers, lived an extended clan of men-at-arms and knights, in the company of their wives, mistresses, and children. Many had relatives among the Perfect; others had been dispossessed by the peace of 1229; still others were mercenaries. The aging Raymond of Pereille had called on a kinsman, Peter Roger of Mirepoix, to be the co-lord of Montségur, mainly because the younger man, from a prominent family of credentes, enthusiastically shared the violent mores of the day. Witnesses would later tell the Inquisition that in lean times Peter Roger was not above such pointedly un-Cathar activities as brigandage, extortion, and theft. He had organized, if not suggested, the murderous evening at Avignonet.

In the spring of 1243, the talents of Peter Roger of Mirepoix became of greater moment than those of Bertrand Marty and his fellow Perfect. In the alpine pastures below the eastern flank of Montségur, warriors from Gascony, Aquitaine, and all parts of a newly subdued Languedoc began arriving and setting up an encampment. These knights and men-at-arms had been summoned to Montségur by Hugh of Arcis, King Louis's seneschal in Carcassonne. The men of Languedoc owed the Crown feudal military service, and the French and their clerical allies had decided that it was time to call up their reserves if ever they were to force the remote stronghold into submission. The siege was fully in place by the Feast of the Ascension, one year after its memorable celebration in Avignonet. The coincidence could not have escaped Peter Amiel, the archbishop of Narbonne, who pitched his richly appointed tent below Montségur and waited for the sanctuary to disgorge its diabolical congregation.

The wait would be long. For all their thousands, the besiegers did not have enough manpower to encircle completely the two-mile perimeter of the mountain's base. In many places, Montségur's steep rock face ended in treacherous, scrubby ravines, their hidden defiles impossible to seal off entirely. Although Hugh's position was not nearly as bad as Simon de Montfort's at the great siege of Toulouse—there were no Garonne barges replenishing the stores of Montségur—the terrain was such that siege engines were out of the question. Fearsome trebuchets and tall cats were of no use on the hardscrabble slopes of the Pyrenees.

Summer and fall passed in stalemate. Within Montségur, Peter Roger of Mirepoix had dug in and built up his defenses well. As the Perfect could not fight, he had a mere ninety-eight able-bodied combatants on the mountaintop to marshal into an effective defensive garrison. The royal armies repeatedly swarmed up the goat paths leading to the summit, only to be repulsed by a well-directed rain of missiles loosed by crossbow and catapult. Urged on by the seneschal and the archbishop, the attackers tried to cling to the gorse-covered slope but always had to retreat to the safety of the camp far below.

The men of Montségur, crushingly outnumbered, dared not risk a sortie for hand-to-hand combat or ambush; thus they had to keep a constant vigil and sight their fire carefully. Peter Roger could not afford to make a mistake. When any of his men sustained a mortal wound, that meant one fewer pair of eyes to peer down into the morning mists. The casualty was carried to the houses of the Perfect, to receive a deathbed consolamentum witnessed by his grieving family. Over eight months, the hard-pressed defenders lost nearly a dozen men to the deadly flights of enemy archers. As the weather turned colder and the supply of food dwindled, the work of Bertrand Marty gradually became just as important as Peter Roger's, for Montségur desperately needed prayer.

Just before Christmas 1243, Hugh of Arcis saw that the paradox of siege warfare was affecting his shivering army: In the absence of any progress, the besieger grew as demoralized as the besieged. It was time to take a risk, and for that he needed volunteers. A troop of Gascon mountain men heeded Hugh's call, even though the task set before them verged on the suicidal. They were to take the bastion atop the Roc de la Tour, a vertiginous spike of stone rising up on the easternmost point of the summit ridge of Montségur. The bastion, separated from the main castle to the west by a gentle incline several hundred yards in length, could not be approached directly by the easier western route, since that would entail running the gauntlet of the defense. To reach the Roc, the attackers had to scale the cliff to the east.

In the dead of night, the Gascons ascended the rock face, wary lest the sound of pebbles bouncing into the void alert the defenders. It was a long and perilous climb in the blackness, the task of the mountaineers made even more difficult by the weight of their heavy steel weapons. The daredevil tactic worked. The occupants of the bastion were caught off-guard and either killed instantly or wounded and then thrown to their deaths from the top of the cliff. A chronicler relates that at sunrise the victorious Gascons looked down in horror at the dizzying drop and swore that they would never have made the ascent by daylight. The route they had taken was too terrifying.

Within the walls of Montségur, the fall of the bastion was rightly seen as a disaster. Bertrand Marty assembled the treasury of the Cathar village—gold, silver, and coins—and had four Perfect smuggle it down into the valley under cover of night. Peter Roger watched as parts of catapults and mangonels were winched up to the Roc by royal engineers; heavy stone projectiles soon began crashing into the outer barbican of his fortress. As the snow swirled, the attackers drew ever nearer to Montségur, moving inexorably forward up the sloping incline from the Roc, entrenching, then creeping forward again. Each week brought the enemy closer, and the catapults within better range. The giant stones flew into and over the walls, causing death and injury. In February 1244, the final messenger to reach Montségur from the lowlands encouraged the exhausted defenders to hold fast, for Count Raymond might come to their aid. There was even a wild rumor about the Emperor Frederick sending a force to lift the siege. When, at last, the weary Cathars could no longer believe in the chimera of deliverance, Peter Roger walked out of the gate to negotiate. On March 2, 1244, ten months after the banners of the fleur-de-lis and the cross had first fluttered in the meadows below the mountain, Montségur surrendered.

By all accounts, the negotiations did not last long. The capitulation was like no other in the Cathar wars, for the victor showed a measure of mercy to the vanquished, an indication of the sense of finality surrounding the fall of Montségur. A two-week truce was declared, after which the laypeople on the mountaintop were free to go. Their past crimes—including the murders at Avignonet—were forgiven, and their sole obligation entailed a promise to submit to a full interrogation by the Inquisition. The record of the defenders' confessions, compiled by a Catalan inquisitor named Ferrer, provides the basis of our knowledge of the events at both Avignonet and Montségur.

Then there were the Perfect, for whom no clemency was possible. The Albigensian Crusade and the Inquisition in Languedoc had established one dark, immutable axiom: To dedicate one's life to a Christian creed outside the bounds of medieval orthodoxy was a capital crime. Only those who renounced the Cathar creed would be spared the flames of ecclesiastical justice. Bertrand Marty and his 200 companions had a fortnight to think over their stark choice: recant or burn. Not one of the Perfect came forward to beg mercy of Archbishop Amiel. They parceled out their meager belongings among their neighbors on the mountaintop and comforted their weeping relatives. As their time left on Earth dwindled with each passing day, the men and women of the dualist faith steeled themselves for an awful death. From atop the walls of Montségur, the archbishop's men could be seen at work in a field far below, stacking a large enclosure with dry wood scavenged from the surrounding forests.

On Sunday, March 13, ten days into the two-week wait, twenty-one credentes approached the Perfect and asked to be given the consolamentum. They too were willing to brave the fire. It was the most eloquent moment in the whole sad saga of Catharism, a testament to the devotion inspired by the holy men and women whose preaching had convulsed an era. Now, as they were on the threshold of death, twenty-one people stepped forward to join them. It was an act of defiance, solidarity, courage, and, in the end, faith. These companions of the last hour came from all stations of feudal society. Raymond of Pereille's wife, Corba, and daughter, Esclarmonde, decided to leave their noble families for the timeless embrace of the Good. With them went four knights, six soldiers (two with their wives), two messengers, one squire, one crossbowman, one merchant, one peasant woman, and one lady. The Perfect of Montségur administered the consolamentum to all of them and welcomed them into their ranks. They had three days of life remaining.

The lugubrious procession of March 16, 1244, began in the early morning. It wound down the sinuous track leading from

A thirteenth-century drawing of a Cathar's fate
(Archives Nationales, Paris)

the summit to a clearing at the base of the hill. The 220 or so condemned walked past the last patches of snow on the brown winter grass until they reached a palisade of logs. Friend and enemy looked on. The leaders of the Cathar faith, barefoot and clad only in coarse robes, climbed the ladders propped up against the wooden walls. Groups of them were lashed together, their backs to the tall stakes sticking up from the colossal bier. At a sign from the archbishop, his men threw burning brands into the enclosure. The low murmur of prayers was overtaken by the crackling sound of flame, spreading underfoot, curling the first of the fiery twigs and setting the hems of garments alight. Within minutes, the crackling had become one great oceanic roar.

By midmorning, a choking black nimbus billowed through the ravines and valleys leading from Montségur. Shepherds on nearby hills would have seen it rise slowly, heavy with the stench of fear and pain and man's inhumanity to God. The wind took the cloud and, as it had done so long ago at Béziers, lifted it high into the skies of Languedoc. The particles of smoke drifted and dispersed, then disappeared.

18.

Twilight in the Garden of Evil

FAITH GAVE WAY TO FAITHLESSNESS. After the fall of Mont-ségur, the valedictory of the Cathars in Languedoc began in earnest, the sea of words collected by the inquisitors over the next three generations spilling out from one repetitive, destructive source: betrayal. The believers in dualism no longer caused armies to march or monarchs to fall; public acts of battlefield heroism and communal resistance were replaced by sordid deeds of private cowardice and delation, as people turned on their neighbors and families to save themselves from impoverishment, imprisonment, or death. No longer protected by the great and the powerful, the humble Cathar adherent now stood alone before a judge who tolerated neither temporizing nor evasiveness. Not everyone had a taste for martyrdom.

The contagion of treachery spread faster and farther than the teaching of the Perfect ever had. In Toulouse, a Cathar believer named Peter Garcias, a consul and successful money changer, began meeting in 1247 with his kinsman William, a Franciscan friar, to discuss the tenets of their respective faiths. Their conversations took place discreetly in a common room of the Franciscan house—the open debates of Dominic's time forty years earlier were now impossible. Confident in the company of a kinsman, Garcias gave vent to his disdain for the medieval Church and the stern god that it worshiped: "If I got my hands on this God who created so many souls to save but a few and damn all the rest," the Cathar exclaimed, "I'd rip him apart with my fingernails and my teeth." As for the Church's pretensions to equity, Garcias looked back at the bloody recent past, then enunciated a view that is still ahead of its time: "Justice cannot condemn a man to death. An official who judges someone a heretic and has him put to death is a murderer. God did not want a justice of death sentences. It is not right to go on a crusade . . . against the Saracens, or against a village like Montségur that opposed the Church. . . . The preachers of crusades are criminals."

Unfortunately, we know of Peter Garcias's dangerous opinions because he was denounced. His Franciscan kinsman, also ahead of his time, hit upon the medieval equivalent of wearing a wire. Whenever he and Garcias met, four other friars lay hidden in a gallery of the common room, silently scratching notes as the Cathar spoke. The ties of family and friendship counted for nothing in this new, perfidious Languedoc. Betrayal became virtue, as Garcias and others learned to their grief. The Perfect who had not been trapped at Montségur now had to live on the run, their sole refuge gone and their flock scattered, frightened, and pressed into becoming informers.

In the end, Count Raymond VII joined the hunt. Having failed to ride to the rescue of Montségur, the epigone of the once-tolerant Saint Gilles family helped persecute his own peo-

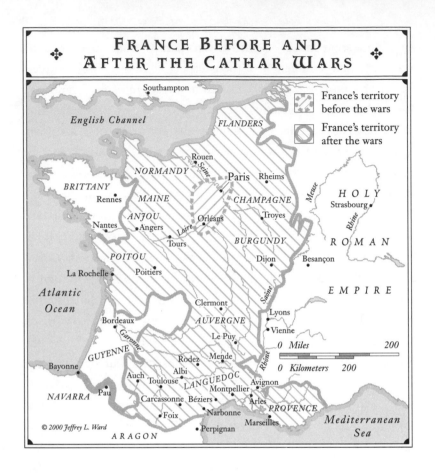

FRANCE BEFORE AND
AFTER THE CATHAR WARS

Southampton

English Channel

FLANDERS

France's territory
before the wars

France's territory
after the wars

Rouen

Seine

NORMANDY

Paris • Rheims

BRITTANY

Rennes

MAINE

CHAMPAGNE

Meuse

H O L Y
Strasbourg •

ANJOU

Nantes • Angers

Orléans

Troyes

Loire

Tours

BURGUNDY

Rhine

R O M A N

POITOU

Dijon

Besançon

La Rochelle • Poitiers

*Atlantic
Ocean*

E M P I R E

Clermont

Saône

AUVERGNE

Lyons

Bordeaux

Vienne

Garonne

Le Puy

0 *Miles*   200

Rodez   Mende

Rhône

0 *Kilometers*   200

Bayonne

GUYENNE

Auch   Albi

Avignon

LANGUEDOC

NAVARRA Pau

Toulouse   Montpellier

Carcassonne Béziers •

Arles

PROVENCE

© 2000 Jeffrey L. Ward

• Foix

Narbonne

Marseilles

*Mediterranean
Sea*

A R A G O N

• Perpignan

ple. In June 1249, he shocked his friends among the surviving
Cathar gentry by ordering eighty people burned in Agen, a city
on the Garonne to the northwest of Toulouse. By September of
that same year, he was dead at fifty-two, shortly after having
contracted a fever in the back-country town of Millau. His body
was taken to Fontevrault, the abbey in the Loire Valley founded
by Robert of Arbrissel, the charismatic preacher of the early
twelfth century. In death Raymond deserted Toulouse, to lie in
Fontevrault alongside his mother, Joan of England, his uncle,

Richard Lionheart, and his grandparents, King Henry II and Eleanor of Aquitaine.

The count who had once vanquished both Simon and Amaury left his homeland defenseless. His daughter Jeanne would die childless in 1271, thereby ending the Saint Gilles line and allowing her husband's family, the Capets of France, to annex Languedoc permanently. After Raymond VII's passing, there was no one to resist the northerners or curb the agents of doctrinal cleansing. In this closing half century of humiliation, even those who had thrown in their lot with the French, notably Roger Bernard of Foix, were as unprotected as those who had remained loyal. In 1269, as a posthumous indignity to the family of Foix, the body of Roger Bernard's wife, Ermessinde, was dug up and thrown out of a Catholic cemetery on suspicion of heresy.

In less than ten years, the Inquisition had gone from being an artisanal undertaking of a fanatical few to a proficient bureaucracy employing hundreds and interrogating thousands. In Catalonia, a conclave of churchmen had assembled in 1242 to compile a glossary of repression:

> *Heretics* are those who remain obstinate in error.
>
> *Believers* are those who put faith in the errors of heretics and are assimilated to them.
>
> *Those suspect of heresy* are those who are present at the preaching of heretics and participate, however little, in their ceremonies.
>
> *Those simply suspected* have done such things only once.

Those vehemently suspected have done this often.

Those most vehemently suspected have done this frequently.

Concealers are those who know heretics but do not denounce them.

Hiders are those who have agreed to prevent heretics being discovered.

Receivers are those who have twice received heretics on their property.

Defenders are those who knowingly defend heretics so as to prevent the Church from extirpating heretical depravity.

Favorers are all of the above to a greater or lesser degree.

Relapsed are those who return to their former heretical errors after having formally renounced them.

The inquisitors had cast their net wide. In the heyday of open Catharism, everyone but the blind and the cloistered in a city like Toulouse or Carcassonne would have qualified as a "concealer," for known heretics had abounded as accepted members of the community. Armed with such catchall lists of offenses, the Inquisition of the 1240s proceeded to intimidate indiscriminately, conducting a head count on a scale that had not been seen since a census of antiquity. The sheer number of people called, and re-called, to testify or confess went far beyond the bounds of previous medieval practice. Historical irony had singled out the Cathars—who believed the material world was an evil irrelevancy —to inspire the forerunner of the police state.

Brother Ferrer, a Catalan Dominican from near Perpignan, took over from the assassinated friars at Avignonet. Aside from showing exemplary ruthlessness, he improved the process by systematizing interrogations and limiting arduous and dangerous travel. Villages came to him, rather than vice versa. Ferrer also

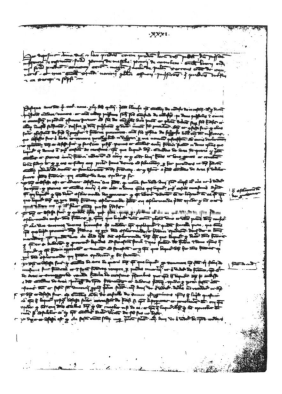

Page from an Inquisition register
(Institut de recherche et d'histoire des textes, Paris)

went back to old registers to ferret out falsehoods in the testimony collected by William Arnald and Stephen of St. Thibéry. He was, in many respects, the most prolific pioneer of mass prosecution and police work, establishing the habit of double- and triple-checking every sworn statement.

In his turn, Ferrer was superseded by two who would gain even greater notoriety: Jean de St. Pierre and Bernard de Caux, the latter earning orthodoxy's fondest compliment, *malleus hereticorum* (the hammer of heretics). In the closing half of the 1240s, Brothers Jean and Bernard compiled a cross-referenced compendium of confessions extracted from tens of thousands of people.

They were, in effect, cartographers of Languedoc's mental landscape. The 5,065 transcripts of their interrogations that have survived represent but a fraction of their work, which mostly took place near the church of St. Sernin in Toulouse and within the walled city of Carcassonne. They filled both dungeons there with hundreds of unfortunates, to be fed, in the words of an admirer, "the bread of pain and the water of tribulation."

The friars' accomplishment would have remained an anecdote in the larger history of organized terror, like Conrad of Marburg's reign of rough justice in the Rhineland, had Brother Bernard not put his investigative expertise in the service of creating a new literary genre: the inquisitor's manual. Designed as guides for the burgeoning number of papal courts throughout Europe, these manuals enlightened the fledgling inquisitor on the pitfalls of the interrogation procedure and recommended a graduated scale of sentences that ranged from burning at one extreme to a mild public penance at the other. Most manuals reminded inquisitors that they were in the business not of punishment but of salvation, a distinction lost on the thousands whose lives were ruined by the friars' judgments.

Bernard de Caux's treatise, known as the *Manual of the Inquisitors of Carcassonne*, stood as the unrivaled authority in the field for a half century and added luster to Languedoc's reputation among churchmen as a laboratory of repression. In the early fourteenth century, the reputation was enhanced even more when a talented inquisitor of Toulouse, Bernard Gui, wrote a hefty manual that would influence the Aragonese and Spanish Inquisitions. Gui, later made a literary villain in Umberto Eco's *The Name of the Rose*, spoke highly of the work of Bernard de Caux and Jean de St. Pierre and acknowledged their contribution to the crushing of Catharism.

Such sterling coercion was made easier by an improved quality of turncoat. The inquisitors managed to persuade a handful of captured Perfect to convert to Catholicism and, in some instances, to sell their services to the court. Outstanding in this work of delation was one Sicard of Lunel, who had been a prominent Perfect in the Cathar diocese of Albi. In the 1240s, Sicard gave the friars an exhaustive list of Cathar sympathizers—he even fingered his own parents. All those who had helped him in any way during his years of secretive missionary work, whether they had offered him a bed for the night or given him a jar of honey, were hauled up for punishment on the strength of his encyclopedic testimony. He and others of his ilk were lodged thereafter in a castle outside of Toulouse, in a type of witness-protection program, where they visited dungeons to coax confidences from prisoners and exhort the obstinate to follow them in the paths of righteous betrayal. Handsomely rewarded by the Inquisition, Sicard apparently lived into a peaceful old age, his activities recorded well into the 1270s.

As a final fillip to inquisitorial power, Pope Innocent IV issued a decree in May 1252 that gave the friars permission to use torture in their search for the truth. The procedure, primly called "putting the question," could be employed at the discretion of the inquisitor, but on no account should the victim, the pope thought prudent to add, have a limb severed, lose too much blood, or expire. The bull, *Ad extirpanda*, also reinforced the Inquisition in Italy, to which many in Languedoc had fled to elude the traps set by the Dominicans. Italian Catharism, which had subsisted in parts of Lombardy, Venezia, and Tuscany, had not yet felt the full force of papal repression. From the time of Mark, the Lombard who went in 1167 to the meeting at St. Félix, to the mid-thirteenth century, the constant struggle between pope and emperor in many Italian towns had created a civic space in which the heresy could survive, even flourish. Although Catharism in Italy would never reach Languedocian proportions in its following or near the "national" allegiance felt by the Occitans, the faith was firmly established there and possessed enough doctrinal sophistication to split into several different "churches" of dualist thought. Innocent IV's bull, in part triggered by the murder of a respected inquisitor in 1252, spelled the beginning of the end for Italian Cathars; in 1278, more than 200 Perfect were burned in Verona.

Despite the presence of their coreligionists, the fleeing Occitan Perfect who took refuge in the isolated Cathar strongholds in Italy found too few of their compatriots to revive the spiritual community that had once thrived under the counts of Toulouse. Worse yet, their numbers dwindled with each successive generation. In Languedoc, the homeland of the heresy, successive waves of highly trained inquisitors, aided by informers and torturers, fired by a totalitarian creed, and instructed by detailed manuals and ever-expanding registers, slowly ground Catharism into oblivion. Thousands of private dramas ended in the darkness of a dungeon. By century's end, only the truly heroic dared to say aloud that the world was evil.

The year 1300 saw the papacy institute the jubilee, the greatest occasion for raising funds and consciousness ever devised in the Middle Ages.* Pope Benedict VIII, the most ambitious and abra-

---

*Originally planned to be held every century, the jubilee came to be declared every fifty, then thirty-three, then twenty-five years, right up until the present, when the prospect of a millennial blast, a jubilee to outshine even that of 1300, has had contemporary Rome on tenterhooks for nearly a decade.

sive pontiff since Innocent III, declared that pilgrims to Rome that year would receive a raft of spiritual indulgence so ample as to render future damnation an utter fluke. Somewhere between one and two million people accepted his offer, an army of the anxious faithful from all over Europe, crossing the Alps on foot and horseback, docking at ports on the Adriatic and the Tyrrhenian, ready to open wide their hearts and purses once in sight of the holy city on the Tiber. The clergy and merchants of Rome exulted. An eyewitness, William Ventura, described the scene in one church: "Day and night two priests stood at the altar of St. Paul's holding rakes in their hands, raking in infinite money." The crowds were so large that papal soldiers had to double as crossing guards by enforcing a keep-right system on the bridge leading to the Vatican.

The hordes of the first jubilee meandered the length and breadth of Italy, on their way to and from the Eternal City, attracting fellow travelers who sought safety in numbers. Homebound Occitans made their way along the rocky shore of the Mediterranean past Genoa, Nice, and Marseilles. At some point during these seasons of spiritual migration, two brothers, Peter and William Autier, slipped into the crowd of pilgrims, their bags laden with knives from Parma which they said they were going to sell in their native Languedoc. Until 1296, the two men had lived a comfortable, sedentary existence in Ax-les-Thermes, a mountain town near Foix where the literate Peter had been a successful notary. In that year, the brothers had sold everything and vanished from Ax. Riding the tide of jubilee pilgrims, the Autiers resurfaced, seemingly content to make their living as itinerant peddlers. The least credulous of their companions may have found it odd that such educated, wealthy men, well into their fifties, should embrace such a lowly station in life.

The Autier brothers no doubt kept to themselves on their journey home. At the many shrines on the well-trodden pilgrimage route, the company stopped to hear mass and pray. Peter must have repeatedly bitten his tongue at these pious moments, for he would later say that making the sign of the cross was useful only for batting away flies. He even suggested alternate wording for the gesture: "Here is the forehead and here is the beard and here is one ear and here is the other." Had such sarcasm defined the outer bounds of his skepticism, Peter Autier's name would be unremembered, like those of the millions whose sacrilegious wit formed a rich part of folk culture. But the notary-turned-knife-salesman was more than a mere wiseacre; Peter Autier was the last great Perfect in Cathar history. After three years of study, fasting, and prayer—and a solemn consolamentum conferred by Italian dualists—Peter and his Perfect brother returned to Languedoc as missionaries. It was a jubilee year for the Cathars, too.

For once, the inquisitors were caught unawares. Or rather, they had their attention turned elsewhere, in a nasty sink of secular politics and ecclesiastical intrigue. In the years surrounding the turn of the fourteenth century, the Dominicans and their episcopal allies had at last run into resistance, as urban leaders reconciled themselves to the French conquest and royal officials began seeing the all-powerful clergy as inimical to the prosperity of the province and the prestige of their monarch. In Albi, Bishop Bernard de Castanet threw many of his secular adversaries into prison, on what were often flimsy charges of latent Cathar sympathies, and insisted that any opposition to him was tantamount to sin. To drive home his point, Castanet began the erection of the red-brick behemoth of Ste-Cécile, the fortress cathedral which still reminds the town of the bishop's might. In Carcassonne, plots were hatched to destroy Inquisition registers; in the hands of unscrupulous bishops and friars, these bound volumes of confession and betrayal had become tools of blackmail and extortion.

While Peter Autier quietly made his way back from Italy to the highlands of Languedoc, civic strife kept the inquisitors on the defensive. Their most eloquent critic was Bernard Délicieux, a Franciscan friar who claimed that the prosecution of a moribund faith had degenerated into an abuse of power. The darling of merchants and magistrates, Délicieux was a gifted rabble-rouser who, at the height of his power in 1303, convinced a royal official to lead a mob in storming the Inquisition's dungeon in Carcassonne and freeing all of its prisoners. The incendiary friar, who went so far as to claim that inquisitors simply made up confessions of fictitious people in order to blackmail the innocent, stood squarely in a purist tradition that despised the Dominicans for their gradual slide into worldliness. Indeed, the brand of apocalyptic piety common to Délicieux and many others, who were known as "Spiritual Franciscans," would be declared a heresy in 1317. They made the mistake of taking up where the Cathars had left off—in decrying too loudly the wealth of the Church. Their less radical brethren, however, weakened the appeal of heresy. Throughout the thirteenth century, the preaching and example of the friars had done much to bring spontaneous, popular piety back into the fold of orthodoxy.

Before the uproar caused by Délicieux died down, the Autier brothers had benefited from five long years of neglect. In the hills of the Sabartès, the up-country near Foix, Catharism once

Bernard Délicieux as depicted by Jean-Paul Laurens
(Musée des Augustins, Toulouse/Art Resource, New York)

again took root. Although nearly three generations had passed since the time of tolerance, there were still vivid memories of the "good Christians" who had once freely walked the mountain meadows and preached in village squares. In the first decade of the new century, Peter Autier recruited about a dozen people to join him in his austere mission, among them the last recorded female Perfect, Aude Bourrel. There were to be no Cathar "homes" or bishops or mountaintops this time around. The acolytes of Autier led a harsh life of perpetual stealth and moonlight travel, always on the move lest they be detected.

The 1,000 or so households won back to the illicit faith stood in constant peril of betrayal; if but one of their family turned traitor and went to the authorities in Toulouse, Carcassonne, or Foix, misery and ruin would have ensued. There were instances of husbands and wives concealing their heretical beliefs from each other, of village gossips ignorant of the dualist missionaries hidden in their neighbors' back rooms, of suspected double agents for the Inquisition found murdered in remote ravines. The credentes spoke guardedly of their faith in coded language: The "scandal" referred to the decades of persecution; the "understanding of the Good" (*entendement de Be*), to their acceptance of the Perfects' message. Unlike their predecessors of a century before, conversant with troubadour, tradesman, and merchant, the Cathars of 1300 lived in a lonely landscape of fear.

The nature of the revival reflected the sadly reduced circumstances of Catharism. Autier's Perfect were metaphysical highwaymen, dimly glimpsed creatures of the night who acted less as pastors of a flock than as visiting angels of death. Administering the consolamentum to the dying became the raison d'être of the Perfect. Credentes had always wanted to "make a good end" so that their next "tunic," or earthly incarnation, would lead them closer to God. Among Autier and his followers, however, the consolamentum at death's door took precedence over other aspects of the faith.

The risks taken to attend to the expiring were immense. Time was short, making subterfuge all the more difficult. Panting messengers sought out the Perfect, or people who knew where they were hiding, then led them back, often over great distances, to the grieving family. Since medieval death, like medieval life, entailed a promiscuous lack of privacy, the Perfect had few occasions to be alone with the dying and perform the sacrament. They frequently spent hours, if not days, concealed in a household, hoping that the stricken believer would not lose consciousness before they had a chance to promote him to a better future life. In one instance, having advised a relative to find a pretext for clearing the sickroom of its milling guests, Peter Autier donned the clothes of the future widow and took care to keep his back to the window as he administered the consolamentum. Those who might linger on for several days were ordered to undertake the *endura*, a hunger strike that ended in death. Nothing could be allowed to corrupt—and thus cancel—the otherworldly grace bestowed by the consolamentum, and the Perfect, for safety's sake, could not risk staying around to keep a vigil over the ill. The endura was a cruel surrogate for the hospice work performed by Cathar Perfect in happier times.

Peter Autier's men must have realized that their obsession with the final consolamentum might give simple credentes a skewed vision of what was a philosophy that embraced all of life. Errors about the faith could flourish. Grazida Lizier, a woman believer from the village of Montaillou, gave the following strange version of dualism to the Inquisition: "I believe God made those things that are helpful to man, and useful too for the created world—such as human beings, the animals men eat or are carried about on—for instance oxen, sheep, goats, horses, mules—and the edible fruits of the earth and of trees. But I don't think God made wolves, flies, mosquitoes, and such things as are harmful to man." Other credentes strayed from Cathar precepts by squirreling away scraps of bread touched by the Perfect, a practice similar to orthodoxy's reverence for relics. Earlier Cathar leaders might have denounced such material magic, but Autier and his fellows blessed the bread crumbs as a souvenir of their passage.

Discovery was inevitable, for thousands of people—especially a grudge-bearing, garrulous peasantry—could not be expected to keep a secret indefinitely. Also, after the middle of the first decade of the fourteenth century, men of exceptional ability were appointed to head the Inquisition. Geoffrey d'Ablis, an incorruptible Dominican, got Carcassonne; Bernard Gui, a brilliant investigator, Toulouse. In the county of Foix, Jacques Fournier, the bishop of the see of Pamiers, undertook an Inquisition that was a model of painstaking thoroughness. Fournier, an intelligent and sensitive Cistercian who would later be elected Pope Benedict XII, brought what can only be termed an anthropological curiosity to bear on the practices and prejudices of the remaining Cathars—to the delight of future historians. He and Gui were not vindictive hacks; both men allowed Christian ideals to inform their work. Many of their hundreds of victims appealed for, and received, clemency. To the Perfect and the unrepentant credentes, of course, the inquisitors showed no mercy.

The Autier network began unraveling in 1305, as the result of a betrayal. The turncoat was one William-Peter Cavaillé, a longtime believer who had kept his mouth admirably shut while serving time in the prison of Carcassonne. Upon his release, he badgered his fellow credentes to lend him a petty sum of money so that he could dispose of a debt he had contracted with a jail guard. For reasons unknown, the money was denied, and Cavaillé, furious, took his revenge by putting the inquisitors onto the scent of the secret revival. Through his efforts, in September 1305, two Perfect were captured and a manhunt begun. The next five years saw the Perfect of Peter Autier's revival—Peter Raymond, Amiel de Perles, William Autier, James Autier, Prades Tavernier, Philip d'Alayrac, Pons Bayle, Peter Sans, Raymond Fabre—picked off and sent to the stake. One of them, Sans Mercadier, committed suicide in despair.

Unprecedented police actions marked the investigation, such as the raid of September 8, 1309, when the village of Montaillou was sealed off by soldiers and all of its inhabitants were arrested by the inquisitor Geoffrey d'Ablis. Although d'Ablis, detecting a recrudescence of the forbidden faith, imprisoned many of the villagers, it would take a far more skillful questioner, Jacques Fournier, to find out a decade or so later that Montaillou had been that rare pearl—a settlement where the heretics formed a majority. Fournier also discovered that its randy priest, Peter Clergue, had wheedled many village women into his bed through a peculiar interpretation of Catharism that called for carnal adventures with the Catholic clergy. Clearly, not all adepts of dualism shared the stern piety of the Perfect.

In the summer of 1309, the elusive Peter Autier was finally caught. Precisely 100 years had passed since the armies of the north marched on Béziers and Carcassonne to begin the extermination of the Cathars. Unfortunately, the transcripts of the interrogations Autier withstood—he was held for nearly ten months—have been lost to posterity. In April 1310, the inquisitors hauled him up in front of the cathedral of St. Stephen in Toulouse and burned him alive. His last wish, which he reportedly cried out as he was being tied to the stake, was to be given a chance to preach to the huge crowd of onlookers. In no time, Peter Autier declared defiantly, he would convert them all. The request was denied.

19.

Bélibaste

THERE WAS NOW ONE CATHAR LEFT in Languedoc. One Perfect in the long line that stretched back through the Inquisitions of Fournier and Gui, the wars of Raymond and Louis, the crusades of Innocent and Simon de Montfort, the debates of Dominic and Guilhabert, and the Cathar International of Nicetas and Mark—the last man in a procession of holy men and women that began, the Cathars believed, in the time of Mary Magdalene and the twelve apostles. His name was William Bélibaste.

As befitted his singular status, Bélibaste was perhaps the most peculiar Perfect in Cathar history. A murderer and adulterer, he nonetheless proved a gentle pastor to his small following of credentes and, when his time came, showed as much courage as his far worthier predecessors. It was the sinner, not the saint, who bade good-bye to the greatest heresy of the Middle Ages.

Believers in the "good men," the Bélibastes were a clan of

landowners in the Corbières, the rugged upland that overlooks the valley of the River Aude. William, one of several brothers, spent his early manhood as a shepherd, wandering the windswept reaches of southern Languedoc with his flock, following the paths of transhumance that had been traced through the mountain passes in antiquity. His descent from the high pastures in the autumn of 1306 had changed his life forever—in the course of a brawl, Bélibaste beat another shepherd to death. Having become notorious throughout the Corbières, he ran from the French king's justice, taking with him a brother who was sought by the Inquisition. The two fugitives eventually came across others hiding in the hills: the hunted Perfect of the Autier revival.

One of them, Philip d'Alayrac, befriended the remorseful shepherd. Recognizing a promising recruit, the Perfect began initiating the murderer into the arcana of the dualist faith. Bélibaste's sin was washed away when, after several seasons of instruction, he was given the consolamentum. Whether he intended to be an active missionary or simply wished to atone for his wrongdoing will never be known. What is certain is that he and d'Alayrac, arrested on suspicion of Catharism, somehow escaped from the prisons of Carcassonne in 1309 and fled over the Pyrenees to Catalonia. When d'Alayrac ventured northward on a mission of mercy the following year, he was captured and burned, leaving Bélibaste alone in Catalonia to comfort the refugees who had deserted Montaillou, Ax-les-Thermes, and other towns in the Sabartès to escape the inquisitors. The former shepherd now had a small flock of souls.

The exiles wandered through Aragon and Catalonia, settling only temporarily wherever they went, always ready to move on when better opportunites beckoned or when the Aragonese Inquisition came too close. To allay suspicion, Bélibaste posed as a married man. Raymonda Piquier, a Languedoc native who had lost track of her husband in the confusion of arrests at home, shared the Perfect's house and, when traveling, his room. The two became lovers. Despite this breach of the vows taken at the consolamentum, Bélibaste kept up appearances of celibacy for nearly a decade, and his indulgent followers feigned ignorance of the real relationship between their Perfect and his house-keeper. In 1319, the shepherd Peter Maury, an inveterate bache-lor from Montaillou, was hectored by Bélibaste into wedding Raymonda. The Perfect performed a hasty marriage cere-mony—yet another innovation for a faith that had no such sacra-ment—and Peter and Raymonda moved in together. Within a week, Bélibaste had released them from their vows and brought Raymonda back under his roof. Several months later, she gave birth to a child; Peter Maury, obligingly, acknowledged pater-nity.

For all his failings, the last of the Cathar Perfect worked hard to edify his flock. The interrogation transcripts of his credentes—most were eventually ensnared by the Inquisition— show that Bélibaste's sermons were remembered for years after his disappearance. The Cathar preached movingly and com-manded respect. He spoke at length of never giving in to the sin of despair, of the need to love one another, of how the good God awaited us all beyond the evil veil of creation. He never wavered in his belief that the world was ruled by maleficent powers and that four demons—the king of France, the pope, the inquisitor at Carcassonne, the bishop of Pamiers—were espe-cially active in keeping people from finding their true salvation.

Knowing himself to be compromised, he refused to administer the consolamentum; it would, he assured his anxious listeners, be given to them freely in the afterlife by a Perfect-turned-angel.

The community at last found permanent homes in Morella and Sant Mateu, towns near the delta of the River Ebro, south of Tarragona. It was a long journey—more than 200 miles—from Languedoc, yet not far enough away for the seemingly serendipitous to occur. One day in 1317, a certain Arnold Sicre, an inhabitant of Ax-les-Thermes, stumbled across the small settlement of his exiled compatriots. The coincidence was hailed as providential. Arnold claimed to have the "understanding of the Good"; his mother, Sibyl Bayle, had been a prominent believer who was burned by the Inquisition, as was his brother, Pons Bayle, one of Peter Autier's inner circle of Perfect. The more suspicious of the villagers pointed out that Arnold's father, a notary, had soured on Catharism and helped organize the raid on Montaillou. Even the easygoing Bélibaste had his doubts. Although Arnold boasted of having known the Autier brothers, the newcomer was woefully ignorant of the basic practices of Catharism. He couldn't perform the melioramentum, the ritual greeting extended to the Perfect, and he had the gaucheness to bring red meat to Bélibaste's table.

Arnold Sicre assured the skeptics that he had found what he was seeking. He apprenticed as a shoemaker in Sant Mateu and within weeks was accepted as a member of the secretive Cathar community. He was assiduous in attending the sermons of Bélibaste and soon caught up with the others in his knowledge of dualist mythology and doctrine. He became one of the Perfect's preferred companions; he may even have been considered as a possible successor to Bélibaste, with or without the consolamentum. As the months turned into years, Arnold seemed content with his modest life, his only regret the beloved Cathar relatives he had left on their own in the mountains of Languedoc near Andorra. His rich aunt and beautiful maiden sister were all by themselves, bereft of the spiritual solace he received in Catalonia. Bélibaste at last instructed Arnold to go to Languedoc and fetch them. A nubile Cathar bride was needed for one of the bachelor faithful, and a wealthy benefactress was always welcome.

After several months' absence, Arnold returned, alone, with the news that his aunt, Alazaïs, was now gout-ridden and too frail to travel, and his sister, a loyal niece, had chosen to stay with the old lady. Both women, however, were overjoyed at the news he brought of fellow believers. The aunt, Arnold reported, had bestowed a hefty dowry on his sister and said she was willing to give far more to the struggling exiles. Thanks to her liberality, a free-spending Arnold was able to make the Christmas of 1320 the most pleasant in memory for the outcasts. His failing aunt had opened her purse and made but one request: to be blessed by a good Christian before her death. And his sister, Arnold added, was pining to meet her suitor. Surely, they deserved to be visited.

The longtime companions of the Perfect counseled caution. Bélibaste had barely escaped Languedoc a dozen years ago, and his presence was essential in Morella and Sant Mateu to keep the last ember of Catharism aglow. It would be folly to return to the land of persecution. Arnold quieted their misgivings by pointing out that a safe, short trip to his aunt's estate would benefit the entire community.

In the spring of 1321, William Bélibaste, Arnold Sicre, Arnold Marty, the prospective husband for Sicre's sister, and the ever-faithful shepherd Peter Maury headed north toward home. A soothsayer had warned Bélibaste that he would never return to Catalonia, but the Perfect ignored this advice, as well as the appearance of two magpies—a bad omen if seen in a pair—that swooped across his path while he trudged through the back-country of Barcelona. A mixture of conscientiousness and cupidity impelled Bélibaste forward on his mission to give solace and receive reward at the house of the elderly Alazaïs. Yet as the peaks of the Pyrenees grew taller on the horizon and the dangers of Languedoc neared, the old doubts about Arnold Sicre returned.

Prior to crossing the Ebro on their journey north, as Arnold Sicre subsequently told the Inquisition, Bélibaste and Maury decided to get him drunk as part of the age-old ruse of *in vino veritas*. At the riverside inn where they put their plan into effect, the younger man saw through the scheme and surreptitiously dumped out the goblet that his dinner companions took pains to fill and refill. Faking fall-down intoxication, Arnold eventually let Peter Maury help him off to bed. Once they were in his room, Arnold dropped his trousers and got ready to urinate on the pillow. Maury dragged him outside and as the younger man tottered in the darkness, suggested that they betray Bélibaste and collect the handsome price on his head. To which Arnold protested, "I cannot believe that you would do such a thing! I would never let you get away with it!" He staggered back to his bed and was soon emitting a stream of counterfeit snores. Maury returned to Bélibaste and told him that they should stop worrying.

Within a week, the small party from Sant Mateu had reached an outlying possession of the counts of Foix, a small, exiguous mountain valley on the southern slopes of the Pyrenees near Andorra. They slept their first night in Castellbò; the second, in the village of Tirvia. The next dawn, an armed posse broke down their door and placed them under arrest. Arnold Sicre had

Bishop and Inquisitor Jacques Fournier, who became Pope Benedict XII
(Roger-Viollet, Paris)

tipped off the Inquisition. He was, as Bélibaste moaned in horror from his dungeon, "a Judas."

In fact, he was far worse. Throughout his lengthy stay in Catalonia, Arnold had been working for Bishop Fournier, the inquisitor of Pamiers. The coincidence of his arrival, his devotion to dualism, his generous aunt and willing sister—all had been the invention of a genius of deceit. The money Arnold spent the previous Christmas had come from the treasury of Fournier, an advance on the large reward he would earn by bringing in Bélibaste. But that was not all; the bounty hunter had also struck a bargain with the bishop whereby he would recover the property confiscated from his heretical mother, Sibyl Bayle. Arnold became a rich man. After more than a century of double-dealing—the violated safe-conduct offered to Raymond Roger Trencavel, the perjury trap set by Arnold Amaury, the hostage-taking of Toulouse's ambassadors by Bishop Fulk, the burning of the dying woman by Bishop Raymond du Fauga, the eaves-dropping on Peter Garcias, the sellout of the convert Sicard of Lunel, and the thousands upon thousands of betrayals coaxed, threatened, or tortured out of simple, pious people by more than eight decades of implacable Inquisition—Catholic orthodoxy had found in Arnold Sicre a champion of treachery.

William Bélibaste, the last of the Languedoc Perfect, was led over the Pyrenees in chains. News of his capture spread far and wide, scattering the faithful of Sant Mateu and Morella to the four winds, to be pursued for the rest of their lives. In Pamiers, Bishop Fournier was denied the pleasure of lighting the fire. The pope, ruling that Bélibaste was a native of the Corbières, ordered him tried by the episcopal tribunal of that region and punished by its secular authority. The archbishop of Narbonne combined these functions as spiritual and temporal overlord; "relaxing to the secular arm" involved nothing more than sleight of hand.

The trial, of which no record exists, must have been swift. In the autumn of 1321, an unbowed Bélibaste, the hotheaded shepherd turned homespun pastor, walked into the courtyard of the castle at Villerouge-Termenès, a village in the bald heart of the Corbières. He mounted a pile of straw, vine cuttings, and logs and was tied to a stake. A flaming torch was lowered. The last Perfect heretic of Languedoc was gone.

Epilogue: In Cathar Country

AS YOU DRIVE INTO LANGUEDOC from the north, past such cities as Avignon, Nîmes, Montpellier, and Béziers, it soon becomes obvious that something odd is afoot. Large brown signs on the highway announce, *Vous êtes en pays cathare* (Entering Cathar Country). At one spot, on the cypress-covered hills overlooking Narbonne, there stands a trio of concrete tubes, their uppermost third cut open in the shape of a helmet visor. This specimen of French autoroute art represents *les chevaliers cathares* (the Cathar Knights), an Easter Island–like threesome of gigantic heretics looking impassively over the expressway as thousands of tourists, like the crusaders of yesteryear, invade Languedoc every summer. French pop singer Francis Cabrel was moved to compose a plaintive song about the sculpture in 1983:

Les chevaliers cathares	The Cathar knights
Pleurent doucement	Are softly crying

Au bord de l'autoroute	By the roadside
Quand le soir descend	As the day is dying.
Comme une dernière insulte	As a final insult,
Comme un dernier tourment	As a last torment,
Au milieu du tumulte	They're lost in the tumult
En robe de ciment	Enrobed in cement

The commemorative spirit grows more cheerful farther west, near Carcassonne. This part of Languedoc abounds with signs celebrating Cathar country. There is an official logo, a yin-yang depiction of a half-shrouded disk suggesting the light-and-dark dualism of the Cathar faith. This tourist-board branding—the logo is affixed to everything from hotel price lists to canned duck meat—seems restrained in comparison to what can be found within the walled city, which, from without, still resembles an unspoiled dream. On the main street of Carcassonne, a polyglot pitchman distributes brochures for Torture and Cartoon Museums, adding helpfully that the first is like *The Name of the Rose* and the second like *Cinderella*. Young boys with plastic swords square off on restaurant terraces. Ads for "Catharama," a sound-and-light show held in the nearby town of Limoux, are plastered on the hoardings outside postcard shops. All over Languedoc, the word *Cathar* crops up in unusual places: on cafés, real estate agencies, adult comic books, lunch menus, and wine bottles.

It is exceedingly strange to find chamber-of-commerce boosterism for a faith that was annihilated seven centuries ago, a faith that left no physical trace—no chapel, no monument, no art—of its existence. And it seems perverse, almost Celtic, to celebrate a failed heresy. However much other Europeans revere their past, you do not see roadside attractions elsewhere announcing: "Entering Waldensian Country" or "Welcome to

Spiritual Franciscan Country." A rejected metaphysic is usually an embarrassment, and an obscure one at that.

Although decried with humorless regularity by local Cathar experts, the cheesy pop exploitation of their subject attests to its presence in collective memory. The Cathars of Languedoc defy obscurity because their story has become legend, a tale which belongs to everyone. The story of their defeat has given rise to a collective, international narrative, its various strands picked up and rewoven by a succession of "alternative" movements for more than 100 years. The Cathar country advertised on the signs is an imaginary landscape first created in the nineteenth century and embellished ever since. The father of the myth is indirectly responsible for those giant concrete tubes by the highway and the logo on the hotel. His name was Napoléon Peyrat, and his peculiar legacy deserves study.

Napoléon Peyrat was born in 1809 in the Ariège, the mountainous French *département* of which Foix is the capital. He was the pastor of the Reformed Church of France, in the Parisian suburb of St. Germain en Laye. More important, Peyrat was a formidable and prolific writer, a poet-turned-historian who could mix the prose styles of Chateaubriand, Walter Scott, and Jules Michelet to electrifying effect. Unfortunately, he had very little respect for the truth.

As one of the most eloquent of that anticlerical brotherhood of the French Third Republic known popularly as *bouffeurs du curé* (priest eaters), Peyrat regularly launched broadsides against what he saw as a reactionary, antidemocratic Catholic establishment. Obviously, the story of the Cathars was a godsend to such a man. Until Peyrat published his multivolume *Histoire des Albigeois* (History of the Albigensians) in the 1870s, Cathar historiography had been a fairly low-profile shooting gallery between French Protestant and Catholic historians. The Catholics argued that the Cathars were not even Christians; the Protestants, that they were forerunners of the Reformation. Lay liberal historians, ignoring such doctrinal discussions, usually played up the sophistication of Languedoc troubadour culture and the horror of the crusade. No one work until then, however, had the sheer narrative verve of Peyrat's. Taking the ideas and conjectures that had been floating around in earlier anticlerical, romantic treatments of the Cathars, the polemical pastor went wild.

In his colorful history, medieval Languedoc became the apex of civilization, full of liberty-loving democrats attacked by barbarians who were little better than Norsemen. The spirit of freedom crushed by the crusaders lay dormant for centuries, only to resurface, Peyrat emphasized, among the bourgeois liberals of the French Third Republic, that is, people like himself. In response to the cult of Joan of Arc, an invention of nineteenth-century French nationalists, Peyrat concocted an Occitan equivalent, Esclarmonde of Foix. There was, indeed, a historic Esclarmonde of Foix; she was the sister of Raymond Roger, and she may even have clashed with St. Dominic. Peyrat, however, conflated five separate historical figures to come up with his fanciful, imaginary Esclarmonde. In his treatment, Esclarmonde became a high priestess guarding Cathar treasure and texts, an inspiring warrior like Joan, a preacher of unparalleled persuasiveness and beauty, the godmother of a whole generation of lovely female Perfect, and, ultimately, a martyr who turned into a dove in the flames of Montségur.

Peyrat created the cult of Montségur and made it central to

Cathar country. He spoke of tunnels and grottoes hiding thousands of Cathars. It was, in his words, "our wild Capitoline, our aerial tabernacle, our ark sheltering the remains of Aquitaine from a sea of blood." The following passage sums up his view of Montségur of the Cathars:

> Montségur was an Essenian Zion, a Platonist Delphi of the Pyrenees, a Johannite Rome, condemned and untamed in Aquitaine. Montségur, from its naked rock, looked out sadly but steadily at the Louvre and the Vatican. . . . In its grotto it sheltered three irreconcilable enemies of theocracy: the Word, the Nation and Freedom, those powers of the future. It was from its peak that this sweet and terrible conjuration first took wing, under the name of Spirit, to make its secret way through the winds, its invisible path through the storms; it was this mysterious horseman, mounted on the tempest and the thunder, who would through the religious revolution of the sixteenth century and the political revolution of the eighteenth regenerate Europe and the whole world.

Such was Peyrat's Hegelian republicanism put to use in making myths about a medieval heresy.

Peyrat firmly established the story of a fabulous Cathar treasure, a notion which would have very long legs. In Peyrat's defense, the historical record—in this instance, transcripts of Inquisition interrogations of survivors of Montségur—does speak of four Perfect scurrying down the mountain one night during the siege to hide a sack of gold, silver, and coins—obviously the treasury of the 200 or so Cathars atop the hill. Peyrat, however, made the treasure immense, and not just of monetary value. There were also sacred texts. The treasure was supposedly taken to a cave fifteen miles away called Lombrives, which Peyrat saw as a new Montségur. A large Cathar community, according to Peyrat, took to living like troglodytes in Lombrives until a French royal army discovered them and bricked up the entrance to the cave. Peyrat's passage on the death of the immured Cathars is haunting:

> One day they had nothing left, no food, wood, or fire, or even a wan light, that visible reflection of life. They came together as families, in separate niches, the husband beside the wife, the virgin beside her failing mother, a little baby on her dry breast. For a few moments, above the pious murmur of prayers, one could still hear the voice of the Cathar minister, declaring the Word that is in God and that is God. The faithful deacon gave the dying the kiss of peace, then lay down to sleep himself. All rested in a slumber, and only the drops of water that fell slowly from the roof of the vault disturbed the sepulchral silence for centuries. . . . While the inquisition damned their memory and even their loved ones no longer dared speak their names, the rock wept for them. The mountain, a tender mother welcoming them in her bosom, religiously wove for them a white shroud with her tears, buried their remains in the gradual folds of a chalky veil, and on their bones that no worm would ever profane, she sculpted a triumphant mausoleum of stalagmites, marvellously decorated with urns, candelabras and the symbols of life.

Sadly, for all its beauty, the story is utterly the invention of Napoléon Peyrat.

Peyrat's prose had a bewitching effect on those of his contemporaries enamored of the past. Earlier in the nineteenth century, the troubadour poetry in the Provençal languages had been re-discovered by French and German scholars, inspiring Frédéric Mistral and others to launch a linguistic recovery movement called the Félibrige. The Languedoc branch of this movement—the dialect of Languedoc being called Languedocien or, much later, Occitan—looked on Peyrat's work as a new gospel. The Félibrige glorified the pastor's romanticized Cathars and his glowing portrait of the south before the crusade.

Many in the Languedoc Félibrige were republicans, but federalists, in favor of a decentralized France where regional identities and languages would flourish. They wouldn't get very far against the centralizing bulldozer of the Third Republic. In response to their political failure, they retreated to fiction, music, and poetry based on the Cathars, of which there was a considerable production in the 1890s and 1900s. The ethos of the troubadours somehow became intertwined with the supposed libertarian Cathars. Operas were written about Esclarmonde of Foix, who became the subject of choice for turn-of-the-century southern poetasters. In 1911, there was a fight in her hometown, Foix, over whether to put up a statue for her. The Félibrige lost, and the statue was never commissioned.

Peyrat's Esclarmonde also began showing up in Paris, usually as a disembodied voice at séances frequented by intellectuals and socialites disgusted, at least for an evening, by nineteenth-century materialism. The Cathar Perfect were ideal interlocutors for such groups. Fin-de-siècle France also saw an explosion of theosophy—a rediscovery of the religions of the East that ushered in a tide of orientalism and esoteric thought. In this hothouse of occult salons and secret societies, Peyrat's Cathars prospered. They went from being protoliberals to continuators of a line of preclassical, Eastern wisdom. A neognostic church was founded by one Jules Doinel, who declared himself the gnostic patriarch of Paris—and, significantly, of Montségur.

The treasure of Montségur then became a cache of ancient knowledge. This theory was advanced by an influential occultist named Joséphin Péladan. His friends—Charles Baudelaire, Joris-Karl Huysmans, and others—called him Sar, as befitted his self-proclaimed status as the descendant of the monarchs of ancient Assyria. Péladan-Sar pointed out that Montsalvat, the holy mountain of Richard Wagner's *Parsifal* and *Lohengrin*, had to be Montségur. Thus was born the myth of the Pyrenean Holy Grail, yet another landmark of Cathar country destined for future glory.

The calamity of the First World War, which pulverized rational nineteenth-century certainties, led to a continent-wide upsurge in interest in the paranormal. The call of the Cathars was heard beyond the borders of France. A handful of pioneering British spiritualists descended on Montségur and the caves near Lombrives. There, in the 1920s and 1930s, groups of local Occitanists—heirs of the Félibrige—and erudite occultists welcomed them and worked hard to embroider on Peyrat's narrative.

Foremost among these local lights was Déodat Roché, a notary public from a town near Carcassonne. Roché was a disciple of Rudolf Steiner, the founder of anthroposophy, a system of creative rationality designed to allow its followers a direct and immediate contact with the spirit world. Roché's Cathar-tainted anthroposophy was open to all influences: hinduism, druidism, gnosis, and so on. He made much of cave scratchings near Montségur, claiming that they were pentagrams traced by Cathar fugitives in an attempt to transmit a message to posterity. Indeed, any cave graffito that was not obviously modern was immediately Catharized by Roché. He died in 1978, at the age of 100, his influence in the construction of Cathar country immense.

Gravitating around Roché, especially in the 1930s, was a group of young spiritual seekers, which included, for a time, the philosopher Simone Weil. She used an anagrammatic pen name, Emile Novis, to publish her articles about medieval Languedoc as a moral Utopia. But it was two men, especially, who would best export and distort the legacy of Peyrat. The first was Maurice Magre, a writer of considerable talent who is now almost totally forgotten. In the 1920s and 1930s, this prolific novelist and essayist—as well as prodigious consumer of opium— brought the energy of Paris's Montparnasse to Catharism. Magre's *Magiciens et illuminés* (The new magi) was a magisterial work of speculative history, a lively examination of the secret influence of Eastern sages throughout the ages. The Cathars held pride of place. This book was widely translated and reached audiences in both Britain and the United States.

Among Magre's impressive literary output, there were two Cathar novels, *Le Sang de Toulouse* (The blood of Toulouse) and *Le Trésor des Albigeois* (The treasure of the Albigensians). In the first, he brought the fabulations of Peyrat to modern audiences and recast such stories as Lombrives and the Cathar treasure in a vivid, mystical style that made Peyrat's romantic prose look dated. Magre also took the time to skewer the enemies of the Cathars: Alice of Montmorency, the wife of Simon de Montfort, is described as a creature with rotting teeth, sallow skin the color of "Sicilian lemons," and a big nose. The second, less successful Cathar novel had the Perfect as Buddhists.

In 1930, Magre met a young German graduate student in Paris, Otto Rahn, the second of Roché's circle to internationalize

Cathar country. Magre directed Rahn to his friends in the Ariège, and the result, in 1933, was *Kreuʒʒug gegen den Gral* (Crusade against the Grail). Rahn essentially assembled all of the Pyrenean Grail stories and compared them to the medieval *Parʒifal* written by Wolfram von Eschenbach. Montsalvat became Montségur, Parsifal (or Perceval) became Trencavel, and the guardian of the Grail was none other than Esclarmonde. What she was guarding was a sacred stone that had dropped from heaven during the time that the angels had fallen. Esclarmonde managed to hide the stone in the mountain before the French stormed Montségur and burned the Cathars.

This, then, was the true Grail, mistakenly placed in the fourteenth-century cycle written by Chrétien de Troyes somewhere in the north of France and, more important, wrongly transformed by Christian mythology into a chalice containing Christ's blood. Rahn's Cathars were pagans; they were also—and this was new—troubadours. Rahn's *Kreuʒʒug gegen den Gral* successfully placed the Cathars in the center of esoteric Grail studies.

Rahn and his followers then cast the darkest shadow ever to fall across Cathar country. In 1937, Rahn published *Luʒifers Hofgesind* (The court of Lucifer), another Cathar-Grail book. By this time, the visiting graduate student had moved back to Germany and become a member of the SS. Who then were the Cathars, in Rahn's new formulation? It isn't hard to guess:

> We do not need the god of Rome, we have our own. We do not need the commandments of Moses, we carry in our hearts the legacy of our ancestors. It is Moses who is imperfect and impure. . . . We, Westerners of nordic blood, we call ourselves Cathars just as Easterners of nordic blood are called Parsees, the Pure. Our heaven is open only to those who are not creatures of an

inferior race, or bastards, or slaves. It is open to Aryas. Their name means that they are nobles and lords.

Rahn's benign Grail speculations and his later Hitlerian take on the Cathars inevitably became combined. After the Second World War and well into the 1970s, a cottage industry of former Vichy collaborators churned out an astonishing amount of rumors concerning the connection of the Nazis to the Cathars, such as:

* On March 16, 1944, the 700th anniversary of the burning at Montségur, Alfred Rosenberg, the Nazi theorist, was said to have overflown the peak as a gesture of homage.
* Hitler and his closest advisers were said to have been part of a neo-Cathar pagan secret society.
* German engineers were said to have excavated Montségur during the Occupation and come away with the Holy Grail. In this last tale, which prefigures *Raiders of the Lost Ark*, Esclarmonde's precious Cathar stone—or, according to some far right-wingers, a non-Jewish tablet of commandments—was buried in a glacier in the Bavarian Alps just before the fall of Germany.

These rumors, while universally recognized as false, showed stubborn staying power in Languedoc. In 1978, there was a minor diplomatic incident when a group of rowdy German boy scouts was accused by locals of trying to steal blocks of stone from Montségur. The alleged prank was taken as proof that the boys had neo-Nazi leanings.

There would be no officially sponsored Cathar country signs in Languedoc if the legacy of Peyrat had solely degenerated into nostalgia for the Third Reich. Fortunately, Otto Rahn's competition eventually overwhelmed him. First, there was the obvious comparison of Cathars to members of the French Underground, fighting an invading force. This trope came up again and again in works published in the 1950s. The Cathars—bourgeois liberals, Buddhists, gnostics, Nazis, and whatever else they were—had now joined the *maquis* (the Resistance).

Also, the propaganda of Roché and Magre began to bear scientific fruit. Serious archaeologists and engineers started examining Montségur for signs of hidden chambers and tunnels. They found nothing. This did not stop one author, Fernand Niel, from publishing a chart-laden study showing Montségur to have been constructed as a solar temple. Niel even included one of these diagrams in a volume he wrote about the Cathars for the French "Que Sais-Je" collection, a series of handbooks destined for schools and reference libraries. His learned explanation of the solar nuances of Cathar construction has since been overshadowed by the rigorous scientific conclusion that the ruined castle now atop Montségur was built long *after* the Cathar crusade. (The original castle was demolished in the thirteenth or fourteenth century, then replaced.) The same conclusion about other ruined castles in the Corbières and the Pyrenees has not prevented their becoming *les châteaux cathares* (Cathar castles)— evocative remnants regularly visited by eco-hikers convinced that they are looking at solar temples destroyed by Catholicism.

The 1960s brought the counterculture to the Cathars and updated the lore surrounding them. The *babas-cool*, the French word for back-to-the-land hippie types, made the Ariège one of their prime targets for returning to nature and making goat cheese. When they began arriving in the late 1960s, they were met by Dutch Rosicrucians, neognostics from Belgium, and other groups who had already moved south to Cathar country summer camps. The babas-cool found in the Cathars several appealing qualities: They were vegetarians; they disapproved of marriage—therefore they were pro–free love; women could be Perfect—therefore they were feminists; and they were part of the troubadour love culture of Occitania. The Cathars, in short, became groovy. Rock groups serenaded crowds at the foot of Montségur, where the billows of smoke now came only from reefers.

In the English-speaking world, British psychiatrist Arthur Guirdham gained notoriety in the 1960s and 1970s through a series of occult books that inspired many Britons to explore southwestern France. Guirdham described how several of his patients independently exhibited signs of being reincarnated Cathar Perfect. He, himself, is/was Guilhabert of Castres. Why so many of these Cathar spirits congregated in Bath, England, the home of Guirdham's practice, is not answered in his books, but his New Age updating of Parisian salon séances has proved enduring.

By the late 1970s, Cathar country had truly come of age. People measured the cosmic vibrations at Cathar castles. Occitan nationalists gathered for ceremonies at Montségur. Weekend archaeologists turned up what they inevitably claimed were Cathar crosses, pendants, and stone doves. Replicas of these objects became the staples at craft fairs throughout Languedoc. Stonehengers and other assorted neopagans began taking an interest. French and British television did specials on the various enigmas of the Cathar story, all of which were more or less inherited from the circles of esotericism animated by Déodat Roché in the

1930s. Roché was now in his nineties, a frail Cathar pope to a growing entourage.

Shortly after Roché's death, the Anglo-American trio of Michael Baigent, Richard Leigh, and Henry Lincoln published the most successful book ever to hit Cathar country: *The Holy Blood and the Holy Grail,* now past its thirty-fifth printing in English. The threesome made Catharism a truly mass phenomenon and turned the international Glastonbury Arthurian crowd on to a new form of medieval romance. The writers took the legacy of Magre, Roché, and others and wrote a thoroughly entertaining occult detective story. The mystery is this: At the turn of the twentieth century, a country priest in the remote parish of Rennes-le-Château, near Carcassonne, suddenly took to living very well and constructing additions to his church and residence. He was spending millions of francs. Where did he get them?

The short answer is that he had masterminded a system of mail-order fund-raising and conned several local notables into leaving him money in their wills. The long answer is told in the more than 500 pages of *The Holy Blood and the Holy Grail.* The priest, it turns out, found the treasure that the Cathars had smuggled out of Montségur during the siege. He began selling off parts of it, as well as blackmailing the Vatican. The Cathar treasure, aside from its incalculable hoard of Visigothic gold, was nothing less than the proof that Jesus was not god but a king who had married Mary Magdalene. Their son founded the line of Merovingian kings, who were, incidentally, Jewish. This secret, along with others debunking Jesus' divinity, was found below the Temple of Jerusalem during the Crusades. It had been transmitted to both the Cathars and Knights Templars. After the treasure's narrow escape at Montségur, an occult society had kept the secret to themselves until the priest's discovery at Rennes-le-Château. In the past, the secret society had been headed by, among others, Leonardo da Vinci, Nicolas Poussin, Isaac Newton, Victor Hugo, and Claude Debussy. The book shrewdly hints that not all of the treasure has been found. Since its publication, the land around Rennes-le-Château has become pockmarked with the spadework of treasure hunters. A landing pad for UFOs has been constructed (in truth, a mown meadow), and tours are now conducted through what is a very ordinary country church.

The imaginary landscape first outlined by Napoléon Peyrat has become progressively weirder. The Cathars are now a protean bunch, ready to transform into just about anything the soul desires. Religious cults of the 1980s and 1990s used them in murderous delirium: The Order of the Solar Temple, the Franco-Québécois-Swiss suicide cult, based some of their arcane calculations on the nonsense written about the Cathar castles. The Web site of Marshall Applewhite's Heaven's Gate teemed with references to the asceticism of the Cathars and the god hidden behind the god. He eventually persuaded his followers to commit suicide, so as to go to the "level beyond human"—a state not unlike the Perfects'—and, in the end, listen to the message of the Hale-Bopp Comet.

However dubious some of its satellites, Cathar country looks likely to continue expanding. It is promised a bright future on the Internet, a matter-free medium made to be an echo chamber of esoteric thought. There is also a movie in the works, a French film for 2000 or 2001 entitled *La Main de Dieu* (The hand of God). It will deal with the great unsolved murder mystery of the Cathar drama: Who killed Peter of Castelnau? The only other major film about the Cathars dates from the 1940s. *La Fiancée des ténèbres* (The bride of darkness) had a troubled and fetching young woman realize that she was the reincarnation of—who else?—Esclarmonde of Foix. Napoléon Peyrat, the man who created the myths of Cathar country, is no doubt resting in peace.

March 16, 1999, was the last anniversary of the famous bonfire to share the same millennium with the Perfect of Montségur. I left my home near Perpignan and headed toward the Pyrenees, the true legacy of the Cathars uppermost in my mind. That this beautiful corner of France—the national affiliation being a part of that legacy —should have been the theater of such cruel intolerance was still hard to credit, even after two years of travel throughout Languedoc in the imagined company of the Cathars. Yet the villages in the Corbières filed by, their names now familiar from Inquisition registers and chronicles of the crusade. History had happened here; a culture had made a choice. At every bend in the road, it seemed, there was a vista of a ruined castle brooding atop a hill, the site, if not the stones, having witnessed some chapter in the Cathar drama. Languedoc, it occurred to me, teaches a lesson about the dangers of the absolute.

The day was unseasonably warm. I parked in the small lot at the foot of Montségur and walked over to the commemorative stela. A rangy young man shoved a raft of papers into my hand: poems, in Occitan. He was a troubadour, here with his mother. The ticket taker farther up the slope rolled his eyes and told me that they come to Montségur every March 16th.

The path was steep, snaking upward through the rock and

Montségur
(Jean Pierre Pétermann)

undergrowth, making dizzying switchbacks over the void. The snow-specked heaths grew smaller in the morning sunlight. At one spot, leaning against a bench, a middle-aged man knelt in prayer. I passed him wordlessly; I don't think he even heard me.

In the remnants of the castle at the summit, what looked like an extended family—grandmother, parents, teenage children—stood off to one side and sang. The effect was lovely. The eldest boy later explained that they were Filipinos and that his father had always wanted to come here. Why? He didn't know.

I walked through a gap in the walls to where the village of the Perfect had once stood. A few ropes cordoned off the ledges on which archaeologists would be perched once the fine weather returned. I rounded a corner of a rampart and saw, to the south, Mount St. Bartholomew stretching into the sky. I closed my eyes, felt the wind.

Silence. The clamor of Cathar country lay far below, in the souvenir shops and the cities. Albi was so far away that even its awful shout had been stilled.

I opened my eyes. The Cathars had won after all. They no longer existed.

Notes

USAGE AND PRIMARY SOURCES

I opted to anglicize most proper names. Some language groups have no problem with such blanket transformations (the French, for example, can call Michelangelo *Michel-Ange* without a twinge of embarrassment), yet making the switch for *The Perfect Heresy* meant defying present-day Occitan political correctness. May my friends in Languedoc forgive me, but the vagaries of spelling—I've seen the Occitan for *Peter* rendered as *Peire*, *Peyre*, and *Pere*—proved daunting. While it is true that the many Raymonds of the story might have styled themselves *Raimon* or *Raimond* or some other cognate, to my eye such unfamiliar spellings put up obstacles to understanding. (The names of the two troubadours I mention, however, have been left as found.) A few other exceptions to my linguistic imperialism occur, for reasons of euphony, nationality, or avoidance of the ridiculous. *King Peire/Peyre II* of Aragon became *Pedro*, not *Peter* or *Pierre*; the Italian *Lotario* resisted becoming *Lothar*; and *Guilhabert of Castres* simply refused to be called Wilbert. As for the numerous French figures in the text, there too I have anglicized names in the interests of easier comprehension. In this I am not alone: The thirteen-volume *Dictionary of the Middle Ages*, edited by Joseph R. Strayer (New York: Scribners, 1989), has comforted me in many of my decisions. The French *particule* (i.e., de or des) is retained only when a long-standing convention has been established (e.g., Simon de Montfort) or when I have determined the name is a patronymic. Thus the murderers of Avignonet include a William *of* Lahille, a man from the village of Lahille near Fanjeaux, and a Bernard *de* St. Martin, whose last name appears to be just that—a last name. If my desire to make the text more accessible is an insufficient argument in the face of debatable judgment calls, I will gladly fall back on the excuse made famous by French Communists: "Ce sont mes contradictions!" (Such are my contradictions).

In the same arbitrary mood, I have embraced anachronism in geography. For our period, as mentioned in the introduction, it is premature to speak of *France* or *England* as established national states or governments, yet it would be tiresome to continue repeating "that patchwork of feudal arrangements that would one day coalesce into what we now call *x*." A recent book on the Cathars adopts the following nomenclature: Carolingian France is referred to as *Gaul*; the area under the suzerainty of the early Capets is then termed *Francia*; and the confines of the state after King Philip Augustus is called *France*. Masterly distinctions; muddy waters. As long as it's recognized as such, a little anachronism is better than a lot of confusion.

Readers should know of the principal primary sources for the Cathar drama before consulting the notes. First among equals is the thirteenth-century *Canso*, or, as it is now translated, *The Song of the Cathar Wars*. A 10,000-line Occitan-language chanson de geste—that is, a rhymed narrative song—the *Canso* has the peculiarity of being the work of two authors, both of whom witnessed many of the events of the crusade. The first third of the poem was written by the pro-crusade William of Tudela, a cleric assumed to have received the patronage of Baldwin, Count Raymond VI's brother. When the traitorous Baldwin, a partisan of Simon de Montfort, was captured and hanged by his kinsmen shortly after the battle of Muret, William's inkwell ran dry. The story from 1213 on was taken up by an anonymous continuator, who was ferociously pro-Toulouse in his leanings. The *Canso* thus switches sides. The last two-thirds of the poem brings the action up to 1219, as Toulouse is about to repel its third siege in eight years. The continuator, usually referred to as Anonymous, appears to have been a devout Catholic and, most probably, a companion of the young Count Raymond VII. Janet Shirley, in the introduction to her welcome English prose translation of the *Canso* (Aldershot, England: Scolar Press, 1996), distinguishes between the two writers: "Another and considerable difference between these two authors, one that is all but lost in translation, is that William was a good competent writer but his successor was a man of genius. William can tell a good story and is careful to leave us in no doubt that he was a well educated literary man. . . . The Anonymous, however, can toss showers of words into the air and catch them again."

Another primary source of importance is the *Hystoria albigensis*, a Latin chronicle written by the pro-crusader Peter of Vaux de Cernay, a Cistercian monk. The nephew of a prelate who was a faithful friend of Simon de Montfort, Peter took part in many of the crusade's actions and is a valuable, if unswervingly partial, eyewitness. At this writing, the definitive translation was to the French: Pascal Guébin and Henri Maisonneuve, *Histoire albigeoise* (Paris: Vrin, 1951). An English version of Vaux de Cernay's chronicle, translated by W. A. and M. D. Sibly was published in 1998 (Rochester, N.Y.: Boydell).

The last of the trinity of contemporary accounts was written at mid-century by William of Puylaurens, a notary for the Inquisition once in the employ of Count Raymond VII. Telegraphic in style, yet covering a greater chronological span, the *Chronica magistri Guillelmi de Podio Laurentii* backs up the detail found in the *Canso* and the *Hystoria*. Puylaurens appears to have spoken to the survivors of the crusade in their old age. The most commonly used translation from the original Latin was effected by the dean of French-language Cathar studies, Jean Duvernoy (Paris: C.N.R.S., 1976). The *Chronica* is not sympathetic to the Cathar cause, but neither does it spare the crusaders abuse for their often underhanded tactics.

The primary sources used for later periods of the Cathar story are discussed in the chapter notes that follow. Full publishing information on most of the books mentioned in the notes can be found in the bibliography.

The Perfect Heresy was written to be accessible to all readers curious about the past. For points of well-established fact and excerpts of medieval documents to be found in most studies of the Cathars, I did not think it necessary to credit the sources. Serious points of disagreement among them, however, are outlined in the notes, as well as any information that I deemed subsidiary, or distracting, to the flow of the narrative. Some of this "off-topic" information, I like to think, is interesting in its own right.

▣ Introduction

4   There was nothing subtle about the appearance of Ste-Cécile: Lest any admirer of this peculiar church criticize me for neglecting the interior of Ste-Cécile, it should be mentioned that the side chapels and ceiling of the cathedral are a riot of colorful portraiture. Around the choir, occupying fully half of the nave, a pale lattice of carved limestone houses dozens of statues in its niches. This flamboyant Gothic rood screen is among France's finest ecclesiastical treasures—a testament to the wealth of the see of Albi. At the back of the church, however, is an enormous fresco of the Last Judgment, four stories tall and as wide as the building itself. Commissioned by Louis d'Amboise, a late medieval bishop, it is a masterwork of the macabre, teeming with scores of figures in various stages of agony as reptilian demons and slimy toads torture them for eternity. Although the Cathars had long since vanished when Bishop d'Amboise had Florentine artists execute the work between 1474 and 1480, the fresco's grotesque depiction of the consequences of sin seems less than innocent in this red-brick menace of a cathedral. Further queasiness is caused by another accident of art history. A bishop of the baroque era, Charles Le Goux de la Berchère, punched a huge hole in the center of the fresco to build a chapel in the base of the bell tower. In the top half of the painting—that part dedicated to the souls heading heavenward—the modification had the unfortunate effect of obliterating God, the judge of the Last Judgment. The solace of the divine is thus nowhere

to be seen in this horror show, as if the painting sought solely to scare rather than to uplift. Again, given the history of the area, the result is almost too fitting to be a coincidence.

6   Whether Arnold Amaury actually uttered that pitiless order is still a matter for debate: "Kill them all, God will know his own" first appeared in the *Dialogus miraculorum* of the Cistercian monk Caesarius of Heisterbach, who wrote his admiring account of the crusade some thirty years after the fact. It had long been a historian's reflex to shrug off the order as apocryphal and absolve Arnold Amaury of any such brutal eloquence. Recent scholarship, however, has pointed out that the wording echoes passages to be found in 2 Timothy (2:19) and Numbers (16:5). As the scrupulous Malcolm Lambert states in *The Cathars* (p.103): "This makes it a little more likely that these words from the mouth of an educated member of the hierarchy [i.e., Arnold Amaury] were authentic." Whatever the truth of its birth, the expression continues to live on. Culture critic Greil Marcus, in his *Lipstick Traces: A Secret History of the 20th Century* (Cambridge: Harvard University Press, 1990), claims that the expression "Kill 'em all, God will sort 'em out!" was a T-shirt slogan favored by fans of punker Johnny Rotten and, in a Spanish version, by members of Guatemalan death squads. The *New York Times* reported that Karla Faye Tucker, the ax-murderer executed in 1998 in Texas, used to wear a "Kill 'em all" T-shirt in her bad girl days.

6   "a thousand years without a bath": The *mot* is attributed to Jules Michelet.

6   "I'm gonna get medieval . . .": Tarantino's zinger about the Middle Ages is rivaled by the memorable couplet concocted in the 1960s by satirist Tom Lehrer about segregationist Dixie: "In the land of the boll weevil/Where the laws are medieval."

13   the obscene kiss: Even though the tales of turpitude concerning heretics were borrowed from slanders that abounded in classical times (sometimes spread by pagan alarmists about the fledgling sects of Christianity), they were believed by many who should have known better. In 1233, Pope Gregory IX, the sponsor of the Inquisition, issued a papal bull, *Vox in Rama*, that breathlessly repeated old stories about feline orgies. A much-repeated slander was penned in the 1180s by Walter Map, a

deacon of Oxford, who wrote the following of heretics: "About the first watch of the night . . . each family sits waiting in silence in each of their synagogues; and there descends by a rope which hangs in their midst a black cat of wondrous size. On sight of it they put out the lights and do not sing or distinctly repeat hymns, but hum them with closed teeth, and draw near to the place where they saw their master, feeling after him and when they have found him they kiss him. The hotter the feelings the lower their aim; some go for his feet, but most for his tail and privy parts. Then as though this noisome contact unleashed their appetites, each lays hold of his neighbor and takes his fill of him or her for all he is worth" (source: Jeffrey Richards, *Sex, Dissidence, and Damnation*, pp. 60–61).

13   the heretics believed that no one could sin from the waist down: We have Peter of Vaux de Cernay to thank for this titillating fiction about the Cathars.

13   the thirteenth century's culture of lawmaking and codification: It is a commonplace to compare the curiosity of the twelfth century with the reaction of the thirteenth. In a 1948 study of the Plantagenet kings of England, John Harvey summed up the historical consensus elegantly: "The thirteenth [century] was to witness the first riveting of the bands forged by scholasticism upon the minds of scholars, and the barren substitution of authority for empiricism. On the other hand, in the manual arts, such as architecture, sculpture, and painting, great strides were made by lay craftsmen who were sufficiently beneath the notice of the learned world of the schools to be able to carry on a living empiricism of their own. In certain other fields, notably those of law and administration, advances were made in the direction of unity by a process of codification and the hardening of earlier tentative formulae into settled rules of life" (source: J. Harvey, *The Plantagenets* [London: B. T. Batsford, 1948], p. 50).

13   historian R. I. Moore has provocatively seen. . . : In *The Formation of a Persecuting Society*, Moore argues that the persecuting apparatus was a natural but not inevitable outgrowth of the nascent state. He sees the years 1180–90 as a turning point in the development of oppressive institutions. His book, published in 1987, is still making waves.

14   Ironically, it took a twentieth-century Dominican friar, Antoine Dondaine, to dispel the fog: The banner year for understanding Catharism was 1939, when Dondaine discovered several important documents in archives in Florence and Prague: a Cathar catechism in Latin; a thirteenth-century philosophical treatise, *The Book of Two Principles*, written by a John of Lugio; and an exceptionally evenhanded description and rebuttal of Catharism, *Contra Manicheos*, written by Durand of Huesca, a Waldensian thinker who had been converted to orthodoxy during a debate with Dominic in 1207. Prior to these discoveries, Cathar theology had been pieced together solely from what their adversaries had written about the heresy and from two incomplete Occitan manuscripts found in Lyons and Dublin. Naturally, the enemies of Catharism had depicted the faith as a mass of superstition. From these documents it became obvious, especially in the case of John of Lugio (a Cathar scholastic), that the heresy was squarely in the tradition of Aristotelian rationalism. After centuries of being considered a fifth column for a Manichean revival, the Cathars could be studied for what they were: medieval Christians.

14   there were four contemporary chroniclers: For identification of these sources, see "Usage and Primary Sources" above.

16   the forces of American corporate imperialism: The novel in question is *Le Christi*, by René-Victor Pilhes. The author sees American economic leadership as a reincarnation of the totalitarian medieval Church, a view not uncommon in present-day France.

◻ 1. Languedoc and the Great Heresy

19   the outermost fringes of the Romance conversation: Occitan and its cousins were once squarely center stage. Before deciding on composing in his Tuscan vernacular, Dante Alighieri considered writing the *Divine Comedy* in Provençal.

20   often as weavers: Tradition holds that dualism was spread along the trade routes of the south by itinerant artisans. Foremost among these tradespeople were weavers, and for a while the Cathars were known as *tisserands* (weavers). Dissident scholarly opinion questions this occupational proclivity, by claiming that associating the Perfect with the rootless

artisans was yet another way Catholic propagandists had found to slander them.

21   St. Félix en Lauragais: At the time, the village was called St. Félix de Caraman. I have given its modern name.

21   a Cathar International: The capitalized title for the meeting is my invention. As for the meeting itself, a vocal group of revisionists, led by historian Monique Zerner, claim that the heretical conclave never occurred. The skeptics' argument rests principally on the fact that the sole source for the St. Félix meeting is a seventeenth-century document, whose author (Guillaume Besse) claimed to have worked from a now vanished manuscript of 1223. A colloquium was held in Nice in January 1999 to give the revisionists a hearing, yet the crushing weight of consensus among Cathar experts—Anne Brenon, Michel Roquebert, Malcolm Lambert, Bernard Hamilton, Jean Duvernoy, et. al.—continues to come down on the side of St. Félix having witnessed "the most imposing international gathering ever recorded in the history of the Cathars" (source: Malcolm Lambert, *The Cathars*, pp. 45–46). Some, however, argue that the meeting took place in the 1170s, not 1167. For an entertaining summary of many of the arguments pro and con, see Michel Roquebert, *Histoire des cathares*, pp. 58–62.

21   the believers overwhelmingly outnumbered . . . the Perfect: To my chagrin, I felt obliged to opt for the terminology coined by the Cathars' persecutors. I have done this to avoid confusion, for the Cathars simply referred to themselves as Christians, good Christians, good men or good women, or friends of God. A Perfect is so called not because he or she is flawless; rather, one so labeled is a *hereticus perfectus* or *heretica perfecta*—"a completed heretic," in the sense of one who has passed from the stage of sympathizer to the rank of the ordained. I have elected to capitalize the term so it will not be confused with the ordinary sense of "perfect." The term for believers, *credentes*, was also coined by Catharism's enemies.

22   a ritual response to the melioramentum: The exchange of greetings in the melioramentum emphasized the gulf between the simple, earthbound believer and the quasi divine Perfect. Malcolm Lambert, in *The Cathars* (p. 142), draws on Y. Hagman's doctoral work, "Catharism: A

Medieval Echo of Manichaeism or of Primitive Christianity," in describing the exchange: "In the most solemn form of the ceremony, three profound inclinations of the head on to the hands, so far as to kiss them, was accompanied by 'Bless us' (*benedicte*), 'Lord', or 'good Christian' or 'good lady', 'the blessing of God and your own', 'Pray God for us' and on the third inclination, 'Lord, pray God for this sinner that he deliver him from an evil death and lead him to a good end.' The perfect responded affirmatively to the first and second prayers and to the third at great length alluding to the *consolamentum*: 'God be prayed that God will make you a good Christian and lead you to a good end.' "

22 leader of the Cathar faith in northern France: Not much is known of Catharism north of the Loire, save that it was repressed at an early stage and thus never came close to the success it enjoyed in Languedoc. The greatest concentration of dualist heretics in this region appears to have been in Champagne, an area crisscrossed by trade routes and host to the great medieval fairs where goods—and ideas—were exchanged.

23 The very last of the Bogomils: This nugget of surprising information is found in Friedrich Heer's *The Medieval World* (p. 206). I have seen *Bogomil* also translated as "Deserving of the Pity of God."

24 The Catholic precept of *ex opere*. . . : To believe that a corrupt priest cannot celebrate a sacrament is a heresy known as Donatism. Augustine of Hippo (354–430) was merciless in combating the Donatists in his homeland of Roman North Africa.

26 heretical, by every definition except their own: Heresy is a slippery little devil. To label an idea heretical is to know exactly what it is you believe, and precisely what it is that you consider an unacceptable interloper into your patch of the divine. For the great majority of medieval believers, the line between heterodoxy and orthodoxy snaked all over the map. Christianity, like other faiths, was an ongoing argument, and the teachings and practices of the Church wandered in and out of dead-end debates, picking up thoughts that would later be deemed repugnant, dismissing others that might subsequently constitute dogma. To the average Languedoc peasant, no doubt the Cathar holy men and women seemed to be completely orthodox in their piety, more orthodox than the

village priest living with his concubine. Scholar Leonard George has nicely defined *heresy* as "a crime of perception—an act of seeing something that, according to some custodian of reality, is not truly there." The word originates in the Greek *hairesis*, the noun formed from the verb *haireomai* (to choose). At base, *heresy* means consciously opting for a set of beliefs, and thus a heretic is—the anachronism is irresistible—pro-choice. It then came to mean choosing an *incorrect* belief system. Given the shifting sands of doctrine, finding the officially approved path to salvation frequently took deft spiritual footwork. Paul admonished his followers about heretics in an oft-quoted passage from the New Testament's Titus 3:9–11: "But avoid foolish controversies and genealogies and arguments and quarrels about the law, because these are unprofitable and useless. Warn a divisive person once, and then warn him a second time. After that you may have nothing to do with him. You may be sure that such a man is warped and sinful; he is self-condemned." In another influential remark about heresy, the thirteenth-century English churchman Robert Grosseteste, one of the rare specimens of medieval humanity to have survived into his eighties, leaves implicit the notion of a single, approved truth. According to him, heresy is "an opinion chosen by human perception, contrary to holy scripture, publicly avowed and obstinately defended." Again, choice and perception were paramount in this definition, with the added proviso of publicity. The wise old Grosseteste was saying that you wouldn't be called a heretic if you just kept your mouth shut. The Cathars, famously, did not. Their creed embraced so many officially proscribed errors—Donatism, Docetism, dualism, Monophysitism, etc.— that to call them heretics seems an understatement. True, the Cathars thought the Catholics were heretics, but the Church, just as famously, won the argument. If the Cathars can't be called heretics, we should just delete the word from our dictionaries. In the text I use the term in the sense of dissent, not depravity.

27   Ephemeral messiahs and cranky reformers: My quick review of colorful charismatics of the twelfth century should be supplemented by reading, in order of palatability, Norman Cohn's *The Pursuit of the Millennium*, R. I. Moore's *The Origins of European Dissent*, and Malcolm Lambert's *Medieval Heresy*. The jungle of dissent is lush.

27 revered him so much that they drank his bathwater: The charge against Tanchelm's followers, complete with details of how they adored his toenail clippings, may or may not be true, given the partisan nature of the pro-Catholic medieval sources. What is more certain is that the tale, even if it is a canard, continues to intoxicate with its perverseness. In the *New Yorker* of November 29, 1999, John Updike writes about Shoko Asahara, the head of the cult that released nerve gas in Tokyo subways: "His followers were also privileged, when he was at liberty, to kiss his big toe and to pay upward of two hundred dollars for a drink of his used bathwater."

29 Mystical, anorexic, brilliant, eloquent and polemical: The mention of anorexia may surprise, but the great Bernard was voluble about his ills, imagined or real. An entertaining depiction of the man—and of his nemesis, Peter Abelard—can be found in Christopher Frayling's *Strange Landscape*, in which he devotes a chapter titled "The Saint and the Scholar" to their famous twelfth-century feud. Frayling writes (p. 123) of Bernard's gastric troubles: "Bernard was permanently ill—which was hardly surprising given the way he punished his body and the damp surroundings he lived in. He seems to have suffered from a form of extreme anorexia nervosa—rejecting food so regularly that he was sometimes paralysed through lack of nourishment; and he stank continually of stale vomit. 'I have a bad stomach,' he wrote, 'but how much more must I be hurt by the stomach of my memory where such rottenness collects.' "

29 The great man was laughed out of town: The story is alluded to in Geoffrey of Auxerre's medieval *Life of Saint Bernard* and expanded upon in the first chapter of William of Puylaurens's chronicle.

30 dualists were sighted everywhere: Perhaps the strangest incident of heresy detection in the twelfth century occurred near Rheims, when a cleric named Gervase of Tilbury, out riding with the archbishop and some senior prelates, spotted a pretty girl working alone in a vineyard. A chronicler, Ralph of Coggeshall, relates: "Moved by the lewd curiosity of a young man, as I heard from him myself after he had become a canon, he went over to her. He greeted her, and asked politely where she came from, and who her parents were, and what she was doing there alone, and then, when he had eyed her beauty for a while, spoke gallantly

to her of the delights of love-making." She turned him down, saying that she would always remain a virgin. His suspicions now aroused as well, Gervase learned that the peasant girl believed, on heretical religious grounds, that her body must not be corrupted. He tried to get her to change her mind, in the timeless manner of one who will not take no for an answer. Their arguing finally attracted the attention of the archbishop, who rode over and soon became scandalized. Not by Gervase's conduct, but by the girl's faith. He had her arrested and brought back to Rheims for questioning. The farm girl refused to recant, and she was burned. (Source: R. I. Moore, *The Birth of Popular Heresy*, pp. 86–88.)

30   labeled the unfortunates *Cathars*: The name originated in Eckbert of Schönau's *Thirteen Sermons against the Cathars*, written in 1163. Eckbert also called the Cathars "wretched half-wits."

30   the question of oath taking: The refusal to swear oaths was frequent among heretics, and not just of the Cathar variety. One justification is found in Matthew 5:33–37: "Again, you have heard that it was said to the people long ago: 'Do not break your oath, but keep the oaths you have made to the Lord.' But I tell you, Do not swear at all: either by heaven, for it is God's throne; or by the earth, for it is his footstool; or by Jerusalem, for it is the city of the Great King. And do not swear by your head, for you cannot make even one hair white or black. Simply let your 'Yes' be 'Yes,' and your 'No,' 'No;' anything beyond this comes from the evil one."

31   Cathar dioceses were drawn up: Among those who concede that the St. Félix meeting took place, there is further argument about what happened there. Some believe that Nicetas (often styled *Niquinta*) laid down the dualist law, convincing the Languedoc Cathars to move from "mitigated dualism" to "absolute dualism"—the latter being a more hard-core belief positing an almost co-equal evil divinity. Others hold that the tale of Nicetas's dogmatic authority is baseless, caused by a misreading in the 1890s (by historian Ignaz von Döllinger) and repeated unwittingly by generations of historians throughout the twentieth century. What *is* certain is that Nicetas warned the Languedoc Cathars against divisiveness and approved their diocesan organization.

⊠ *2. Rome*

33   the pontiff's superiority over all the crowned heads of Christendom: The chutzpah of Gregory VII can still take one's breath away.
In a volume of his correspondence, historians found a list that contains
the following statements: "The pope can be judged by no one; the Roman
church has never erred and never will err till the end of time; the Roman
church was founded by Christ alone; the pope alone can depose and
restore bishops; he alone can make new laws, set up new bishoprics, and
divide old ones; he alone can translate bishops; he alone can call general
councils and authorize canon law; he alone can revise his own judge-
ments; he alone can use the imperial insignia; he can depose emperors; he
can absolve subjects from their allegiance; all princes should kiss his feet"
(source: R. W. Southern, *Western Society and the Church in the Middle
Ages*, p. 102).

37–38   the church of SS. Sergio and Bacco: The church of Lotario's
cardinalate no longer exists. Neither does the tower that was erected on
top of the arch of Septimius Severus.

37   The church was a treasure house of relics: There may be a six-
or seven-year anachronism in the list of some of the relics to be found at
the Lateran in 1198. A lot of relics came on the market following the
crusader sack of Constantinople in 1204; thus some of the objects listed
may not have found their way to Rome until after that event. For example, Enrico Dandolo, the wily old doge of Venice, brought back from
Constantinople the lions that stand in front of St. Mark's, as well as a
piece of the True Cross, the arm of St. George, a vial of Christ's blood,
and a chunk of John the Baptist's head (source: Marc Kaplan, "Le sac de
Constantinople," in *Les Croisades*, ed. R. Delort).

38   it was he who definitively nudged the papal court to . . . the
Vatican: Innocent would eventually wind up back at St. John Lateran,
however, when a disgruntled nineteenth-century papacy moved his body
to the church as a symbolic riposte to constitutional liberalism. He now
lies in the transept, his recumbent stone effigy a study in lordly calm,

guarded by a pair of statues depicting women. One holds the light of wisdom; the other, the banner of crusade. It is rumored that his remains were transferred from Perugia to Rome in the suitcase of a seminarian traveling in the second-class compartment of a train.

38 Lotario must have absorbed the lesson behind that beatification: There is no documentary evidence proving that the young Lotario was impressed by the canonization of Thomas Becket in neighboring Segni. It is, however, a fairly reasonable assumption and one that is repeated by several of Innocent's biographers. Jane Sayers, in her *Innocent III*, states that Lotario toured the saint's shrine in Canterbury on a student visit to Britain (p. 19). Historian Edward Peters, in "Lotario dei Conti di Segni becomes Pope Innocent III" (from *Pope Innocent III and his World*, ed. J. C. Moore) dates the visit at 1185 or 1186 (p. 10).

38 5,000 ounces of gold: In Paul Johnson's *A History of Christianity* (p. 267), the visit in 1511 of the Dutch scholar Erasmus to the shrine of St. Thomas in Canterbury is evoked: "Erasmus's account makes it clear they were deeply shocked by what they saw. The riches which adorned the shrine were staggering. Erasmus found them incongruous, disproportionate, treasures 'before which Midas or Croesus would have seemed beggars;' thirty years later, Henry VIII's agents were to garner from it 4,994 ounces of gold, 4,425 of silver-gilt, 5,286 of plain silver and twenty-six cartloads of other treasure."

⊠ 3. The Turn of the Century

40 "To be always with a woman . . .": This nugget of misogyny is quoted in R. W. Southern's classic *Western Society and the Church in the Middle Ages* (p. 315). Southern makes his point about the Church turning its back on women with other selected quotations. One of the most remarkable was penned by a Premonstratensian abbot: "We and our whole community of canons, recognizing that the wickedness of women is greater than all the other wickedness of the world, and that there is no anger like that of women, and that the poison of asps and dragons is more curable and less dangerous to men than the familiarity of women, have unanimously decreed for the safety of our souls, no less than that of our

bodies and goods, that we will on no account receive any more sisters to the increase of our perdition, but will avoid them like poisonous animals."

42   ". . . We cannot. We have been reared in their midst.": The Catholic knight who made this oft-cited admission to Bishop Fulk was Pons-Adhémar of Roudeille. The anecdote is related by William of Puylaurens.

42   entirely free of the prejudices of its time: Peter Autier, the leader of the Cathar revival in the early 1300s, taught that one had to be a male in one's last incarnation if one was to join the good god. The idea that women were sinks of corruption and carnality, an oft-repeated theme in medieval Catholicism, appears to have cropped up in Catharism during the time of its persecution. For a levelheaded and exhaustive examination of Cathar beliefs, see Anne Brenon's excellent *Le Vrai Visage du catharisme*.

43   Noblewomen, especially, founded, managed, and led Cathar homes: Again, the work of historian Anne Brenon should be consulted, especially her *Les Femmes cathares*. The role of women in Catharism, long neglected by Catholic and Protestant historians feuding over the doctrinal implications of dualism, is now seen as one of the most remarkable sociological aspects of the heresy. Of the great Cathar matriarchs, Blanche of Laurac was undoubtedly the most notorious. On becoming a widow, Blanche and her youngest daughter, Mabilia, received the consolamentum and ran a Cathar home in Laurac, the town that gave its name to the Lauragais region. Another daughter, Navarra, left her husband, Stephen of Servian, when he repented of his heresy to Dominic. Navarra moved to Montségur. Another of Blanche's daughters, Esclarmonde, married into the Niort clan and became the mother of the most dangerous family in Cathar history. The last of Blanche's daughters was Geralda of Lavaur, a Cathar believer murdered by the crusaders in 1211. Blanche's only son was Aimery of Montréal.

44   the elder man invited a bevy of prelates to sniff out Catharism in his capital of Toulouse: The unsuccessful mission of 1178 included the head of the Cistercians, Henry of Marsiac, a powerful cardinal, Peter of Pavia, as well as the bishops of Bourges and Bath. Marsiac returned in 1181, at the head of an armed force and captured the town of Lavaur, a settlement between Albi and Toulouse that had a reputation for heresy.

Although Marsiac's occupation of Lavaur was fleeting, an ominous precedent had been set.

45   a troubadour named Peire Vidal: Vidal was by no means the only troubadour in Raymond's court. Indeed, the count's secretary for many years was Peire Cardenal, a troubadour who was an accomplished composer of *sirventes*—rhymed songs that usually skewered the enemies of the man who commissioned them.

46   hotly contested sources of money: The splintering effect of partible inheritances that worked wonders for low-maintenance female Perfect was disastrous for their petty noble kinsmen, on whom Raymond should have been able to call for support. By the first decade of the thirteenth century, many towns and villages had thirty to fifty "colords"—fifty in Lombers, thirty-five in Mirepoix (source: Walter L. Wakefield, *Heresy, Crusade, and Inquisition in Southern France, 1100–1250*, p. 52)—the result of successive pie splitting, and thus everyone involved was more or less broke or quarreling with each other over a few far-flung acres of vines. Not many nobles could stable a military establishment. The recourse to freelance *routiers* (armed mercenaries) as a means of resolving disputes only added to the anarchy. These routiers, often landless younger sons from the neighboring kingdom of Aragon, were notorious for overstaying their welcome and wreaking havoc with a terrified peasantry.

46   approximately 150 in all at the turn of the millennium: The estimate stands for the year 975 (source: Michael Costen, *The Cathars and the Albigensian Crusade*, p. 5).

46   led the Christian armies into Jerusalem: Raymond IV of Toulouse wrote to the pope of the holy massacre perpetrated by his crusaders on storming the mosques and synagogues of Jerusalem in 1099: "And if you desire to know what was done with the enemy who were found there, know that in Solomon's Porch and in his temple our men rode in the blood of the Saracens up to the knees of their horses." Christian sources put the number of victims at 10,000; Arab sources claim 100,000 were killed. (Source: Friedrich Heer, *The Medieval World*, p. 135.)

51   "The chief cause of all these evils is the archbishop of Narbonne . . .": Innocent's famous feud with Archbishop Berengar lasted

well over ten years. The corrupt prelate, who used mercenaries to collect his tithes, was able to hang on to his lucrative post so long in the face of papal displeasure primarily because of his splendid family connections. He was the illegitimate son of a count of Barcelona and the bastard uncle of King Pedro II of Aragon.

51 "I'd rather be a priest.": The anecdote is told by William of Puylaurens in his prologue to the *Chronica*. William, perhaps exaggerating the plight of the Church in order to justify the subsequent calling of a crusade, went on to say: "When the clergy showed themselves in public they concealed their small tonsures by combing the long hair forward from the back of their head" (source: Zoé Oldenbourg, *Massacre at Montségur*, trans. Peter Green, p. 54).

52 *Stadtluft macht frei*: The expression also had the literal meaning of freeing serfs. In Germanic custom, any serf who took up residence for one year and one day in a town would automatically be exempted from his former manorial obligations (source: Charles T. Wood, *The Quest for Eternity*, p. 88).

52 "for reason of adultery . . .": For scholarly evaluations of medieval Toulouse's remarkable climate of freedom, see the work of J. H. Mundy, particularly his *Men and Women at Toulouse in the Age of the Cathars*.

⊠ *4. The Conversation*

56 "O dolorous case . . .": The lamentation comes from William of Puylaurens. His chronicle is the major source for our knowledge of the debates.

56 "Go back to your spinning, Madame . . .": Scholarly opinion is divided over whether the female Perfect so rudely addressed was Esclarmonde of Foix. Proponents of the "Cathar country" myths outlined in the epilogue naturally assume that it had to be Esclarmonde who was doing the talking. Others believe that it was her cousin.

56 "the mother of fornication and abomination": In a debate of 1207, Arnold Hot loosed an impressive volley. The St. John to whom he refers is not the evangelist but John of Patmos, the mystic who authored

Revelations: "[The] Roman Church is the devil's church and her doctrines are those of demons, she is the Babylon whom St. John called the mother of fornication and abomination, drunk with the blood of saints and martyrs. . . . neither Christ nor the apostles has established the existing order of the mass" (cited in Joseph R. Strayer, *The Albigensian Crusades*, p. 22).

57   Innocent attempted again and again to organize a punitive campaign: Historian Michel Roquebert has effectively exploded the notion, long held by the apologists of orthodoxy, that Innocent's hand was forced by the murder of Peter of Castelnau. In fact, Innocent was trying to organize a crusade against Languedoc from the very outset of his pontificate. See Michel Roquebert, *L'Epopée cathare*, vol. 1, pp. 132–33.

63   The paper then wafted upward, charring a ceiling beam: When I visited Fanjeaux in the summer of 1998, a Korean Dominican nun kindly showed me around her convent and indicated where the miracle had taken place. As I was leaving, she asked me to sign the guest book. I saw that the last visitor had been a Spaniard, whose entry dated from several months previously. He/she had written: "Te perdono, Domingo, burro, no supiste lo que hacías" (I forgive you, Dominic, you mule, for you knew not what you did).

64   "the conversation of old ladies . . .": Dominic's deathbed admission about liking the company of pretty young women is related in Georges Bernanos's *Les Prédestinés*, p. 77.

64   The Spaniard's ceaseless wanderings . . . brought him deep within dualist country: Those old enough to remember the warbling Belgian nun who performed a hit song of 1963 about St. Dominic may be surprised to learn that one verse dealt with the Cathars. The chorus and verse in the original French: "Dominique, nique, nique/ S'en allait tout simplement/ Routier pauvre et chantant/ En tous chemins, en tous lieux/ Il ne parle que du bon Dieu/ Il ne parle que du bon Dieu. . . . A l'époque où Jean-sans-Terre/ D'Angleterre était le roi/ Dominique, notre Père/ Combattit les Albigeois." The same again, in the English version: "Dominique, nique, nique/ Over land he plods along/ And sings a little song/ Never asking for reward/ He just talks about the Lord/ He just talks about the Lord. . . . At a time when Johnny Lackland/Over England

was the king/ Dominique was in the backland/ Fighting sin like anything." Unfortunately, Noel Rigney's English adaptation neglects the mention of *Albigeois* found in the original. Then again, finding a snappy rhyme for the English equivalent—*Albigensian*—is not terribly obvious.

64 "I should beg you not to kill me at one blow . . .": Dominic's first biographer, a Dominican friar named Jordanus of Saxony, emphasized the Spaniard's saintly pacifism. Others were not so sure. Stephen of Salagnac, a Dominican from the middle of the thirteenth century, wrote that an exasperated Dominic once preached at Prouille: "For several years now I have spoken words of peace to you. I have preached to you; I have besought you with tears. But as the common saying goes in Spain, Where a blessing fails, a good thick stick will succeed. Now we shall rouse princes and prelates against you; and they, alas, will in their turn assemble whole nations and peoples, and a mighty number will perish by the sword. Towers will fall, and walls be razed to the ground, and you will all of you be reduced to servitude. Thus force will prevail where gentle persuasion has failed to do so." Whether Dominic actually said something this prescient can only be a matter of conjecture. It sounds like the invention of someone who is looking back on, and perhaps trying to justify, the Albigensian Crusade.

◙ 5. Penance and Crusade

67 the northern chronicler who recorded the episode . . . must have been pleased to see Raymond so thoroughly humiliated: There can be no doubt that our source, Peter of Vaux de Cernay, would have been delighted at Raymond's predicament. Elsewhere in his *Hystoria albigensis*, the chronicler calls the count of Toulouse "a limb of Satan, a child of perdition, a hardened criminal, a parcel of sinfulness."

68 an unsolved murder mystery: The question of who, if not Raymond, ordered the killing of Peter of Castelnau can still inflame some imaginations, in much the same way that Oliver Stone got overheated with *JFK*. In Jean-Jacques Bedu's historical novel, *Les Terres de feu*, the conspiracy theory circulating in neo-Cathar circles is clearly outlined.

The accused stands as none other than Arnold Amaury, Peter's colleague. If Arnold was at Peter's side on that day—as some believe—then why did the murderer kill just one legate? And how did the murderer know who to stab? And why didn't he get rid of the witnesses? Who sprang the perjury trap so that Raymond could not clear his name? And why wasn't Raymond charged? Finally, who profited most from the murder? Certainly not Raymond. Who, as a result of the murder, got to lead a crusade, crush the Trencavels, and use armed force to place himself in a very lucrative position as archbishop of Narbonne? Arnold Amaury. It's not impossible, though no jury outside of Languedoc would convict.

68   Innocent called for a crusade: The clergy did not use the term *crusade*. It was known as *negotium pacis et fidei* (the enterprise of peace and faith).

70   "naked in front of the tomb of the blessed martyr . . .": The source is Vaux de Cernay. The tomb can still be viewed.

73   the Christian city of Zara: It is now known as the Croatian port of Zadar.

73   European Jewry, in particular, was subject to slaughter: The First Crusade initiated what would become a sorry tradition. In marching across Europe in 1096, the crusaders murdered 12 Jews in Spier, 22 at Metz, 500 at Worms, and 1,000 at Mainz (source: Paul Johnson, *A History of Christianity*, p. 245).

73   "You ask us urgently . . .": This duplicitous scheme of Innocent's was followed to the letter. The correspondence is cited in most works on the Cathars. I have used Joseph R. Strayer's translation from *The Albigensian Crusades*, pp. 58–59.

▣ 6. *Béziers*

75   he had rebuffed Count Raymond's proposal of a defensive alliance: The deviousness of Raymond of Toulouse was not bottomless. In the winter of 1208–9, he tried to reach a common defensive agreement with Raymond Roger Trencavel, but, for reasons unknown, the negotiations broke off and each man went his own way. Whether Count Ray-

mond was *sincere* in trying to form this alliance still divides historians of the crusade.

78   one of them, William of Tudela, conceded: The three chroniclers for Béziers were Tudela, Vaux de Cernay, and Puylaurens. None of them was an eyewitness to the events. In this chapter, unless otherwise stated, the fullest account—that of William of Tudela in the *Canso*—forms the basis of the narrative. I have used Janet Shirley's excellent translation (pp. 19–22) for direct quotations about the incidents at Béziers.

79   222 names: Debate rages over whether this list included all of the Cathars of the town or just the Perfect. Most believe that the number is too low to encompass all the credentes of Béziers, which was a fairly sizable town at the time. Notations appear alongside a couple of names indicating that some of the heretics sought may have been Waldensians rather than Cathars.

80   Mary Magdalene had an even better reputation among the gnostics: As described in Elaine Pagels's landmark *The Gnostic Gospels*, the ancient writings unearthed in 1945 at Nag Hammadi, Egypt, attest to the wide range of Christian beliefs that were squelched by the emergent orthodoxy of Rome. Of particular interest concerning the Magdalene's status as the first of the apostles are the Gospel of Mary, the Gospel of Thomas, and Dialogue of the Saviour, the last stating that Mary was "the woman who knew the All."

85   Not even Count Raymond: There is a rock-solid consensus among historians that Raymond did not participate actively in the actions of the crusaders. Given his subsequent military incompetence, it is unlikely that he saddled up and rode anywhere when battle beckoned. Also, he seems to have been universally beloved in Languedoc; had he joined in the massacre at Béziers, there would have been Occitans who bore him a grudge. Lastly, Raymond always showed a reluctance to harm fellow southerners.

🔲 *7. Carcassonne*

90   "To horse, my lords!": The direct speech is reported by William of Tudela, author of this section of the *Canso* (p. 22 in Janet Shirley's

translation). Unless indicated in the text, the quotations are from the *Canso*.

90   Peter Roger of Cabaret: Cabaret is now called Lastours, after the ruins of the four castle keeps (towers) that dot its hillside.

90   "stupider than whales": The expression is William of Tudela's. Translator Shirley wryly states in a footnote: "*La balena*, the whale, is the rhyme word; there is no reason to suppose medieval whales were a by-word for stupidity" (p. 20).

95   "In Jesus's name, baron . . .": Again, the direct speech is reported by William of Tudela in the *Canso*.

100   the discretion of the pro-crusade chroniclers: Although all sources skate suspiciously fast over the incident, they are at variance over what precisely was offered to Raymond Roger. In the *Chronica*, William of Puylaurens states it was the young Trencavel who lost his nerve and agreed to be held hostage. Peter of Vaux de Cernay, who makes no mention of King Pedro's failed attempt at mediation, implies that the crusade always intended to keep the viscount a captive indefinitely. The *Canso* seems to be missing a passage at this crucial juncture. For a full discussion of the incident, see volume 1 of Michel Roquebert's *L'Epopée cathare*, pp. 275–78.

⊠ 8. Bad Neighbors

104   "Et ab joi li er mos treus . . .": The Occitan text is taken from Ernest Hoepffner's *Le Troubadour Peire Vidal, sa vie et son œuvre* (Paris: Les Belles Lettres, 1961). The French translation is in Michel Roquebert's *L'Epopée cathare*, vol. 1, p. 314. The English translation, from the French, is my own.

106   the grotesque march: Some of Simon's defenders, most recently Dominique Paladilhe in *Simon de Montfort et le drame cathare* (pp. 115–19), point out that it was not the northerner who started this awful practice of mutilation during the crusade years. In the winter of 1210, a particularly ferocious Occitan noble by the name of Gerald of Pépieux cut off the facial features of a handful of crusaders he had captured. The

sheer scale of Simon's riposte at Bram—as well as his presence at the sack of Béziers—has usually silenced those who seek excuses for his behavior.

107   Simon's fourth son, another Simon de Montfort: It is the younger Simon de Montfort who is better known to students of British history. A leader of the baronial party opposed to the foreign adventurism and spendthrift ways of King Henry III, Simon got his monarch to agree to the Provisions of Oxford (1258) and the Provisions of Westminster (1259), which held that a council of nobles would exercise some control over the treasury and royal appointments. The king broke the agreement, and civil war ensued in 1264. Before being killed in the decisive Battle of Evesham in 1265, Simon began summoning lesser knights and townsmen to his parliament—thereby initiating the institutional practice that would mature as the House of Commons.

107   a great mane of hair: The champion of homoerotic Montfort idolatry is without a doubt Peter of Vaux de Cernay. The author of the *Hystoria albigensis* speaks of Simon's "elegant face," his "broad shoulders," "muscular arms," "gracious torso," "agile and supple limbs" (source: Paladilhe, *Simon de Montfort*, p. 25).

115   the more zealous northern pilgrims complained: In a nice lexical coincidence, the leader of the grumblers who were worried that the heretics might escape was a French baron, Robert of Mauvoisin, a name that resembles that of the infamous trebuchet, Malvoisine. Unless indicated in the text, all of the incidents and speeches following the surrender of Minerve are attributable to the *Hystoria*.

115   Three of the women, however, abjured the dualist faith: Curiously enough, the person responsible for changing their minds was Mathilde de Garlande, the mother of Bouchard de Marly, the crusader held captive in Cabaret. Mathilde apparently yanked them off the bonfire as the flames were just getting going.

☒ *9. The Conflict Widens*

118   the Toulousains left for Rome: Before going to Rome to complain to the pope, Raymond had gone to Paris to complain to the king.

Philip Augustus gave him a sympathetic hearing but did nothing to help out the beleaguered count.

119 "foxes in the vineyards of the Lord": Innocent was not the only churchman to use this image. It was a fairly common trope for heresy in the Middle Ages, echoing a passage from the Song of Songs (2:15).

126 tears welled up in the count's eyes: Peter of Vaux de Cernay notes the tears of Raymond but is quick to attribute them to "rage and felony" rather than "repentance and devotion."

127 King Pedro of Aragon tried to prevent the war: Pedro bent over backward to keep the peace and, in the process, keep both sides off-balance. He offered his son in marriage to Simon's daughter. War would break this betrothal. At the same time, he wed his sister to Raymond's son. Since Raymond VI was already married to another sister of Pedro's, he (Raymond) and his son became brothers-in-law—a relation which raised a few eyebrows. In the Trencavel matter, Pedro behaved as decently as could be expected. In exchange for getting Simon to agree to pay a pension to Agnes of Montpellier—the widow of Raymond Roger Trencavel—Pedro recognized Simon's legitimacy. Agnes and her infant son Raymond then moved to Aragon, where they lived with the royal family. The disinherited son would twice roar back over the Pyrenees and try to reclaim Carcassonne after he had grown to manhood.

128 Arnold did not disappoint: Arnold's outrageous offer occurs only in the *Canso*, leading some historians to question the reality of the proposal. One of the more influential doubters is Joseph R. Strayer, who, in *The Albigensian Crusades*, calls William of Tudela a "not entirely trust-worthy writer" (p. 78). In the same passage, however, Strayer concedes that the general tenor of the demands makes sense.

129 Enguerrand of Coucy: The great barons of the crusade of 1211 included Robert of Courtenay (a first cousin of Raymond VI of Tou-louse), Juhel of Mayenne, Peter of Nemours, and Enguerrand of Coucy. The last should be familiar to readers of Barbara Tuchman's *A Distant Mirror*, her account of the Coucy family in the "calamitous 14th century." The Enguerrand at Lavaur is an ancestor of Tuchman's hero of the same name. It was our Enguerrand who, in 1225, began the construction of the

great castle at Coucy-le-Château-Auffrique that figures so prominently in Tuchman's tale. The Coucy fortress—the grandest medieval castle in France—was blown up by the Germans during their strategic retreat from the Noyon Salient in 1917, in one of the most devastating, and gratuitous, acts of vandalism of the Great War.

130   under the direction of Bishop Fulk of Toulouse: The number of Fulk's contingent of singers and soldiers swells according to the sources consulted, from a few hundred to 5,000. What is certain is that these men were firebrands of orthodoxy. In a nettlesome question of usage, I have opted to follow Joseph Strayer's example and have referred to the bishop throughout as *Fulk*. He appears in some histories as *Foulquet* when a troubadour and *Foulque* or *Foulques* in his later incarnation as bishop.

130   Montgey: The mass murder at Montgey deeply shocked chroniclers and churchmen throughout Europe. For one, it was the only slaughter en masse of pilgrims during the entire twenty years of the crusade. Also, the job of mutilating and finishing off the wounded was left to peasants and villeins—which was an almost intolerable transgression of the social order. This might, if one were disposed to make excuses, account for Simon de Montfort's savagery toward Lady Geralda and the eighty knights at Lavaur, which violated all customary practices toward captives of noble birth. Near Montgey today, there is a plaque at a roadside calvary in the village of Auvezines, memorializing the lost column of armored pilgrims. To embrace anachronism for a moment: The plaque must be unique in France for deploring the demise of an invading German army.

130   The leader of the defeated defenders was Aimery of Montréal: The village of Montréal bears no relation to the great city on the St. Lawrence River. First garrisoned by the Romans, the gentle height became a village in the ninth century and owes its name to a corruption of the Latin *Mons Regalis* (royal mount) or *Mons Revelatus* (bare mount). Its sister in Catharism, Fanjeaux, is said to derive its name from *Fanum Jovis* (temple of Jove). The tale of Aimery's hulking corpse bringing down the gallows originates in the *Hystoria* of Vaux de Cernay. The average height of the warriors of thirteenth-century France was five-foot-two or five-foot-three. As for Geralda, a later Catholic chronicler claimed

that she and Aimery had several children borne of their incestuous couplings, a fairly standard libel leveled at heretics.

▧ *10. A Time of Surprises*

132   led by four Christian kings: Kings Alfonso VIII of Castile, Sancho VII of Navarra, Alfonso II of Portugal, and Pedro II of Aragon.

141   his historic flip-flop: Innocent threatened Pedro at the end of his letter dated May 21, 1213: "Such are the orders which your Serene Highness is invited to obey, in every last detail; failing which . . . We should be obliged to threaten you with Divine Wrath, and to take steps against you such as would result in your suffering grave and irreparable harm" (source: Zoé Oldenbourg, *Massacre at Montségur*, p. 163). It is amazing that Pedro should have gone from being Christendom's hero— the battle of Las Navas de Tolosa took place in July 1212—to the pope's nemesis, all in the space of ten months.

141   Simon . . . had made his last will and testament that morning: Peter of Vaux de Cernay recounts this telltale act on the part of a nervous Simon. Much of our information about the actions of Simon comes from his chronicle. It should be noted that from January 1213 to May 1214 Vaux de Cernay was in France; thus he was not present for the fateful battle. However, he would have spoken to Simon and his men about the events once he had returned to Languedoc and rejoined the crusade.

142   Pedro . . . relaxed with his mistress: There are two dubious historico-erotic tales told of Pedro's actions before the battle. The first has Pedro writing a letter to a married lady of Toulouse in which he proclaims that his sole reason for fighting is to impress her enough to get into her bed. Vaux de Cernay tells of Pedro's letter being intercepted by a prior in Pamiers and shown to Simon de Montfort as he marched to Muret. There is much tut-tutting by Simon about the indecency of the king's motives. Historians, while not doubting the existence of the intercepted letter, believe Pedro's missive was a standard, poetic greeting couched in the courtly language of the day, and addressed to one of Pedro's sisters in Toulouse—it will be remembered that Raymond the elder and Raymond the younger had both married into the Aragonese

royal house. Vaux de Cernay, significantly, does not give the identity of the addressee. The other rumor has Pedro so tired after his amorous activities on the eve of the battle that he can barely stand up in the morning. This originated in the *Llibre dels feyts*, a chronicle that Pedro's son commissioned when he had reached manhood and become King Jaume (or James) the Conqueror. Although delightful (and unlikely), the story is thought to be the invention of a Catalan chronicler who wanted to explain how the otherwise unbeatable Pedro could have been slain on the field of battle. The poor fellow was exhausted, so it wasn't a fair fight.

143   "It is a great pity that you who have lands to live on should have been such cowards as to lose them": The insult is recorded in the *Canso*. Just prior to Muret, the chronicler known as Anonymous (see "Usage and Primary Sources" above) takes over from William of Tudela. The man who spoke so woundingly to Count Raymond was Michael of Luesia, who died fighting alongside Pedro later in the day.

143   Simon de Montfort ordered his knights to . . . get ready for battle: The prelude and aftermath of the battle are rich in contemporary accounts. There is, however, a remarkable paucity of sources concerning the actual fighting at Muret. There is also a remarkable lack of agreement about where exactly the battle took place and how the forces were arrayed. The work of Michel Roquebert, in the second volume of his *L'Épopée cathare*, is exemplary for its exhaustiveness and its evenhanded consideration of different theories. His conclusions, including a set piece on the battle (pp. 167–236), guided my brief evocation of the fight. The route taken by the crusaders along the towpath, for example, is Roquebert's hypothesis.

143   "If we cannot draw them a very long way from their tents . . .": Simon's speech is set down by Anonymous in the *Canso*.

143   Masses were said, confessions heard: Pious legend—backed up by a plaque in the main church of Muret—has Dominic inventing the Catholic prayer cycle known as the Rosary during the vigil before the battle. Church historians have long since proved, alas, that Dominic was not among the clergymen at Muret on that fateful September day.

146   "Across the marshes . . .": The descriptive passage is from the *Canso* (in Janet Shirley's translation, p. 70).

148   A mass grave would be unearthed in the nineteenth century: The riverside spot is called Le Petit Jofréry. Floods of 1875 and 1891 uncovered makeshift cemeteries and thirteenth-century armor (source: Dominique Paladilhe, *Les Grandes Heures cathares*, p. 154).

◙ *11. The Verdict*

150   the vicar of Christ stalked out of his cathedral: For the events at the Lateran Council, I relied on the work of Brenda Bolton ("A Show with a Meaning: Innocent III's Approach to the Fourth Lateran Council, 1215," *Medieval History* 1 (1991), pp. 53–67), which in turn led to S. Kuttner and A. Garcia y Garcia's article "A New Eyewitness Account of the Fourth Lateran Council," *Traditio* 20 (1964), pp. 115–78. There was another eyewitness, the chronicler Richard of San Germano.

153   A chronicler told of how the session . . .: The chronicler is Anonymous of the *Canso*. It is possible that he attended the Lateran Council in the entourage of the Raymonds. At the very least, he talked to many of the principal participants. The speeches are all to be found in the *Canso* and are widely thought to give an accurate picture of the verbal sparring that must have occurred there. The version used is Janet Shirley's translation.

156   "you take away Montauban and Toulouse . . .": Montauban, a city on the River Tarn to the northwest of Toulouse, was the only other major center to resist Simon de Montfort's rule.

◙ *12. Toulouse*

158   Any unlucky besieger captured . . . according to a chronicler: In his *Hystoria albigensis*, Peter of Vaux de Cernay lists an impressive number of atrocities committed by the Toulousains. There is no reason to disbelieve him.

161   "When the count entered through the arched gateway . . .": The eyewitness here is not Vaux de Cernay but Anonymous. In this chapter, the direct quotations relating to the siege are taken from the *Canso*, but much of the background material is found in the *Hystoria* and

the *Chronica*. All three sources are prolix about the great siege of Toulouse; only the *Canso*, however, has women operating the mangonel that killed Simon de Montfort. That twist of fate is too lovely not to be repeated.

167   As was the custom: It is William of Puylaurens who states that the boiling of the corpse was a French funerary custom.

168   "The epitaph says . . .": The epitaph to which this remarkable passage refers has been lost. As for the funerary stone depicting Simon de Montfort, now affixed to a wall in the transept of Carcassonne's St. Nazaire, it is now considered a hoax. Experts from Toulouse established in 1982 that the stone was carved between 1820 and 1829, at the behest of Alexandre Dumège, a local historian with an overheated romantic imagination (source: Michel Roquebert, *L'Epopée cathare*, vol. 3, p. 143).

⊠ *13. The Return to Tolerance*

169   Every man, woman, and child in Marmande: The massacre provoked almost as much comment as Béziers and became a staple among northern chroniclers. Anonymous, in the *Canso*, lets out all the stops in his description: "But clamour and shouting arose, men ran into the town with sharpened steel; terror and massacre began. Lords, ladies and their little children, women and men stripped naked, all these men slashed and cut to pieces with keen-edged swords. Flesh, blood and brains, trunks, limbs and faces hacked in two, lungs, livers and guts torn out and tossed aside lay on the open ground as if they had rained down from the sky. Marshland and good ground, all was red with blood. Not a man or a woman was left alive, neither old nor young, no living creature, unless any had managed to hide. Marmande was razed and set alight" (Janet Shirley's translation, pp. 188–89).

170   "*Roma trichairitz* . . .": The troubadour's song appears, with a translation by Roger Depledge, in Yves Rouquette's *Cathars.*, pp. 162–63.

176   his body was denied a public Christian burial: Discredited legend long had it that the remains of Raymond VI were left to rot outside a cemetery gate, picked over by rats, but the truth of his ultimate fate may yet turn out to be less unseemly. Just before Christmas 1997, some

775 years after the count's death, workmen restoring a medieval building in old Toulouse discovered a hitherto unsuspected hollow in a wall containing the hidden sarcophagus of a thirteenth-century nobleman. At this writing, DNA tests are being done to determine whether its occupant is the long-vanished Raymond, and the ever loyal city of Toulouse has formally petitioned the current pope to lift the excommunication that still hangs over his soul. There is a slim hope that the bones found might turn out to be, plausibly, those of Raymond VI. In the side of the great church of St. Sernin in Toulouse is a portal known as the Counts' Door, where tenth- and eleventh-century members of the Saint Gilles clan had been laid to rest. Some of these sarcophagi have been pried open, and the jumble of 900-year-old bones therein is being genetically mapped. If some of these bones produce a familial "match" to the jumble found in 1997 in the sarcophagus hidden in the niche of the former Toulouse headquarters of the Knights Hospitallers (later the Knights of Malta), then the metropolis on the Garonne will no doubt build a worthy mausoleum for its beloved count. Toulouse's mayor, Dominique Baudis, is somewhat of a Cathar enthusiast. His novel, *Raimond "le Cathare,"* tells a first-person story of Raymond VI and, on its publication in 1996, was fairly well received in neo-Cathar circles. One such group based in Toulouse, La Flamme cathare, is circulating a petition—*Manifeste pour la Réconciliation*—asking Pope John Paul II to come to the church of St. Sernin in the year 2000 and apologize to Languedoc for the actions of his predecessors. The first signatory of the petition was Mayor Baudis.

177   through diplomacy, guile, and feats of arms, he had subdued his enemies: As his barons were helping out Simon de Montfort, King Philip Augustus had been thrashing his enemies in the field. In the year after Muret, he repelled an English force under King John, who had used the upheaval of the Cathar struggle to try and enlarge his holdings in northwestern France. In the decisive battle of Bouvines on July 27, 1214, the French routed the forces of Otto IV, the Holy Roman Emperor. The Germans were neutralized; the English thrown into disarray.

178   Amaury had, in fact, lost everything given to his family nine years earlier in Rome: In a bar at Montségur, I was assured by several

patrons that *un amaury* or *un maury* is a local dialect word meaning "a loser." Alas, I was unable to find a similar entry in any regional dictionaries of the Midi.

⊠ *14. The End of the Crusade*

181   in 1216, Louis had briefly accepted the crown of England at the invitation of the barons: On the death of King John of England in 1216, his successor, the future Henry III, was only nine years old. The ever-rebellious barons of Britain saw their chance to unseat the Plantagenets by inviting in Louis.

183   Michel Roquebert has argued convincingly. . . . : Roquebert makes his case for a collective panic in chapter 22 ("Le Printemps de la grande peur") of volume 3 of his *L'Epopée cathare.*

185–86   Romano and Blanche sharing more than just prayers: The long-lived rumor was apparently spread by the irreverent students of the Latin Quarter. Romano's power at the Louvre and in the Cité was resented by the schoolmen of the Left Bank. The rumor was reported by the English chronicler Matthew Paris (source: Krystel Maurin, *Les Esclarmonde*, p. 88). In any event, Blanche, as a mother of eleven, might have grown leery of the consequences of close male company.

186   Gregory IX, a nephew of Innocent III: It is almost certain that Ugolino dei Conti di Segni was Lotario's nephew. More in dispute is his birthday. In the past, historians have relied on information provided by the chronicler Matthew Paris, who held that Gregory was nearing his hundredth year at his death in 1241. It is now thought more likely that the nephew of Innocent was ten years younger than his uncle, which would place his birth year at around 1170.

188   "It was a great shame . . .": The comment is from William of Puylaurens, who was once in the employ of Raymond VII. Of the three main chronicles about the Cathars, his is the only one that covers these years.

190   the county of Toulouse automatically became a part of France: Perhaps the most astounding clause of the treaty concerned the future of

Languedoc. Raymond's daughter Jeanne was forced to marry Louis's brother Alphonse of Poitiers. They were to inherit at Raymond's death— even if Raymond had fathered other children. Succession would then pass through the Capets. Raymond died in 1249, after having spent the last twenty years of his life trying to find a way to beget a legitimate male heir—who, in any case, would have had to fight to regain his birthright. Toulouse was then governed in absentia by Count Alphonse. He and Jeanne died childless, within three days of each other, in 1271, and Languedoc was definitively annexed to the royal domain.

190   a university was to be established: The university, founded in 1229, is still going strong. The city of Toulouse counts a postsecondary student population of about 100,000.

190   Eleanor of Aquitaine: The justly celebrated Eleanor shaped the dynastic politics and culture of twelfth-century Europe. The granddaughter of the first troubadour, William of Poitiers (Guilhem de Poitou), and endowered with the immense duchy of Aquitaine, she first married King Louis VII of France. She bore him two daughters, accompanied him on the disastrous Second Crusade preached by Bernard of Clairvaux, then, on returning to France, had her marriage annulled on grounds of consanguinity. This ruse to get rid of an unwanted spouse was common practice among noblemen—Eleanor pioneered its practice among women. She then married Count Henry of Anjou, eleven years her junior, who became King Henry II of England. She bore him a brood of children, fiercely guarded her independence, and eventually left England to preside over a brilliant court for troubadours and scholars in Anjou. Her life has inspired a flood of scholarship and art. In Norman F. Cantor's *Medieval Lives*, a series of imagined vignettes with emblematic figures of the Middle Ages, the chapter devoted to Eleanor ("The Glory of It All") demonstrates her importance in an entertaining fashion. Her connection to the Cathar drama is fairly straightforward: Her daughter Joan of England married Raymond VI and produced Raymond VII; another daughter, Eleanor, married Alfonso VIII of Castile (who fought at Las Navas de Tolosa) and produced Blanche of Castile. Raymond and Blanche were thus first cousins. *Their* children, respectively Jeanne of Toulouse and Alphonse of Poitiers, were married under the terms of the treaty.

⊠ *15. Inquisition*

191 a wealthy old lady of Toulouse: This story is told by the Dominican William Pelhisson in his *Chronica*, translated into English by Walter L. Wakefield as *The Chronicle of William Pelhisson* in *Heresy, Crusade, and Inquisition in Southern France, 1100–1250*, pp. 207–36.

195 "It often happens that bishops . . .": Innocent's stern sermon is quoted in Friedrich Heer's *The Medieval World* (p. 220). Heer also finds a passage in Innocent's *De contemptu mundi*, written before he became pope, in which he complains of bishops who "by night embrace Venus and next morning honor the Virgin Mary."

195 Robert le Bougre . . . Conrad of Marburg: There seems to be a consensus among historians that Conrad was a dangerous sociopath who burned many innocents. Heer, a German-language historian writing in the 1950s, makes an implicit comparison between Conrad and Hitler. The evidence against Robert le Bougre, instigator of a massive bonfire at Mont Aimé, in Champagne, is slightly more ambiguous. As Malcolm Lambert states in *The Cathars*, "Acquittal of Robert as an arbitrary, wilful inquisitor is not yet justified: a verdict of not proven best fits the existing evidence" (p. 125).

196 "We marvel . . .": Pope Gregory's disingenuous missive is quoted in Heer, *The Medieval World* (p. 217).

197 "The accused shall be asked . . .": From Bernard Gui's *Practica Inquisitionis*, cited in Zoé Oldenbourg's *Massacre at Montségur*, pp. 307–8.

200 Qui aytal fara. . . : This lugubrious chant is related by William Pelhisson in his chronicle.

⊠ *16. Backlash*

201 John Textor lay in chains: The imprisonment quickly became a cause célèbre in Toulouse, inciting formerly quiescent citizens to denounce the actions of the inquisitors. Awkwardly, the average-Joe John Textor publicly converted to Catharism while in prison—receiving the

consolamentum from a captive Perfect—and thus made his erstwhile defenders appear foolish. William Pelhisson, who tells the story, fairly chortles at the embarrassment of Textor's partisans. Many of them were subsequently jailed, or worse.

202   At the behest of the city's conservative Jews: The bonfire of 1234 in Montpellier may have been the only instance of the Inquisition doing anything for the Jews. By 1240, the wind had definitively turned; the Talmud was tried, found guilty, and burned in Paris. This was a mere prelude for several centuries of anti-Jewish activities by inquisitors (sources: R. I. Moore, *The Formation of a Persecuting Society*, p. 10 and L. Poliakov, *The History of Anti-Semitism, vol. 1, From Roman Times to the Court Jews*, London: Elek Books, 1966, pp. 68–70).

204   Stephen of St. Thibéry: The appointment may also have been an attempt to wrest the institution of inquisitor away from the Dominicans. In later years, the Dominicans and the Franciscans would engage in unseemly turf wars that would stall the cause of doctrinal purity. In the Balkans in the thirteenth century, the competing friars quarreled bitterly over precedence for nearly a decade before an inquisition was set up.

208   On May 28, 1242, Stephen of St. Thibéry and William Arnald stopped in Avignonet: The story of Avignonet, like most events to follow in the narrative, was culled from Inquisition interrogations, in this instance those of Brother Ferrer, the inquisitor who questioned the survivors of the siege of Montségur some two years afterward. The story of Brother William's skull comes from the same source.

⊠ *17. The Synagogue of Satan*

212   Henry had made landfall in the southwest with a derisively small force of knights: Still, some did make the journey. One of the barons who sailed to fight the French, and thereby indirectly help Raymond VII, was the English king's brother-in-law, Simon de Montfort. His father, the Simon de Montfort of the Albigensian Crusade, and his oldest brother, Amaury, who had died in 1241 after a decade's service as High Constable of France, were no doubt spinning in their graves at this switch in allegiance.

213   Raymond and Louis signed a treaty: The Treaty of Lorris.

215   In the spring of 1243. . . : The most scrupulous examination of the siege of Montségur, without recourse to the mythmaking that usually shrouds the citadel of "Cathar country," is, once again, the work of Michel Roquebert: *Montségur, les cendres de la liberté.*

217   A chronicler relates that at sunrise. . . : The Gascons' retrospective fright is reported by William of Puylaurens.

219   These companions of the last hour came from all stations of feudal society: Not all of the credentes to join the Perfect of Montésegur on the bonfire were saintly. William of Lahille had been one of the three faidits to lead the murderous posse into the inquisitors' quarters at Avignonet. Lahille was the son of a Perfect noblewoman whom Guilhabert of Castres had consoled, along with Esclarmonde of Foix and two other high-ranking ladies, in the well-attended ceremony at Fanjeaux in 1204. Lahille was grievously wounded at Montségur just before the surrender and decided to accompany his Perfect aunt, India, into the afterlife. One of his accomplices, Bernard de St. Martin, also elected to receive the consolamentum and thereby doom himself. The third leader of the Avignonet raid, William de Balaguier, had been captured in the lowlands well before the siege of Montségur. For his complicity in the murders, he had been dragged behind a horse, then hanged. See Jean Duvernoy's annotations to his translation, *Guillaume Pelhisson Chronique (1229–1244)*, pp. 103–04.

⊠ *18. Twilight in the Garden of Evil*

222   a Cathar believer named Peter Garcias: Extended quotations from the hidden friars' testimony—a well-documented event in these years of treachery—may be found in Carol Lansing's epilogue to Joseph Strayer's *The Albigensian Crusades*, pp. 225–28.

225   "*Heretics* are those who remain obstinate in error. . . : The litany of crime was compiled at the Council of Tarragona. Translated and cited by Edward Peters in his *Inquisition*, p. 63. Peters argues that the actual Inquisition was not nearly as fearsome as the myth of the Inquisition created by Enlightenment and romantic imaginations. He lowercases

inquisition when describing the historical institution and capitalizes the word when discussing the myth. I have elected to follow accepted usage and capitalize the word throughout.

228   "the bread of pain . . .": The felicitous expression was penned by inquisitor Bernard Gui, cited in Laurent Albaret's *L'Inquisition: Rempart de la foi?* p. 53.

230   the murder of a respected inquisitor: A cult quickly grew around the victim, Peter of Verona, a Cathar-turned-preacher-turned-inquisitor. A speaker of great charisma and a miracle-worker, Peter was assassinated by credentes near Milan. Legend has it that as he lay dying, he wrote out the word *credo* in his own blood. One of the most popular medieval saints, he was venerated as St. Peter the Martyr. This book, I should add, was written while I was living in a very old Occitan farmhouse called Mas D'En Pere Martre. To my enduring embarrassment, it took me at least a year to realize that my address contained the name of the most famous figure in Italian Cathar history.

230   The year 1300 saw the papacy institute the jubilee: For details of the jubilee, I am indebted to Paul Hetherington's *Medieval Rome*, pp. 78–81.

234   The 1,000 or so households won back to the illicit faith: This estimate, arrived at by historian J. M. Vidal in 1906, is cited in Malcolm Lambert's *The Cathars* (p. 259). Lambert considers the number too low but concedes there is no way of determining a precise head count. See his chapter "The Last Missionary" (pp. 230–71) for the best account, in English, of the Autier revival.

238   Fournier also discovered that its randy priest: The surviving Inquisition registers of Jacques Fournier were translated into the French in their entirety by Jean Duvernoy in the 1960s. Using Duvernoy's translation, Emmanuel Le Roy Ladurie delivered a memorable portrait of the social, religious, and sex lives of fourteenth-century peasants in *Montaillou*. On the Web site of San Jose State University, Nancy P. Stork has helpfully translated some excerpts from the Fournier register into English; they can be accessed directly at www.sjsu.edu/depts/english/Fournier/jfournhm.htm. For immediate gratification of prurient curiosity, go to the testimony of Béatrice de Planissoles.

⊠ *19. Bélibaste*

239   There was now one Cathar left. . . . : The remarkable detail it is possible to employ in telling the sad story of Bélibaste is due, once again, to Inquisition registers. The transcript of Bélibaste's questioning has not survived, but the debriefing that Arnold Sicre gave Fournier in October 1321 provides a wealth of detail. So too does the testimony of the shepherd Peter Maury, who had been rashly released by the men who arrested Bélibaste in Tirvia. Maury was recaptured on Majorca two years later. The story of the last Languedoc Perfect was transformed into an accomplished French-language novel, *Bélibaste*, by Henri Gougaud.

246   the castle at Villerouge-Termenès: The castle still stands today and has not been much modified since the days of the Cathars. The picturesque village holds a well-attended medieval weekend every July, during which poor old Bélibaste is burned in effigy.

⊠ *Epilogue: In Cathar Country*

247   *"Les chevaliers cathares . . ."*: The song appears on Francis Cabrel's album, *Quelqu'un de l'intérieur*. The translation is my own. The roadside art is also called *les chevaliers d'Oc*.

249   *bouffeurs du curé*: Napoléon Peyrat's anticlerical credentials were severely dented when, shortly after his death, his widow, Eugénie, made a very public conversion to Catholicism. Still, he is making a comeback, as witnessed by the collective scholarly work devoted to Peyrat in 1998: *Cathares et camisards—l'œuvre de Napoléon Peyrat (1809–1881)*.

250   The Catholics argued that the Cathars were not even Christians: The nineteenth-century position staked out by Catholic historians has found a frequent echo in the twentieth century, to wit, that the Cathars were adepts of the religion founded by Mani, the self-proclaimed messiah from third-century Babylon. Many of the Cathars' medieval opponents referred to any dualists—indeed, any heretics—as Manichees, and the affiliation was taken for granted. The masterly 1947 work of

Steven Runciman in *The Medieval Manichee*, which traced a *direct* line from gnostic to Manichean to Paulician (ninth-century dualists of Armenia and Thrace) to Bogomil (tenth-century dualists of the Balkans) and thence to the early medieval heretic, is now seriously questioned by historians of Cathar thought. Contemporary consensus holds that the Cathars were Christians, that dualism has always been an "underground" strand of Christian thought, and that proving a direct link between the dualists of antiquity and those of the Middle Ages is an impossible, if not irrelevant, task. The thrust of debate now is over whether Catharism constituted a church, that is, an independent hierarchy with coherent rules, dogma, and organization.

250   an Occitan equivalent, Esclarmonde of Foix: For a thorough examination of the Esclarmonde myth, as well as the place of other female historical figures (Blanche of Castile, Etiennette de Pennautier, Agnes of Montpellier, Alice of Montmorency, and others) who appear in the neo-Cathar delirium, see Krystel Maurin's immensely entertaining *Les Esclarmonde*.

251   "our wild Capitoline . . .": Cited in Charles-Olivier Carbonell, "D'Augustin Thierry à Napoléon Peyrat: Un Demi-siècle d'occultation," *Cahiers de Fanjeaux* 14 (1979), p. 161. My translation.

251   "Montségur was an Essenian Zion . . .": Cited in Jean-Louis Biget, "Mythographie du catharisme," *Cahiers de Fanjeaux* 14 (1979), p. 279. My translation.

252   "One day they had nothing left . . .": Cited in Michel Roquebert, "Napoléon Peyrat, le trésor et le 'Nouveau Montségur' " *Hérésis* 7 (1998), p. 365. My translation.

253–54   A neognostic church was founded: For a full discussion of this weird fin-de-siècle bloom, see Suzanne Nelli, "Les Néo-gnostiques. Jules Doinel évêque de Montségur," *Hérésis* 7 (1998), pp. 121–29.

254   Joséphin Péladan: Péladan-Sar's 1906 Grail work was titled *Le Secret des Troubadours: De Parsifal à Don Quichotte* (The troubadours' secret: from Parsifal to Don Quixote). It is out of print.

255   Emile Novis: The pedantic might say that *Emile Novis* is not an anagram of *Simone Weil*. It is close, and works phonically in French.

Weil's association with Roché is briefly evoked in Biget's "Mythographie du catharisme," p. 317.

255   Magre also took the time to skewer the enemies of the Cathars: Magre was not alone in constructing an imaginary portrait gallery of historical figures that became particularly vivid when women were the subjects. Krystel Maurin, in *Les Esclarmonde*, examines the pride of place given to Esclarmonde of Foix in neo-Cathar mythology, but also gives a description of the secondary female characters to fall on one or other side of the Cruella/Cinderella divide erected in pro-Cathar novels and plays. Among those particularly vilified, aside from Alice of Montmorency, were Agnes of Montpellier and Blanche of Castile; the women glorified were Geralda of Lavaur, Loba, and Béatrice de Planissoles.

255   Otto Rahn: The definitive work on the bizarre trajectory of Otto Rahn is a 400-page book of painstaking research by Christian Bernadac, *Montségur et le Graal*. A more concise summing up of the phenomenon is Marie-Claire Viguier's "Otto Rahn entre Wolfram d'Eschenbach et les néo-nazis," *Hérésis* 7 (1998), pp. 165–79. The speech of the Aryan Perfect, taken from Rahn, appears in Viguier's article (p. 179). My translation from the French. The rumors about Rosenberg's and Hitler's attachment to Montségur were principally spread by *Nouveaux Cathares pour Montségur*, a quasi-historical novel about Rahn published in 1969 by the extreme-Right French writer Marc Augier under the pseudonym of Saint-Loup. The story of the 1978 incident involving German boy scouts and stolen stones from Montségur is well told by Charles-Olivier Carbonell in "Vulgarisation et récupération: Le Catharisme à travers les mass-média," *Cahiers de Fanjeaux* 14 (1979), pp. 361–80.

260   The short answer is that he had masterminded a system of mail-order fund-raising: In fact, the mysterious country priest, Bérenger Saunière, had a simony-by-correspondence racket, whereby he would place ads in small publications throughout Catholic Europe offering to say—that is, sell—masses. He raked in the cash. The story of his discovery of a treasure is decisively debunked in *Rennes-le-Château, autopsie d'un mythe*, by Jean-Jacques Bedu, who pores over Saunière's account

books. As for *The Holy Blood and the Holy Grail*, it heavily embroidered on a 1967 work, *L'Or de Rennes*, by Gérard de Sède, a prolific author of occult works who found credulous readers throughout France. *Holy Blood* internationalized Sède's hoax and, to the delight of everyone involved, called into question the foundations of Judeo-Christian civilization.

Selected Bibliography

This list is by no means exhaustive, or intended for scholars. Books are in French or English only, and the editions cited are those I consulted. *N* indicates a novel. Asterisks precede and brief comments follow a dozen or so entries that nonspecialists could profitably consult to satisfy a curiosity that, it is my hope, *The Perfect Heresy* has aroused. Books unmarked by an asterisk, it should be added, are not necessarily dry.

ALBARET, LAURENT. *L'Inquisition: Rempart de la foi?* Paris: Gallimard, 1998.

BAIGENT, MICHAEL, RICHARD LEIGH, AND HENRY LINCOLN. *The Holy Blood and the Holy Grail.* London: Arrow, 1996.

BALDWIN, MICHAEL. *The Rape of Oc.* London: Warner, 1994. *N.*

BAUDIS, DOMINIQUE. *Raimond "le Cathare."* Paris: Michel Lafon/Ramsay, 1996. *N.*

BEDU, JEAN-JACQUES. *Rennes-le-Château, autopsie d'un mythe.* Portet-sur-Garonne: Loubatières, 1990.

————. *Les Terres de feu.* Portet-sur-Garonne: Loubatières, 1994. *N.*

BERLIOZ, JACQUES. *"Tuez-les tous, Dieu reconnaîtra les siens," le massacre* de Béziers (22 juillet 1209) et la croisade contre les Albigeois vus par Césaire de Heisterbach. Portet-sur-Garonne: Loubatières, 1994.

BERNADAC, CHRISTIAN. *Montségur et le Graal: Le Mystère Otto Rahn.* Paris: France-Empire, 1994.

BERNANOS, GEORGES. *Les Prédestinés.* Ed. Jean-Loup Bernanos. Paris: Seuil, 1983.

BIRKS, WALTER, AND R. A. GILBERT. *The Treasure of Montségur.* Wellingborough, England: Crucible, 1987.

BOGIN, MEG. *The Women Troubadours.* New York: Norton, 1980.

BOLTON, BRENDA. *Innocent III: Studies on Papal Authority and Pastoral Care.* Aldershot, England: Variorum, 1995.

*BRENON, ANNE. *Le Vrai Visage du catharisme.* Portet-sur-Garonne: Loubatières, 1988. Far and away the best examination of Cathar beliefs for the general reader. Unfortunately, it has yet to be translated from the French. No readily accessible English equivalent exists, though Lambert, Moore, and Wakefield deftly cover the ground in a scholarly fashion.

———. *Les Femmes cathares.* Paris: Perrin, 1992.

———. *Les Cathares: Pauvres du Christ ou apôtres de Satan?* Paris: Gallimard, 1997.

Cahiers de Fanjeaux, no. 14, "Historiographie du catharisme." Toulouse: Privat, 1979.

*CANTOR, NORMAN F. *The Civilization of the Middle Ages.* New York: HarperCollins, 1993. An accessible introduction to the entire millennium of the Middle Ages.

———. *Medieval Lives: Eight Charismatic Men and Women of the Middle Ages.* New York: HarperCollins, 1994.

CAUVIN, ANDRÉ. *Découvrir la France cathare.* Alleur, Belgium: Marabout, 1993.

*COHN, NORMAN. *The Pursuit of the Millennium.* Rev. and expanded ed. New York: Oxford University Press, 1972. A classic of scholarship on medieval apocalyptic cults.

COSTEN, MICHAEL. *The Cathars and the Albigensian Crusade.* Manchester, England: Manchester University Press, 1997.

DELORT, ROBERT, ed. *Les Croisades.* Paris: Seuil, 1988.

DUVERNOY, JEAN. *Le Catharisme.* Vol. 1, *La Religion des cathares.* Toulouse: Privat, 1976.

————, trans. *Guilhem de Puylaurens, chronique; chronica magistri Guillelmi de Podio Laurentii.* Paris: C.N.R.S., 1976.

————, trans. *Le Registre d'inquisition de Jacques Fournier, Evêque de Pamiers (1318–1325).* 3 vols. Paris and The Hague: Mouton, 1977–78.

————. *Le Catharisme.* Vol. 2, *L'Histoire des cathares.* Toulouse: Privat, 1979.

————, trans. *Guillaume Pelhisson Chronique (1229–1244).* Paris: C.N.R.S., 1994.

FRAYLING, CHRISTOPHER. *Strange Landscape: A Journey Through the Middle Ages.* London: Penguin BBC, 1995.

FRIEDLANDER, ALAN. *The Hammer of the Inquisitors: Brother Bernard Délicieux and the Struggle Against the Inquisition in Fourteenth-Century France.* Leiden, The Netherlands: Brill, 2000.

GARDÈRE, MICHEL, trans. *Rituels cathares.* Paris: La Table Ronde, 1996.

*GEORGE, LEONARD. *The Encyclopedia of Heresies and Heretics.* London: Robson, 1995. Lively writing, impressive scope, crammed with detail. A nonstuffy compendium of spiritual dissent. Eminently readable.

GOUGAUD, HENRI. *Bélibaste.* Paris: Seuil, 1982. *N.*

————. *Les Cathares et l'éternité.* Paris: Bartillat, 1997.

GRIFFE, MAURICE. *Les Cathares: Chronologie de 1022 à 1321.* Le Cannet: Editions T.S.H., 1997.

GUÉBIN P., AND H. MAISONNEUVE, trans. *Histoire albigeoise de Pierre de Vaux-de-Cernay.* Paris: Vrin, 1951.

*HEER, FRIEDRICH. *The Medieval World: Europe, 1100–1350.* Trans. Janet Sondheimer. New York: Penguin NAL, 1961. Still a great sweeping read.

Hérésis, no. 7, "Catharisme: L'Édifice imaginaire." Carcassonne: Centre d'Etudes Cathares, 1998.

HETHERINGTON, PAUL. *Medieval Rome: A Portrait of the City and Its Life.* New York: St. Martin's, 1994.

JOHNSON, PAUL. *A History of Christianity*. London: Penguin, 1988.

JOULIN, MARC. *Petite Vie de saint Dominique*. Paris: Desclée de Brouwer, 1989.

KELLY, J. N. D. *The Oxford Dictionary of Popes*. Oxford: Oxford University Press, 1986.

KRAUTHEIMER, RICHARD. *Rome: Portrait of a City, 312–1308*. Princeton: Princeton University Press, 1980.

LAMBERT, MALCOLM. *Medieval Heresy: Popular Movements from the Gregorian Reform to the Reformation*. Oxford: Blackwell, 1992.

*————. *The Cathars*. Oxford: Blackwell, 1998. The latest scholarly tome on the Cathars. Special attention devoted to Catharism in Italy and the Autier revival. Authoritative, but for the stouthearted only.

*LE ROY LADURIE, EMMANUEL. *Montaillou: The Promised Land of Error*. Trans. Barbara Bray. New York: G. Braziller, 1978. A justifiably famous examination of Pyrenean peasants infected by Catharism.

MARROU, HENRI-IRÉNÉE. *Les Troubadours*. Paris: Seuil, 1971.

*MAURIN, KRYSTEL. *Les Esclarmonde: La Femme et la féminité dans l'imaginaire du catharisme*. Toulouse: Privat, 1995. Maurin, an academic with a lyrical writing style, delivers a fascinating work of cultural archaeology about the image of woman in the Cathar mythmaking of the nineteenth and twentieth centuries. In French. Exceptional.

MOORE, JOHN C., ed. *Pope Innocent III and his World*. Aldershot, England: Ashgate, 1999.

*MOORE, R. I. *The Formation of a Persecuting Society*. New York: Blackwell, 1987. A groundbreaking work in the study of heresy. Brief, crisp, and revolutionary in its assertions that Western civilization forged its institutions through persecution at the end of the twelfth and beginning of the thirteenth century. An important book, and not just for medievalists.

————. *The Origins of European Dissent*. Toronto: Medieval Academy of America Reprints, University of Toronto Press, 1994.

————, ed. *The Birth of Popular Heresy*. Toronto: Medieval Academy of America Reprints, University of Toronto Press, 1995.

MUNDY, J. H. *Men and Women at Toulouse in the Age of the Cathars*. Toronto: Pontifical Institute of Mediæval Studies, 1990.

————. *Society and Government at Toulouse in the Age of the Cathars.* Toronto: Pontifical Institute of Mediæval Studies, 1997.

NELLI, RENÉ. *La Vie quotidienne des cathares en Languedoc au treizième siècle.* Paris: Hachette, 1975.

————. *Les Cathares.* Paris: Marabout, 1981.

NIRENBERG, DAVID. *Communities of Violence: Persecution of Minorities in the Middle Ages.* Princeton: Princeton University Press. 1996.

*OLDENBOURG, ZOÉ. *Massacre at Montségur.* Trans. Peter Green. London: Weidenfeld and Nicolson, 1997. Reedition of the impassioned 1959 work of popular history. Many of Oldenbourg's conclusions have been superseded by subsequent research, but the book is still a stirring read. Oldenbourg's greatest contribution remains the historical novel, of which she was a peerless practitioner in the 1940s and 1950s. In 1998 and 1999, three of her superb, atmospheric novels were reissued by Caroll and Graf, New York: *The Cornerstone, Destiny of Fire,* and *The World Is Not Enough.* The last, which bears no relation to 007, was described by the *New York Times* on its release as "the finest historical novel about the Middle Ages in this century, little short of a masterpiece." Although it does not deal with the Cathars, the novel could be read by anyone seeking an imaginative escape into the Middle Ages.

PAGELS, ELAINE. *The Gnostic Gospels.* New York: Random House, 1979.

PALADILHE, DOMINIQUE. *Simon de Montfort et le drame cathare.* Paris: Perrin, 1988.

————. *Les Grandes Heures cathares.* Paris: Perrin, 1995.

PERNOUD, RÉGINE. *Pour en finir avec le Moyen Age.* Paris: Seuil, 1977.

PETERS, EDWARD. *Inquisition.* Berkeley: University of California Press, 1989.

PILHES, RENÉ-VICTOR. *Le Christi.* Paris: Plon, 1998. *N.*

*RICHARDS, JEFFREY. *Sex, Dissidence, and Damnation: Minority Groups in the Middle Ages.* London: Routledge, 1991. Brief, lively, and scholarly, the study gives hair-raising details of the persecution of Jews, heretics, and lepers. Instructive but appalling.

ROQUEBERT, MICHEL. *L'Epopée cathare.* 5 vols. Toulouse: Privat, 1970–89 (vols. 1–4); Paris: Perrin, 1998 (vol. 5).

————. *Montségur, les cendres de la liberté.* Toulouse: Privat, 1998.

————. *Histoire des cathares: Hérésie, Croisade, Inquisition, du onzième au quatorzième siècles.* Paris: Perrin, 1999.

*ROUQUETTE, YVES. *Cathars.* Trans. Roger Depledge. Portet-sur-Garonne: Loubatières, 1998. One of the few recent French populariz-ers of Catharism to be translated. Title presumably meant to be read: "Cathars. Period"—as if this were the last word. Rouquette is pro-vocative in claiming to be a Cathar, polemical whenever he turns to history, and downright chatty in his tour of Languedoc literary cir-cles. For Catharophiles only.

RUNCIMAN, STEVEN. *The Medieval Manichee.* Cambridge: Cambridge University Press, 1991.

SAYERS, JANE. *Innocent III: Leader of Europe, 1198–1216.* Harlow, Eng-gland: Longman, 1994.

SHIRLEY, JANET, trans. *The Song of the Cathar Wars, A History of the Albigensian Crusade, by William of Tudela and an Anonymous Succes-sor.* Aldershot, England: Scolar Press, 1996.

SOUTHERN, R. W. *Western Society and the Church in the Middle Ages.* New York: Penguin, 1970.

*STRAYER, JOSEPH R. *The Albigensian Crusades.* Ann Arbor: University of Michigan Press, 1992. Originally published in 1971, Strayer's account remains the most readable scholarly examination of the crusade in English. The paperback edition has a splendid epilogue by Carol Lansing, which outlines recent trends in English-language Cathar historiography. If you wish to deepen your knowledge of the Cath-ars, start here.

SUMPTION, JONATHAN. *The Albigensian Crusade.* London: Faber and Faber, 1978.

THOUZELLIER, C., trans. *Une Somme anti-cathare: Le Liber contra manic-heos de Durand de Huesca.* Louvain: Université catholique, 1964.

————, trans. *Livre des deux principes.* Paris: Cerf, 1973.

VICAIRE, M. H. *Histoire de saint Dominique.* 2 vols. Paris: Cerf, 1982.

*WAKEFIELD, WALTER L. *Heresy, Crusade, and Inquisition in Southern France, 1100–1250.* New York: Allen and Unwin, 1974. A solid introduction to the beliefs and the misfortunes of the Cathars and the Waldensians.

WAKEFIELD, WALTER L., and AUSTIN P. EVANS, eds. *Heresies of the High Middle Ages*. New York: Columbia University Press, 1991.

WOOD, CHARLES T. *The Quest for Eternity: Manners and Morals in the Age of Chivalry*. Hanover, N.H.: University Press of New England, 1983.

*www.cathares.org. The best on the Web by far. Not at all flaky, like too many of its fellow Cathar sites. Thousands of pictures available, biographies, time lines, maps, interactive facilities, etc. Updated weekly. Much of it has been mirrored in English.

ZERNER-CHARDAVOINE, MONIQUE. *La Croisade albigeoise*. Paris: Gallimard, 1979.

Acknowledgments

It is customary in acknowledgments sections to start with the professional, then move to the personal. A new millennium is beginning—let's get our priorities straight this time.

I owe a very large debt of gratitude to Jill Pearlman, who has helped me at every stage of this project, as a fellow writer, an editor, a companion, a cheerleader, a spouse, and, perhaps most important, a cosurvivor of living in the middle of the countryside with two young and alarmingly vocal daughters, one of whom decided to come into our rural world on a memorable winter's night. Without Jill's support and astonishing ability to do several things at once, I could not have summoned the monomania necessary to complete this book.

My warmest thanks go to our hosts in French Catalonia, Vladimir and Roselyne Djurovic, who were unfailingly kind to the aliens in their midst. Our neighbor Henri Fabresse put his tractor in the service of sanity by plowing the land behind our farmhouse for a vegetable garden that had blessedly nothing to do with flaming heretics. Let no one ever belittle Catalan hospitality or wisdom.

In Languedoc, Jean-Pierre Pétermann was invaluable for giving me Catharized guided tours of Carcassonne and Toulouse that conveniently ignored any irrelevancies built in the last 800 years. Jean-Pierre even managed to sneak me into an off-limits archaeological dig to view the alleged bones of Count Raymond VI.

In Rome, the American Academy made available its resources to a seeker of Innocent III. Eli Gottlieb and Danella Carter, my hosts at the academy and longtime pals from New York, were gracious and patient with my medieval garrulity. Eli risked his eyesight by reading the entire manuscript in E-mail format in time to beat a deadline. While not a Perfect, he's close.

My thanks as well to my immediate family—my parents for their support, my brother Kevin (my companion at Albi) for his unstinting encouragement of projects past and present, and my brother Donal for faxes of obscure troubadour lore—and to the many people who have helped along the way. Foremost among them is the late Matt Cohen, a friend who gave me hope, laughter, and one big push. Others helped in ways that are too diverse to detail: Liz and Kevin Conlon, Sandy Whitelaw, George Haynal, Doris Pearlman, Audrey Thomas, Valérie Chassigneux, Jean-Jacques Bedu, Bruce Alderman, Henri Salvayre, Heidi Ellison, Ruth Marshall, Randall Koral, Dawn Michelle Baude, Susan Adams, Patrick Cox, Zia Jaffrey, Mitchell Feinberg, Edward Hernstadt, Helen Mercer, Mark Hunter, Scott Blair, Niels Stoltenborg, Robert Sarner, Charles F. MacDonald, and Yovanka Djurovic. I would also like to acknowledge the invisible presence of two uncles who have been looking over my shoulder: Fathers Elisha and Damien O'Shea. It is a great pity that this book comes too late for us to sit down over a glass of brandy and have a meandering conversation about the Albigensians.

Thanks are also in order to the courteous librarians of the new and quirky Bibliothèque Nationale in Paris, who, against all odds, never once failed to find the books I was seeking.

Publisher Scott McIntyre deserves my gratitude for once again making a leap of faith, as does publisher George Gibson, who, along with editor Jacqueline Johnson, trained a textual trebuchet on the weak spots of my exposed prose. Any errors or lapses left standing are the result of my obstinacy.

Lastly, a tip of my hat to the café owners, restaurateurs, tourist office employees, hotel keepers, booksellers, museum guards, bartenders, and nuns of Languedoc, all of whom seem to have well-developed theories on who the Cathars were.

Index

A

M

N

O

P

Q

R

PÉRIGORD

Bordeaux

Dordogne

Dordogne

Bergerac

Sarlat

Rocamadour

Garonne

QUERCY

Figeac

Marmande

Lot

Cahors

AGENAIS

N

Agen

Garonne

Moissac

Aveyron

Cordes

Cers

Montauban

All

Rabastens

Adour

Lavaur

Hers

Auch

Verfeil

Toulouse

LAURAGAIS

Puylaurer

Gimone

Baziège

Montgey

Muret

St. Félix

Save

Laurac

Avignonet

Saiss

Arcège

Castelnaudary

Gave du Pau

Bram

Tarbes

COMMINGES

Garonne

Montréal

Prouilles

Lourdes

Pamiers

Fanjeaux

FOIX

Mirepoix

Lir

Foix

Puivert

P Y R É N É E S

SABART

Montségur

Montaillou

Ax-le

ANDORRA

Tirvia

Castellbò

0 Miles   50

0 Kilometers   50

A R A G O N

© 2000 *Jeffrey L. Ward*

to Saragossa